Designing and reporting experiments in psychology

Designing and reporting experiments in psychology

THIRD EDITION

Peter Harris

Open University Press

Open University Press
McGraw-Hill Education
McGraw-Hill House
Shoppenhangers Road
Maidenhead
Berkshire
England
SL6 2QL

email: enquiries@openup.co.uk
world wide web: www.openup.co.uk

and Two Penn Plaza, New York, NY 10121-2289, USA

First published 2008

Copyright © Peler Harris

A catalogue record of this book is available from the British Library

ISBN-13: 978-0-335-22178-3
ISBN-10: 0-335-22178-5

Library of Congress Cataloging-in-Publication Data
CIP data applied for

Typeset by Graphicraft Limited, Hong Kong
Printed in Great Britain by Bell & Bain Ltd, Glasgow

Fictitious names of companies, products, people, characters and/or data that
may be used herein (in case studies or in examples) are not intended to
represent any real individual, company, product or event.

To Antony and Richard, my sons

Contents

Contents of the Web site

Preface

This is a book about how to write undergraduate practical reports. It is designed to help students with every stage of the report writing process by giving them clear and detailed advice about what to put in each section of the report and describing broader issues of format, style and other issues involved in producing good reports of their practical work. As this book is first and foremost about how to write reports, this material forms the focus of the main body of the book, Part 1. Part 2 of this book contains material on design and statistics. It is designed to give students the background they need in key aspects of design and statistics to help them better understand what is required of them in report writing. Material in both parts is supplemented by a Web site that contains additional material on report writing and design. The Web site can be found at **http://mcgraw-hill.co.uk/ openup/harris/**

First published in 1986, this book has been reprinted many times and is now in its third edition, so several generations of undergraduate students have benefited from using it in their studies. I hope that this edition continues to prove a boon to students and look forward to receiving their emails about it.

There are several changes and updates in this new edition. The most obvious is that, for the first time, it has been paired with two statistics textbooks from the same publisher, both of which have been selected because they are comparatively easy to use and have the appropriate breadth of coverage. Both of these are best sellers in their own right. J. Greene and M. D'Oliveira's (2006) *Learning to use statistical tests in psychology* is the more basic and introductory and is suitable for students at the beginning of their careers as undergraduate psychologists. J. Pallant's *SPSS survival manual* (2007) is somewhat more advanced and appropriate for more experienced undergraduate students. You will find references at the end of Chapter 4 and the chapters in Part 2 to further relevant coverage in both statistics textbooks and on this book's Web site. Nevertheless, this book is designed for use alongside any relevant textbook of statistics as well as with either of the above books.

Although the primary emphasis on experimental work is retained in this edition, I also discuss how to write up other forms of quantitative study. So, this book and its Web site should be useful to students writing up any quantitative study, not just experiments.

This edition contains material at the end of each chapter in Part 2 to help students check their understanding and consolidate their learning. For the first time, answers are provided to the diagnostic questions and there are now 50 self-assessment questions. This edition also contains a completely revised section on how to find references, given that so much material is now accessed electronically (Chapter 1), and a greatly expanded section on how to cite electronic references in the REFERENCES section (Chapter 7) that incorporates new guidelines from the American Psychological Association (APA). It also incorporates recent advice from the British Psychological Society about the ethics of conducting studies on the Internet (Chapter 10). I have also compiled a list of things that students continue to do in their reports, despite my advice, and there are now icons in the margin to

indicate where the advice designed to help them avoid these mistakes lies. For the first time, a list of the contents of the Web site is printed in the book and icons are also used to denote where references to further coverage of issues in text occurs on the Web site. The com-

mentary on issues raised in each chapter has also been expanded. This can be found at the rear of the book.

These are the principal changes, but there are many others throughout the text. Nevertheless, retained I hope are the things that both tutors and students liked so much about the previous editions.

To students

This is a book about how to write practical reports. It is designed to help you at undergraduate level write good reports of your studies. Writing reports of practical work is an important part of many courses in psychology, from school level to degree work. This book provides advice on how to go about writing reports of quantitative studies in psychology (i.e., studies where the data are numbers), with an emphasis on the reports you will most often be asked to write – reports of *experiments*.

It is a guide to *design* as well as to report writing. Why? Because these elements are inextricably linked. It is hard to write a good report of a study without understanding the whys and wherefores of its design. In order to fully understand what is required of you in the report, therefore, it helps to have an idea of the function that the report of a study serves in the scientific world. This, in turn, requires you to understand something about the nature and purpose of empirical studies – such as experiments. Yet more than this, of course, many of the problems and difficulties you may face with report writing involve questions such as how to report the features of your design, or how to report adequately the outcomes of your statistical analyses. The answers to such problems depend on knowledge, of both the conventions of report writing and of the logic and terminology of design. Consequently, this book attempts to provide an introduction to both aspects of your practical work.

How to use this book

In this book I have aimed to write something that will serve both as an introduction to design and report writing and as a handy reference source throughout your career as a student of practical psychology. I see it being used much like a thesaurus or dictionary – something that you turn to as the need arises. In particular, you may find yourself having to go over some of the sections a number of times before full understanding dawns. Do not be above doing this – it is what the book is for. Moreover, although you should never let yourself be overawed by the practical report, do not underestimate the task that confronts you either. Report writing is not easy – but I hope that this book will make it easier.

It is essential that you take an active part in assimilating the text rather than being a passive receiver of information. After all, you are in an extremely good position to diagnose what you already know and what you need to learn. I will have failed if the information remains on the page rather than ending up in your head. To help you with your learning, you will find that the chapters in Part 1 typically begin with a number of "diagnostic questions". Test yourself on these to see whether you already have the knowledge to tackle the chapter. If you have any difficulties answering these questions, then you will be directed to another section of the book for assistance. Throughout the book you will find 50 **Self-Assessment Questions** (SAQs) at various points in the text. Attempting these SAQs will give you feedback on your learning and a better general understanding, and will help you to be more of an active participant than a passive reader. The answers to these questions are at the rear of the book. In Part 2, you will find a section at the end of each chapter to help you check your understanding and consolidate your learning. If you are using either Greene and D'Oliveira's *Learning to use statistical tests in psychology* or Pallant's *SPSS survival manual*, you will also find references in that section and at the end of Chapter 4 to relevant coverage in each of those books. If you are using a different statistics textbook, that is no problem – the list of concepts provided at the end of the chapters in Part 2 will help you locate what you need to know in your textbook. There is also a Web site for this book that contains additional material on report writing and design. The Web site can be found at **http://mcgraw-hill.co.uk/openup/harris/**

The summaries at the end of each section recapitulate the main points and so provide a useful aid to revision. The Index of concepts that appears at the end of the book indicates the place in the text where each concept is introduced and defined. Entries in the index are in **bold** print in the text. You will find icons in the margin that flag up things like coverage to be found on the Web site or a piece of advice that students continue to ignore. You can find recommended reading at the rear of the book.

Part 1 is about writing reports. This comes first because it is the principal focus of the book. You will find there chapters for each of the principal sections of the report. Part 2 is about design. The chapters in Part 2 progress, that is, in writing each chapter in Part 2 I have assumed that you are familiar with the material in the previous chapter. So, make sure that you are happy with the material in each chapter before you move on to the next one. In particular, make sure that you are comfortable with the material in Chapters 9–11 before tackling Chapters 12 and 13.

To help you to develop and extend your knowledge of report writing and design, I have included a separate commentary on various issues and points in the text. The commentary is designed to extend your understanding by expanding on points and issues that I do not have the room to cover in detail in the core text or by clarifying something that I have written. You will find this commentary towards the rear of the book. The presence of commentary is indicated by an icon in the margin.

The Web site is likewise intended to help you to develop your knowledge of how to design studies and write reports. You should find yourself looking to the Web site for material more and more as you become experienced and need to write more sophisticated reports. You will find on the Web site fuller coverage of some of the material in this book and also coverage of issues that I have not been able to talk about in the book. You can find a listing of the contents of the Web site at the start of the book. *Do* go and look at what is there. Tell your fellow students about it.

I hope that you will find this book useful and that it will help you to produce good reports. However, please remember that it is designed to *supplement* adequate supervision – not to replace it. The advice in this book is based on the conventions in the *Publication Manual of the American Psychological Association*, fifth edition (APA, 2001). Nevertheless, it is quite possible that I will have written or recommended something with which your tutors disagree. If so, I hope they make clear to you what they want from you instead and that they will not experience fits of apoplexy or direct torrents of abuse at me in the process. So, be alert to places where your tutors expect you to depart from my suggestions.

Please *do* give me feedback. Let me know whether you like the book or not, about the bits that you found useful and any bits that you found hard to follow. This will help me when I come to produce any further editions. It will also help me to develop the material on the Web site.

To tutors

This book is designed both for use as an introductory text for those having to write reports for the first time and also as a resource for students as they progress through the years of a degree course.

The academic world has changed significantly since I wrote the first edition of this book. In the UK the number of students studying psychology has expanded enormously and the numbers that we admit onto degree courses are many times greater than once they were. This has inevitably changed the ways in which we teach our students. If my experience is anything to go by, students receive less experience of report writing and less feedback on their efforts than once was the case. The need for a guide such as this has therefore increased.

Developments in technology continue to change how students work. This edition of the book has been updated to provide students with advice relevant to how they now seek out information. There continue to be changes in custom and practice and I have written this edition to reflect these as best I can. For instance, the move in published work towards dealing with issues of power and effect size continues, as does the need, therefore, to educate and train our students in dealing with and reporting these issues.

Previous editions were used by more advanced students than I had expected. (I know of postgraduates who used the book to help them to prepare their theses, which I had not expected.) Certainly it was not uncommon to find final year students using it extensively to help them to write their projects. In the light of this, I have expanded the commentary and provided other pointers to help such students move towards writing the more sophisticated reports expected of them. A key element in this is the Web site that accompanies this book. The Web site can be found at **http://mcgraw-hill.co.uk/openup/harris/**. There I have placed fuller coverage of various issues discussed in this book and also material relevant to more advanced students. You can find a listing of the Web site's contents at the start of this book. Material on the Web site covers statistics from using and reporting chi-square through to multiple linear regression. It is designed to be of use both to relative beginners and more advanced students who may need to run and report statistics of effect size, multiple comparisons, tests of simple effects, and so on. For each statistic there is a section on things for the student to watch out for when using the statistic or reporting the outcome of the analysis.

Please note that each chapter in Part 2 has been written on the assumption that students are familiar with the material in the previous chapter. The material in Chapters 9–11 covers the core material on design and analysis contained in a "traditional" introductory course on these issues. This book can therefore be used with such courses by omitting the material in Chapters 12 and 13.

The recommendations in this book are based on those in the fifth edition of the *Publication Manual of the American Psychological Association* (APA, 2001). Although not a primer in APA style *per se*, the aim is to encourage students from the outset to produce reports that are generally consistent with APA style. Those tutors for whom this is less of a concern will, I hope, find that much of what I recommend here nevertheless still suits their students' needs. I would appreciate feedback on what works and what might be done differently.

I have continued in this third edition to use the terms *unrelated samples* and *related samples* independent variables. However, for those who wish to use alternatives, I have highlighted this issue to the students (Section 10.2) and told them about the principal alternatives. I have also tried to write in such a way that the above terms could easily be replaced without the students losing sight of the conceptual and methodological issues involved in choosing between these types of independent variables.

This book has been written on the assumption that most of the students who use it will still be asked to test for statistical significance, albeit typically within a broader understanding of issues to do with estimation, power and effect size. Nevertheless, it should be possible to use this book even if you do not want your students to test for statistical significance. I have also expanded the section (Section 13.8) on the use of variables that are not "true" independent variables. In the interests of clarity and simplicity, especially for introductory students, it is assumed that they will generally be testing the traditional "no effect" null hypothesis rather than "minimum-effect" ones (e.g., Murphy & Myors, 2004).

Although this book has been written primarily for students of Psychology, many of the rules and conventions are shared by related disciplines – such as Biology – and so it may prove useful to students of these subjects too.

I hope that much that was good in the previous editions of the book remains and that at least most of the changes are again improvements. I did not get much feedback on the previous editions, but take comfort in their healthy sales. I have had letters and emails from students who found previous editions of the book useful and these have been very gratifying.

Acknowledgements

The call for this new edition came round much quicker than the previous one. I am grateful to the various commissioning editors at McGraw-Hill who were patient but persistent, and latterly to Natalie Jacobs for her support and input. I am also grateful to four anonymous reviewers of the second edition – their reviews greatly influenced me as I worked on this revision. I am also grateful to two colleagues, Paul Norman and Richard Rowe, who commented on some parts of the text. Yet again, I'd like to thank all those who have put up with me over the years and especially while I hid away working on this. Distinguished service awards go to those for whom this was for the second or third time of asking.

Part 1   Writing reports

1 Getting started

When you first signed up for a psychology course, the chances are that you did not really expect what was coming, particularly the emphasis on methodology and statistics. For some of you this may have been a pleasant surprise. For most, however, it will undoubtedly have been a shock to the system.

No doubt in other parts of your course you will examine critically academic psychology's scientific aspirations. My task in this book is to help you as best I can to face up to one of its major consequences for you. This is the prominence given in many psychology courses to doing practical work (especially *experimenting*) and the requirement in most instances to write up at least some of this work in the form of a highly structured and disciplined *practical report*.

All a report is (really) is the place in which you tell the story of your study; what you did, why you did it, what you found out in the process, and so on. In doing this you are more like an ancient storyteller, whose stories were structured by widely recognized and long-established conventions, than a modern novelist who is free to dictate form as well as content. Moreover, like the storytellers of old, although you will invariably be telling your story to someone who knows quite a bit about it already, you are expected to present it as if it had never been heard before. This means that you will need to spell out the details and assume little knowledge of the area on the part of your audience.

The nature of your story – the things that you have to talk about – is revealed in Box 1.1.

> 1 What you did
> 2 Why you did it
> 3 How you did it
> 4 What you found (including details of how you analysed the data)
> 5 What you think it shows

Box 1.1   The information you should provide in your practical report.

Our first clue as to the nature of the conventions governing the report comes with a glance at its basic structure. The report is in *sections*, and these sections (by and large) follow an established *sequence*. What this means is that, in the telling, your story needs to be cut up into chunks: different parts of the story should appear in different places in the report. The typical sequence of the sections appears in Box 1.2.

Most of the sections are separated from each other by putting their titles as headings in the text. The exceptions are the TITLE and INTRO-DUCTION, neither of which needs headings to introduce them.

The exact relationship between the elements of your story and the sections of the report is shown in Box 1.3.

The METHOD is composed of a number of subsections (Box 1.4). There is some disagreement over the precise order in which these subsections should appear and over which are essential and which optional. In this guide I will use the order in Box 1.4. You may be

> Title
> Abstract
> Introduction
> Method
> Results
> Discussion
> References
> Appendices (if any)

Box 1.2   The sections of the practical report.

Introduction	What you did
	Why you did it
Method	How you did it
Results	What you found (including details of how you analysed the data)
Discussion	What you think it shows

Box 1.3   Where the information in Box 1.1 should appear in the report.

Method

Design
Participants
Apparatus (or) *Materials*
Procedure

Box 1.4   Specific subsections of the METHOD.

advised to employ a different one. This is fine: the important thing is that you report the appropriate material in the right way in those subsections you include.

The report, therefore, is a *formal* document composed of a series of sections in which you are expected to provide specific bits of information. I will discuss the specific conventions governing each section in the rest of Part 1 of this book. There are, however, certain general rules that I can introduce you to straightaway.

The first of these concerns the person for whom you should write your report. Let's call this person your **reader**. Who should this person be? That is, what kind of reader should you have in mind as you write? A very common mistake, especially early on, is to assume that your reader is the person who will be marking the report. In reality, however, the marker will be assessing your report on behalf of someone else – an idealized, hypothetical person who is intelligent, but unknowledgeable about your study and the area of psychology in which it took place. Your marker will, therefore, be checking to see that you have written your report with this sort of reader in mind. You need to make sure, therefore, that you have:

- introduced the reader to the area of psychology relevant to your study;
- provided the reader with the background necessary to understand what you did and why you did it;
- spelt out and developed your arguments clearly;
- defined technical terms;
- provided precise details of the way in which you went about collecting and analysing the data that you obtained.

In short, you should write for someone who is psychologically naive, taking little for granted about your reader's knowledge of things psychological. So, when in doubt, *spell it out!*

If you find this difficult to do, then a useful approach is to write the report as if it will be read by someone you know who is intelligent but unknowledgeable about psychology; a friend of yours, say, or your partner. Write it as if this person were going to have to read and understand it. Indeed, it is a good idea, if you can, to get just such a person to read your report before handing it in (Section 8.6).

? SAQ 1   In which sections of the report are you expected to give an account of (a) what you found in your study?; (b) what you think your findings have to tell us?

? SAQ 2   "The people who mark your reports are professional psychologists. As they know quite a bit about the subject already, you can safely assume that they will understand what you did and why you did it without having to spell this out in the report. You should, therefore, direct your report at the expert, specialized reader." True, or false?

1.1   Experienced students, inexperienced students, and the report

The demands and expectations placed upon you will of course vary with your experience of report writing. Early on in your career as an author of practical reports less will be expected of you than later, especially in what are really the key sections of the report – the

INTRODUCTION and DISCUSSION. At this early stage you will be expected principally to show that you understand what you did in your practical and its implications, together with evidence that you have at least a basic grasp of the demands of the report's format.

In particular, less may be expected of you here in the "why you did it" part of the INTRODUCTION (Box 1.3). There are a number of reasons for this, but the main one is that the early studies that you do in your practical course tend not to be justifiable in the terms that we use here – that is, in *research* terms. Generally speaking, these early practicals are chosen for you and, more often than not, are chosen for reasons other than their earth-shattering research significance. It would be rather perverse of us, therefore, to expect you to fabricate some plausible research justification for undertaking such studies.

Later on, however, (e.g., as you begin to take more responsibility for the design of your study) you will be expected to pay more attention to the research significance of what you did. This why part will then become more important – because, in being responsible for the choice of topic and design, you will be expected to be able to justify this choice. So, you must be able to tell us *why* it is that, given the options available to you, you decided to conduct your particular study. Moreover, these will need to be research justifications, not merely ones of expediency! You will need, therefore, to develop the habit of thinking about how the ideas you are entertaining for your study will look in the report, paying particular attention to how they will fit into the INTRODUCTION. Specific dangers that you must watch out for here are, first, a lack of adequate material (*references*) to put in this section and, second, undertaking a project that lacks any research justification (because it is based on assumptions that are contradicted by existing findings in the area). Thinking clearly in advance will help you to avoid making these mistakes.

Summary of Section 1.1

1 The practical report is made up of a series of separate sections in which you should report specific pieces of information. Your task in the report is to tell your reader all about the study that you conducted.

2 You must write, however, for someone who knows nothing about your study or the area of psychology in which it took place.

3 This means that you should spell out the precise details of your study and provide your reader with knowledge of the background relevant to it (previous findings in the area) when writing the report.

4 The demands placed upon you with regard to this task may vary with your experience as a student of practical psychology. In particular, as you progress you will need to get into the habit of thinking about how the ideas that you are entertaining for your study will fit into the report. In particular, pay attention to how you will be able to develop and defend your arguments in the INTRODUCTION.

1.2 Writing the report

Before running your study, you should really have a good idea of exactly how you are going to do it, as well as why it is worth doing, and how it relates to previous work in the area. However, you will have no real idea of what you are going to find and, therefore, no precise knowledge of the implications of your study. Thus, you could write the INTRODUCTION and METHOD before you conduct your study, because these sections report material that you should have decided upon in advance. You cannot, however, write the RESULTS and DISCUSSION in advance, as these depend critically upon the outcome of your study.

As you can see from Box 1.2, the order of the report's sections reflects the historical sequence described above. However, I advise you not to *write* the sections in the order described in Box 1.2. For some of the sections – such as the INTRODUCTION and DISCUSSION – require more thought and effort to do properly than others. Consequently, you would be wise to work on these sections when you are at your freshest, leaving the more straightforward ones – such as those in the METHOD – to those moments in which your interest in what you are doing is at its lowest ebb. In particular, never leave the DISCUSSION until last. I have had too many reports from students who have clearly devoted the better part of their time to the earlier sections, and lost interest in what they were doing by the time they reached the DISCUSSION. The consequence is a perfunctory DISCUSSION, and a poorer mark than they would have received had they budgeted their time more sensibly. Always bear in mind that the DISCUSSION is the key section of the report; it is there that the true value of what you have done in your study will be revealed in all its glory, when you come to assess the *implications* of your findings. How much have your findings added to the stock of knowledge that you described in the INTRODUCTION? The whole process – from design through to the writing of all of the other sections of the report – is intended to clear the ground for the DISCUSSION. So, write your report with this in mind. (Again, this will become more and more important as you come to play a larger role in designing your own studies.)

Finally, the ABSTRACT is invariably better left until last, even though it is the first section to appear in the report. (Indeed, it is difficult to imagine writing an abstract of an unfinished report.)

? SAQ 3   Which sections of the report could you – at least in principle – write *before* you conducted your study? Why?

? SAQ 4   Which is the key section of the report?

1.3 The importance of references in text

Whenever you write in psychology – whether practical reports or essays – you must *substantiate all factual assertions*. A **factual assertion** is simply anything that could prompt your reader to ask "who says?" or "what's the evidence?". A factual assertion is a claim about the psychological universe and few such claims are undeniably, self-evidently true. For example, "people want to be happy", "memory deteriorates with age", "children grow into adults". Only the last of these statements is undeniably true, and only if we take adult to mean "grown up *physically*". Be alert to this issue: you will be making many factual assertions when you write and most of these will require substantiation. You will be expected to tell your reader at least *who* presented evidence or arguments for the claim and *when*. So, if you make a firm statement about any aspect of the psychological universe (however trivial), you must attempt to support it.

In practice, this means that statements such as: "Emotion interferes with the ability to reason logically" or "Anxiety enhances the impact of a persuasive message" are not acceptable. However, statements such as: "Emotion interferes with the ability to reason logically (Dwyer, 1972)" and "Anxiety enhances the impact of a persuasive message (Dale & Stant, 2009)" *are* acceptable. The reason is that they contain what we call **references**, whereas the first two statements do not.

References are the preferred method of substantiating factual assertions in psychology, because references provide direct answers to the questions *who* found, argued or claimed something and *when*. If they wished to, your reader could look up the source referenced to see if it really does say what you claim it says. So, wherever possible, you should cite a reference (at least a name and date) for all *findings, definitions*, and *quotations* at all times, even where you have made the citation before. It must be clear to which author, and to which particular piece of their work, you are referring at *any given time*. For example:

> Chopra (2006) found that emotion impaired participants' ability to reason logically. Emotion did not, however, affect female participants any more than the male participants. Indeed, the reasoning performance of the women was superior to that of the men when the emotional arousal was positive. On the basis of these data and previous findings (Legg, 1999), he argued "the traditional viewpoint that emotion disrupts the reasoning abilities of women, but not those of men, is untenable" (Chopra, 2006, pp. 12–13).

I cannot emphasize enough the importance of citing references in scientific writing. You can find out more about how to reference in psychology in Chapter 8. You must reference properly in your reports and indeed in everything that you write in psychology.

In most cases you will be given at least some references to read for your practical. As you become more experienced, however, more will be expected of you in terms of reading around the area and hunting down your own references. You can find advice about how to locate references in Section 1.5.

In psychology you should *never* find yourself having made a claim about an aspect of the psychological universe without attempting in some way to shore it up. Whatever happens, therefore, *you should attempt to substantiate your viewpoint*. This is particularly true of what you will come to know as the *experimental hypothesis*. You should always attempt to justify the experimental hypothesis (or hypotheses), especially as you become more experienced.

SAQ 5   If you make a statement that might prompt your reader to ask "who says?", what should you do?

Summary of Sections 1.2–1.3

1 The DISCUSSION is the key section of the report. It is there that you reveal the true value of your study, for it is there that you come to assess the implications of your findings. You should therefore budget your time when writing the report so that you devote sufficient thought and attention to this section.

2 When writing the report you will be expected to substantiate all factual assertions, preferably by using *references*.

1.4   The practical report and the research paper

So far, therefore, I have introduced you to the basic requirements of the report and given you some idea of how to go about writing it. Yet *why* does the report take this form: why is it in sections? Why do these sections come in a particular order? Why are there restrictions on what material is to be mentioned, where it is to come, and how it is to be expressed? These are good questions. The answers to them require you to understand something about the function of the report in its **research context**.

Those of you who have already written reports may well have found yourselves confused and frustrated at some stage or other by the format and rules that strike you as being rigid, restrictive, inhibiting, and perhaps even arbitrary. One of the main reasons for this is that you meet the report in a strange environment. For the report is primarily a *research* tool. Its natural habitat is the academic *journal*. The rules and conventions that govern it have evolved for the purpose it serves there. In its educational setting, therefore (where you meet it) these conventions are often difficult to understand, because you have inherited the report divorced – at least at first – from its principal function.

What is a journal? When, as a naive undergraduate, I first encountered this term and was packed off to the library to start work on my first practical report I didn't know what people were talking about. Bewildered, I wandered around the library trying to work out in what ways a journal might look different on a shelf from a book. To me a journal was a dusty old, handwritten thing kept by some intrepid Victorian travelling though the Congo or awaiting the relief of Mafeking. Quite what psychology had to do with such things was beyond me. Now, of course, I know better. Academic journals are the main way in which researchers inform each other about their work and, therefore, the places in which much of a discipline's knowledge and understanding are found. Journals contain a selection of what are thought to be the best articles submitted to them and are published, electronically or in paper form, at regular periods (and are therefore also sometimes referred to as *periodicals*). Most of the studies that you will cite in a report will be published in journals. (Just to add to the confusion, these published reports are also called *papers*.)

In its research context, a journal article serves to inform those who may be interested in a researcher's work of its *nature*, *purpose*, and *implications*, in as *clear*, *thorough*, and *concise*, a way as possible (note the conflicting demands). To this end, the idea of a general format, with clearly labelled sections that provide clearly defined pieces of information, has developed (Box 1.5). Using this format it should be possible for readers to establish quickly and with the minimum of effort whether the reported work is of interest to them and to locate any particular piece of information they want. Ideally, readers should be able to rerun your study (to conduct what we call a "replication")

Introduction:	1	Summarize state of area prior to study. (Why you did it)
	2	Sketch study in broad outline. (What you did)
	3	State the *experimental hypothesis* (or hypotheses) and associated predictions (Section 9.1.4)
Method:	4	Outline precise details of study. (How you did it)
Results:	5	Present relevant data, together with outcomes of appropriate inferential statistical analyses. (What you found)
Discussion:	6	Summarize and interpret findings.
	7	Assess implications for area (i.e., return to 1). (What you think it shows)

Box 1.5   The requirements of the research report.

based solely on the description in your report. This is the level of description that you should aim for, within the constraints imposed by the word limit for your report.

The conventions that govern the construction of the report, therefore, have been developed for the purpose of conveying information clearly, precisely, efficiently, and concisely, to those who are interested. To a large extent, these are the conventions that you must obey in report writing, even though very few of you are ever likely to have your work published. In essence, these conventions have been *transplanted* from the research world into the educational one.

 SAQ 6   What are the main purposes served by the conventions of the *research* report?

As you progress, you will be expected more and more to emulate the research process – to design your studies with their research implications in mind and write your reports with greater emphasis on the implications of what you have done for existing findings and ideas. As a result, more will be expected of you in the report, particularly in the INTRODUCTION and DISCUSSION. So, those of you who will be expected to progress in this way must watch out for this transition. (In the UK, for example, this will probably occur for most of you during the second year of an undergraduate course.)

As this is critical to the way in which you should write your report (and as it affects the way your report is marked), if you have any doubts about what is expected of you, then ask your tutor what you should do. Indeed, this is a general rule for anything in this book: when, in doubt, ask your tutor.

Summary of Section 1.4

1 The practical report is related to the research article. The conventions for writing research articles have developed to convey information clearly, precisely, efficiently and concisely to those who may be interested in a researcher's work.

2 To a large extent, these are the conventions that you must obey when writing your practical reports, particularly as you become more experienced.

1.5   Finding references for your INTRODUCTION

When you start off as a student, knowing what to read for your INTRODUCTION is generally no problem. Your tutor tells you what references to read, you read them, and you write a potted account of what they say. Indeed, in your early reports there may not be much space for anything expansive. As time goes by, however, expectations change. You will be expected to know more, write about more, and find out more for yourself. You need to learn how to find useful, informative and up-to-date things to read so that you can design studies that ask interesting questions based on an *informed* understanding of what has already been found and to help you write a good introduction to your study.

1.5.1   How to structure your reading and what to look for

Most of you, most of the time, do not read enough. However, some of you read too much. Reading just the right amount to give you an informed understanding of the area, but leaving you still able to see the wood for the trees, is an important skill. So rule one, for most of you, is: *read enough*! Rule two, for some of you, is: *know when to stop*!

When doing your reading, take it in stages. Differentiate articles that are readily available to you – ones that you can access online or find in the library – from those you will need to order, which will cause delays. Also budget your time so that you are able to do enough reading.

Start by reading something general if you can. For example, a decent, up-to-date textbook chapter will give you an overview of the themes and issues in the area and a sense of what are the key studies. More advanced students should see if they can find a relevant article in a journal. A recent article in a decent journal will contain some sort of review of the area. If you need further references, you could try to get hold of any promising-looking articles contained in the references sections of such an article. There are also journals and other sources dedicated to reviews: if in doubt, ask your tutor where you might look and what might be suitable for your level of study. Ask also what journals s/he considers to be the best in the field and look for articles in these.

In some cases there will be an obvious starting study or studies on which your experiment is based. If so, start there.

When thinking about what to read, make sure that you differentiate primary from secondary sources. A **primary source** is the original piece of work: the paper in which the authors argued something or first published their findings. Anything in which people give a second-hand account of another piece of work is a **secondary source**. Textbooks are secondary sources. In these the author(s) provide potted accounts of people's work. Such secondary sources are useful starting points, but detail is lost and sometimes mistakes and misinterpretations creep in. As you progress as a student, you should expect more and more of your reading to be of primary sources.

If you do need to generate further references, bear in mind that the process of generating lists of potential things to read is relatively easy; getting hold of the actual articles themselves may not be.

1.5.2 Generating potential references

Electronic resources, such as online catalogues of abstracts or Internet search engines, are a great boon, but not without their problems. It is easy to generate a huge list of potentially relevant references from such sources. However, it can take a lot of sifting through them to find the really useful ones and you can miss some key references altogether if your *search terms* have been inadequate. (A **search term** is the word or phrase you type into the search field of the source you are searching, such as a bibliographic database, like PsycINFO, or a Web site.) Here is some advice about how to find references and some things to watch out for.

1 If you have access to a college or university library, see what advice it has available on where and how to search and *especially* on choosing appropriate search terms. Often, the more specific you can be in your choice of search terms, the better. The library may provide a leaflet or some Web pages or perhaps even a class on searching: make use of whatever is on offer.

2 Your library will give you access to electronic catalogues of abstracts, such as Web of Knowledge or PsycINFO. These contain titles, abstracts, and reference lists of articles in psychology journals and other disciplines that you can search for relevant articles. Depending on your request, the computer will look for your search terms in the title, abstract, author names, and references section of the articles on the database and provide you with a list of the ones

it has found. Be warned, however, that this can (a) generate many hundreds – perhaps thousands – of "hits" but (b) still miss key references, especially if these lie far back in time. Do not make the mistake of assuming that the only things you can or should read are on such lists! For undergraduate practical reports (and essays for that matter), such catalogues are probably best used to help you locate a few up-to-date references.

3 If you do not have access to either of the above, but do have general access to the Internet, then of course Internet search engines can be helpful. Preferably, use an academic search engine, such as Google Scholar, to help you get a list of recent relevant references. For reports (and essays) in scientific psychology, you need articles and other academic material that has been what we call in the trade, "peer reviewed". Such material has been checked for accuracy. It is read by other psychologists and rewritten by the author(s) in the light of their criticisms and comments before being accepted for publication. Academic search engines help you to locate this material among the wealth of unedited, unreviewed and potentially misleading material out there on the Internet.

1.5.3   Locating the references

Once you have identified which articles you want to read, you need to access them. Again, electronic sources are a great boon, but don't forget that libraries have books and journals on shelves and in store as well!

1 Internet search engines, such as Google Scholar, can of course also help you to access some of the papers themselves. You can try searching using author's names or keywords from the title or abstract. You can also use such search engines to find the authors' Web sites. Locating their Web sites can be very useful, as they might not only have the article available for you to download but also other relevant papers and descriptions of their research. Be careful, however, as some articles you may find on the Internet may not be legally available for downloading and you should not download material illegally. When in doubt, check with your tutor.

2 You may have access to a college or university library's electronic journals. If so, search these for the *name of the journal* (not the title

of the article or authors' names). If you find the journal listed, you may be able to download the article you want. If a journal is not available electronically, check whether the library holds paper copies. I sometimes get students telling me a paper is unavailable when the journal is sitting on the library's shelves because they have searched for the author or title of a paper and not the name of the journal.

3 If you are searching a library's catalogue electronically, do not confuse books and journals. To see whether the library has a *book* called *The Psychology of Communication* by an author called George Bush you can type in Bush or communication or both. However, to see if it has his paper on this topic in the May 2008 edition of a journal called *The Journal of Communication Studies*, you need to type in *The Journal of Communication Studies* to see if the library takes the journal. This is because the library catalogue lists what journals are available, *not* the journal's contents.

4 On the other hand, if an Internet search or the library catalogue takes you to a journal's Web site, you will be able to search for Bush's paper by his name or the paper's title. This is because such Web sites *do* list the journal's contents. However, you may find that you are only able to access the ABSTRACT of the paper and not the entire paper. This is because ABSTRACTS are public documents (see Chapter 6) but most journals are commercial enterprises, so someone has to pay a subscription to the publisher to access the papers. Check whether the journal is on your library's list of electronic journals – if so, then your library has paid a subscription and you may be able to get access to the paper through their electronic list (see above).

5 Remember that downloading, printing, photocopying, or highlighting an article are *not* the same thing as reading it!

Overall, strive for a balance between old and new sources. One of the first things I do when I look at a project or practical report *from more advanced students* is to scan the references section to see what proportion of references are from the last two or three years. I want to see a good mix of references: classic sources and recent, up-to-date material published in decent journals.

Finally, if you have accessed material electronically, this may affect how you cite it in the REFERENCES section. You can find out more about this in Chapter 7.

1.5.4   Rubbish and temptation on the Internet

Watch out for two things on the Internet, rubbish and temptation:

- *Rubbish* – be sensible about the material available on the Internet. It may be easy to get access to lots of information, but some of it will be rubbish. Use the Internet mainly to locate material that has been checked for accuracy. Cite material that has not been peer-reviewed, such as someone's blog or Web pages, only when you have a special reason for doing so.
- *Temptation* – as in life, this comes in many forms on the Internet and two forms in particular you need to be wary of here. First, you may come across material that you have not written yourself but that you are tempted to pass off as your own. This is *plagiarism* and it is a serious offence. You should avoid any risk of being accused of plagiarism. I discuss this further in Section 8.3. Second, you may come across material (e.g., an article or scale) that is under copyright and that you should not have been able to access. Hard though it may be, you should not use such material.

Summary of Section 1.5

1 As you progress as a student of psychology, you will be expected to find relevant things to read yourself and to read more primary sources.

2 You can use searches of electronic databases and hand searches of books and journals to help you to get additional references to read. The Internet also contains potentially useful information, but also much that has not been checked for accuracy – so you should use this material sensibly.

3 More advanced students should attempt to read a good mix of references to classic articles and up-to-date ones from decent journals.

1.6   Ethics

Before you even begin to think about designing and running your own studies, let alone writing them up, you need to learn how to treat your participants ethically. Any investigation involving humans or animals is governed by a set of ethical principles and you are required to act in accordance with these. It can be very easy when designing your studies to get caught up in the details and the science and to lose sight of the potential for insult, upset or distress in your procedures. When you first start out, your tutor will play the major part in keeping an eye on this aspect of your work. Nevertheless, you too have a responsibility to make sure that your experiments and other studies are run ethically. Make sure, therefore, that you obtain, read and understand the ethical principles adhered to in your department. At some stage you may undertake project work for which you need prior ethical approval. Make sure that you know how to obtain approval under these circumstances and do not start without it! You will find more on ethical issues in Section 10.10.

1.7   The rest of the book and the book's Web site

Once you have familiarized yourself with the issues covered in this chapter, you can turn to the rest of Part 1 of this book. Chapters 2–7 describe in detail what material you should put in each section of the report. Chapter 8 provides advice on how to produce the final version of the report, including topics such as writing style, how to reference in text, and the use of tables and figures. If at any stage you find yourself puzzled by a statistical term or uncertain about a methodological issue, you can turn to the relevant sections of Part 2 to find out more. You can also find further coverage of report writing, design and statistical issues on the book's Web site at: **http://mcgraw-hill.co.uk/**

 openup/harris/

You can find a full listing of the Web site's contents at the start of this book.

Finally, although – as its title implies – much of this book is about designing and reporting *experiments*, where relevant, I also discuss how to write up other forms of quantitative study (i.e., where the data are numbers). So, this book and its Web site should be useful to you when you are writing up any quantitative study during your time as a student of psychology, not just experiments. (For more on the different types of quantitative research, see Chapter 9.)

2 The INTRODUCION section

 Diagnostic questions on design for Chapter 2

Before reading this chapter, check that you can answer correctly the following diagnostic questions:

1 What is a *variable?*

2 What is the name of the variable that we *manipulate* in an experiment?

3 What is the name of the variable that we *measure* in an experiment to assess the effects of our manipulation?

4 From which hypothesis can we predict that there will be *no difference* between the conditions in an experiment? Is it (a) the experimental hypothesis or (b) the null hypothesis?

5 What is a *nondirectional* prediction?

You can find the answers at the rear of the book (p. 273). If you had difficulties answering any of these questions, read Chapter 9.

The first major section of the report, then, is the INTRODUCTION. As its name implies, the purpose of this section is to *introduce* something. Which raises two questions, both of which you should be able to answer on the basis of your reading of Chapter 1.

? SAQ 7   So, in the INTRODUCTION, you introduce *what* to *whom?*

Essentially in the INTRODUCTION to your report you should do the following, *in the following order*:

1 Review the background material (existing findings and theoretical ideas) relevant to your study.
2 Outline the precise problem that you chose to investigate and how you went about investigating it.
3 Outline the predictions derived from the experimental hypothesis (Section 9.1.4).

This means that your INTRODUCTION is effectively in two parts: (1) a part in which you deal with work that pre-dated your study (which will generally be the work of other people); and (2) a part in which you finally introduce and describe your own study, albeit briefly. You must move, therefore, from the *general* to the *specific*. That is, you do not start with a description of your study – you build up to it. Why, should become clearer as we go along.

As the INTRODUCTION is logically in two parts, I shall deal with them separately here. So, let us turn to the first part of your INTRODUCTION, the part in which you review the background material relevant to the study that you conducted.

2.1   The first part of the INTRODUCTION: reviewing the background to your study

 First, let me issue a word of caution. If you have read around your subject, there is a great temptation, whatever your level as a student, to let your marker know this by hook or by crook. Most frequently this is achieved by weaving every little morsel into the INTRODUCTION, regardless of how contrived this becomes. *Resist this temptation*, for it is counter-productive. The material that you mention should be *directly* relevant to the problem under investigation. Moreover, you should avoid the more trivial details of the studies you report, emphasizing instead their major findings and conclusions. Your task in this part of the report is primarily to put your study into its research context, by showing its relationship to previous work in the area. Consequently, you should mention material *only* if it is relevant. So, if you end up having read something that turns out to be tangential, drop it from the report, however much heartbreak this causes you. Learning to write concisely and yet clearly is one of the key skills that you are trying to develop. Trust me on this: the more desperate you feel about wanting to let your marker know how hard you have worked, the more alert you need to be to this danger.

At the same time, however, bear in mind that you are under no obligation to treat published work as "gospel". From the start of your time as a student of psychology, you are as entitled to disagree with the viewpoints of others as they are with you; this is one of the great things about studying psychology. However, the manner in which you do this is important. Do not be afraid to disagree with what you read if you believe you have good grounds for doing so. However, make sure that you can provide plausible support for your viewpoint. That is, *you must seek to substantiate your point of view* by showing how the evidence supports it. You must get into the habit not merely of asserting things, but of *substantiating* them.

2.2   Inexperienced students, experienced students, and the INTRODUCTION

If you are studying to go to university, taking your first course in psychology, or in the first year of a degree course, you will probably be considered to be a novice. At this stage in your career as psychologists you are basically learning your trade. Consequently, your marker will generally be looking to see whether you have understood the study you conducted and whether you have a grasp of at least the basic demands of the practical report format. So, s/he will assess such things as whether you have put the right material in the right sections, referenced, quoted and defined properly (Chapter 7), and obeyed the other main conventions of report writing.

 For you, then, the more important part of your INTRODUCTION will be the second part – where you talk about your study. The first part of your INTRODUCTION will be an orienting section that gives your reader some idea of the area in which your practical took place. In order to do this you will generally need to include accounts of one or two of those studies most directly relevant to the one that you conducted. However, you probably will not be expected at this stage to spend much time attempting to *derive* your study from the work that went before it.

It is difficult to give general advice here because studies vary so much, as do markers' expectations. However, if you're completely bewildered, one general strategy that you might employ runs as follows:

1 Perhaps open with a statement about the general area or phenomenon under investigation (e.g., memory, attention, attitudes, rumour).
2 Then talk about the particular aspect of this topic that your study specifically addressed (e.g., the impact of mnemonics, the "cocktail party" phenomenon, attitude change, how rumours are spread).
3 Then, with the problem nicely set up, you are ready to introduce your own study to your reader.

This has been done in outline in the following example:

Memory has been defined as "the retention and use of prior learning" (Glassman & Hadad, 2004, p. 472). One aspect of memory of both theoretical and practical interest is how to improve it (Kavanagh, 2005). Over the years people have developed a number of techniques for improving memory (Toshack, 1965; Warboys, 1970). Collectively, these techniques are called *mnemonics*, from the Greek for "memory" (Glassman & Hadad, 2004).

The *method of loci* is an example of a mnemonic. This method involves mentally placing material that needs to be later recalled at various locations, such as on a well-known route or in a familiar building. Subsequently, a mental "walk" around that location can retrieve the material located there. The method of loci is thus particularly suitable for recalling material in sequence.

Investigations of the method of loci were among the earliest experiments in psychology (e.g., Keenor, 1911; Wilson, 1899). For instance, Ferguson (1927) reported significant improvements in participants' ability to recall a list of everyday objects when using this mnemonic. In 1971, Clark found that the technique also enhanced recall of words. Moreover, participants in Clark (1971) recalled significantly more words high in imageability (i.e., words that readily suggested visual images) than words low in imageability.

Recently, however, Earnshaw, Nugent, Ford, and Young (2007) failed in their attempt to replicate the findings of Clark (1971). In their study, Earnshaw et al. manipulated . . . [Continue by telling your reader succinctly the key points of Earnshaw et al.'s study and findings.]

Notice that what you are doing here is *homing in* on your study. Rather than dropping your reader in cold by starting with your study, you are taking it step by step and easing them in gently. Now, it may not be possible to do it quite so neatly each time, but you should always *try* to lead up to your study. This is a good rule: do not *start* with the details of your study; build up to them.

 SAQ 8

Why is it a good idea to build up to the details of your study, rather than starting the INTRODUCTION with a description of what you did?

Starting with such an approach from the outset will result in you developing good habits for later when – at least for those of you who must progress – more will be expected from you in the first section of the report. For, as you become more experienced, this first part of your INTRODUCTION will become longer. It will also take on some of the functions that the INTRODUCTION has in a research paper. By this stage you should be beginning to undertake studies that have at least some limited research justifications – or at least you must write them *as if* they had research justifications.

In the INTRODUCTION to a research paper the author will summarize the state of the area *prior* to the study that s/he conducted. Subsequently, s/he will readdress this material in the light of the study's findings, to see whether the position has changed at all (i.e., whether the study itself has allowed us to make much progress). S/he does this in the DISCUSSION. Essentially, therefore, the report spans two separate time periods – the time immediately *before* the study was undertaken (reported in the INTRODUCTION), and the time immediately *after* the study had been completed and the data analysed (dealt with in the DISCUSSION). The report therefore embodies progress because we essentially revisit the area, looking at the problems and issues addressed in the INTRODUCTION with the benefit of the new knowledge gleaned from the study's findings. It's a bit like one of those "before and after" adverts in which the advertiser is at pains to illustrate the contrast between circumstances prior to and after the use of the product. The INTRODUCTION is the equivalent of a *before* picture. The DISCUSSION is the equivalent of an *after* picture. You can see this process built into the sections of the research report summarized in Box 1.5.

It is now time for the INTRODUCTION you write to ape this function. Thus, at this stage in your career, you should be attempting in the first part of your INTRODUCTION to show how gaps left by previous work – such as flaws in the studies conducted, or simply questions and issues that have yet to be addressed – form the basis of the study you undertook. For it is your task to describe here the advance you propose to make – the gap in our knowledge that your study is designed to plug. At this stage, therefore, not only should you be starting to give a rather more detailed account of the previous work of relevance to your study, but you should also be looking to derive your study from this work. That is, you should aim to show how your study builds on the previous research.

 SAQ 9   How does the research report, in principle, "embody progress"?

This requirement has obvious implications for how you should conduct yourself at the *design* stage. Essentially, you will be ill advised to dream up and run your studies without first doing the background reading and thinking about how you will go about justifying your study in the INTRODUCTION. Remember that studies evolve from the time at which you start thinking about interesting research questions, to the time at which the first participant takes part in your study. Thinking about how your study fits into the existing literature is a critical part of this process. In particular, you should never find yourself having undertaken a study that flies in the face of existing findings without having sound arguments for doing so. For you will, of course, need to be able to make these arguments in your INTRODUCTION.

What this means in practice is that you must *do your preparatory reading* and design your study *in the light of what you find there!* Do not jump straight into your study, or you will run the risk of conducting something for which there is no theoretical justification and which, therefore, is going to be exceedingly difficult, if not impossible, to write up. Always bear in mind that your practical work does not begin and end with the study itself – it ends with the completion of your report. You will, therefore, have to be able to give an account of what you did that shows this to have been justified.

You should attempt to be both clear and concise when writing this part of the INTRODUCTION. Keep to the point. Discuss the most relevant previous work only. Do not attempt to write an exhaustive review of everything that has been done on the topic. Stick to the key features of the studies that you *do* cite – the most relevant findings and conclusions, and any methodological issues that you think are relevant.

Summary of Sections 2.1–2.2

1 The purpose of the INTRODUCTION is to put your study into its research context, by providing your reader with an introduction to the background material (existing findings and theoretical ideas) relevant to it.

2 This material is presented in the first part of the INTRODUCTION. The second part of the INTRODUCTION presents the reader with a brief description of your study.

3 Increasing emphasis is placed on the first part as you become more experienced and the reports that you write begin to emulate research papers.

2.3   Your own study

In the second part of the INTRODUCTION you turn – *for the first time* – to your own study. Here at last you are free to move away from talking about other people's work and are able to introduce your own. However, note that the emphasis is firmly on *introducing* your study. You will not be expected at this stage to give a detailed account of what you did; there is room enough elsewhere in your report for that. Here all that is required is a paragraph or two succinctly outlining the following features of your study:

1 Briefly state the problem that you chose to investigate. This should, of course, be clear from what you have written in the INTRODUCTION so far. Nevertheless, it is good policy to confirm the problem. Then neither you, nor your reader, should be confused over the issue that you tackled.

2 Give your reader a *general* idea of how you went about tackling it. There are always different ways to test the same issue. Here you need to describe in general terms the way that you actually chose to do it.

3 State clearly and accurately the predictions that you derive from the experimental hypothesis (or hypotheses) and clarify how your experiment tests these.

Please note that this is directed at all of you. Although I made exceptions in the first part of the INTRODUCTION for "inexperienced" students, *all* of you – regardless of level – should include the above material in the final part of your INTRODUCTION.

Do not be put off by this – it all sounds much more complicated than it is. You can, in fact, generally achieve it in one or two short paragraphs. Below is an illustration of the sort of approach that you can adopt. This is an extract from the introduction that we began earlier. To recap, the experiment examines whether varying how easy it is to construct mental images from words affects the usefulness of a mnemonic (an aid to memory). The three features described above are all in this example. The first paragraph brings the discussion leading up to it to the point and summarizes the issue in question (requirement 1). The opening sentences of the final paragraph give the reader the general idea of how the problem will be tackled (requirement 2). The final sentences spell out the predictions and their rationale (requirement 3):

> . . . However, as pointed out earlier, Earnshaw et al. (2007) found no evidence that the nature of the material affected their participants' ability to memorize lists of words using the method of loci. Yet, Earnshaw et al. did not allow their participants much time to become accustomed to using the mnemonic. It may be that their findings simply illustrate the need for practice before significant improvements in memory performance are revealed.
>
> Consequently, the current study replicates Earnshaw et al.'s (2007) study. This time, however, those in the mnemonic condition were allowed to practise the method of loci prior to the start of the experiment. If the method depends for its success upon the imageability of the material, then those using the mnemonic should recall more of the easily imaged words than do those not using the mnemonic. Those using the mnemonic should not, however, recall more of the hard-to-image words than do those not using the mnemonic.

Note that although the INTRODUCTION is in two parts, this is *not* indicated in the format of the section itself. That is, you *do not* separate the part in which you introduce your own study from the earlier part of the INTRODUCTION by things such as a separate title or by missing a line. Simply start a new paragraph.

No doubt some of you are still rather confused by all this. If so, don't worry – remember that good report writing is a skill.

Consequently, it takes time to develop. You should not be surprised, therefore, if at times you find yourself uncertain and confused about what is required of you. Just do your best to develop this skill by practising it – by writing reports and getting feedback on your efforts from your tutor. If you are really stuck, look for examples of how other people have solved the problems that confront you. So, if you have access to a university or college library or the Internet, look up some journal articles and see how their introductions have been ended.

At the beginning of this section I stated that the most important thing was for you to make a clear and accurate statement of the findings predicted from the experimental hypothesis. Here is how you go about this:

1 State the predictions clearly; mention in this statement both the independent and the dependent variables. For example, for an experiment to test whether eating cheese before going to sleep causes people to have nightmares (Section 9.1.2), the prediction would be that "those who eat the standard quantity of cheese 3 hours before going to bed will report more nightmares than those who do not consume cheese during this period", rather than "eating cheese will affect nightmares". Note, however, that you do not need to refer to these explicitly here as the independent and dependent variables. You do that in the DESIGN section of the METHOD.
2 State whether the prediction is nondirectional or directional (Section 9.1.4).
3 There is no need to mention here the predictions under the null hypothesis. You can take it for granted that your readers will assume that you are testing a null hypothesis that there is no reliable difference between the conditions in your experiment. You can therefore omit the predictions under this null hypothesis. At this stage of the report you need only mention what your predictions are under the theories discussed in your INTRODUCTION.

For example:

> The experimental hypothesis leads to the directional prediction that those eating the standard quantity of cheese 3 hours before going to bed will report more nightmares than those not eating cheese during this period.

However, your hypotheses must relate clearly to the issues that you addressed in the first part of your INTRODUCTION. That is, they should be linked to what has gone before. So do not, for example, suddenly spring upon your reader a set of experimental hypotheses *contradicting* the ideas you discussed in the first part of your INTRODUCTION. If you wish to disagree with existing arguments or findings in the literature, then include also arguments (ideally substantiated by *references*) in the first part of your INTRODUCTION outlining and *justifying* your own viewpoint. Similarly, do not set up hypotheses that bear no relation to what has gone before – remember that the INTRODUCTION is designed to set the scene for your study, and therefore principally functions to show how you arrived at your predictions. Similarly, never confuse predictions derived from the experimental hypothesis with those derived from the null hypothesis (see Appendix 1). Finally, you must not mention the *results* of the experiment in this section.

? **SAQ 10**   Why not?

? **SAQ 11**   What purpose does the INTRODUCTION serve?

Summary of Section 2.3

1 The second part of the INTRODUCTION outlines the purpose of your own study.

2 After confirming the specific problem you investigated, you need to clarify the way in which your study tackles this problem.

3 Finally, you should describe clearly the predictions that you derive from your experimental hypothesis or hypotheses.

3 The METHOD section

 Diagnostic questions on design for Chapter 3

Before reading this chapter, check that you can answer correctly the following diagnostic questions:

1 What is a *related* samples IV?

2 What is an *unrelated* samples IV?

3 What is a *mixed* design?

4 What is *random assignment* to conditions?

You can find the answers at the rear of the book (p. 273). If you had difficulties answering any of these questions, turn to the relevant sections of Part 2.

The next section in your report is the METHOD. This section is composed of a number of subsections. In these you talk about various aspects of the study that you conducted. The subsections are:

- DESIGN: here you talk about the formal design features of your study, using the appropriate terminology (e.g., for an experiment, things like the name of the design, what your independent and dependent variables were, and so on).

- PARTICIPANTS: here you describe the relevant features of the participants (those from whom you obtained scores on your dependent variables).
- APPARATUS, *or* MATERIALS, *or* APPARATUS AND MATERIALS: here you describe the equipment or materials that you used (or both).
- PROCEDURE: here you give a blow-by-blow account of precisely what you said and did to your participants in the study.

The METHOD, in the form of its various subsections, is designed to give your reader a coherent, clear and precise account of what you did in your study. In this part of the report, therefore, you describe who your participants were, what you said to them and got them to read, how you presented your materials to them, the sequence in which you did things, and so on. In fact, this section is rather like a recipe in a recipe book: the first three subsections (DESIGN, PARTICIPANTS, and APPARATUS/MATERIALS) correspond to the *ingredients* part; the final subsection (PROCEDURE), to the part in which you are told what to do with them.

The watchword of this particular section is *thoroughness*. Your aim should be to provide all the information necessary (and in the right subsections) for your reader to be able to repeat *precisely* what you did – to undertake what we call an exact or direct **replication** of your study.

Why? Well, other researchers might not only disagree with your conclusions – the inferences you draw from your findings – but also question your *findings*. They could argue that your findings were anomalous and that if the study were run again (i.e., were replicated), they would obtain different results. For this reason, you have to present the details of your study in such a way that anyone who thought this – who doubted the *reliability* of your findings – could test it for himself or herself by replicating your study.

This is an important argument. Findings that are not reliable – that are markedly different each time we conduct the same study – have no place in a science. The whole logic of experimental design – of manipulating one variable and looking for the effects of this on another (in order to determine cause–effect relationships) – relies on these relationships remaining constant. It is no good if the causal variables appear to change – that on Monday anxiety impairs memory, but by Thursday it does not. To construct an adequate science of psychology, we have to be able to build on our findings. We must be able to take certain findings as read (as "facts") after evidence has accumulated and use these as *assumptions* in our subsequent research and theorizing.

In other parts of your course you will find debates about whether this is actually achievable. However, that is beyond the scope of this book. Here I am only concerned to give you the skills necessary to design, report and evaluate experiments and other quantitative studies in psychology. Moreover, there are those who argue that more straight replicating work should be undertaken in psychology in order to discover how reliable our findings are. This is another good reason why you *must* be clear and thorough in the various subsections that make up the METHOD.

In this chapter, I describe in detail how to report experiments. Nevertheless, much of what I have to say is relevant to the METHOD of *any* quantitative study. You can find more about this in Section 3.7.

? SAQ 12   What is an exact replication of a study?

Summary

1 The METHOD is composed of a set of subsections: DESIGN, PARTICIP-ANTS, APPARATUS or MATERIALS, and PROCEDURE.

2 It is designed to give a clear and accurate statement of what you did in your study, so that other people can *replicate* it if they wish.

3.1   The DESIGN subsection

There are a variety of ways of going about experimenting in psychology – ways of ordering conditions, using participants, controlling for potentially confounding variables – and your experiment will require you to choose one particular way of putting your ideas into practice. The method you choose is known as the *design* of your experiment. The process by which you come to choose it is called *designing* experiments.

The DESIGN itself is generally one of the briefer subsections of the report. All you need to give here is a brief but formal statement of the principal features of the design you used. In describing the design you should use the terminology that has been developed over the years to enable us to talk accurately about features of experiments. In particular, you will need to state:

1 Which design you used (i.e., whether you used an unrelated samples, related samples, or a mixed design).

2 For *each* independent variable (IV), whether it was a related or unrelated samples IV, how many levels it had, and what these were.

3 What your dependent variable (DV) was and how it was measured, including the units in which participants' scores were measured. You should do this for all of the DVs in your experiment.

While we're on this topic, *please* make sure that you spell the terms correctly! I am surprised how often I get reports that refer to "dependant" and "independant" variables. Misspelling them in this way is unlikely to impress your marker and may well cost you marks. So, remember it is depen*dent* and indepen*dent*. Watch out for this – "dependant" is one of those misspellings that will not be picked up by a computer's spell-checker (see Section 8.7).

However, although students generally get the format of this sub-section right, they sometimes get confused over things like what their IV or DV was, or whether they used *unrelated* or *related* samples. So make sure that you understand these concepts, for you will be expected to write a proper DESIGN regardless of whether or not you played a part in designing the experiment yourself. (This applies to the remainder of the METHOD as well – to the PARTICIPANTS, APPARATUS or MATERIALS, and PROCEDURE.)

Again, as with the description of your study at the end of the INTRODUCTION, this can be done comparatively simply. Indeed, the DESIGN really amplifies and clarifies this earlier statement of the purpose of the experiment.

Here is an example of how this can be done:

Method

Design

The experiment had a two-way, mixed design. The related measures independent variable was the imageability of the words for recall, with two levels (easily imaged or hard to image). The unrelated measures independent variable was instruction in the use of the method of loci mnemonic: the experimental group received instruction and training in the use of the mnemonic, whereas the control group did not. This independent variable thus also had two levels (mnemonic or no mnemonic). The primary dependent variable was the number of words of each type correctly recalled by the participant after 10 minutes' delay. Misspellings counted as errors. Other dependent variables were the number of words correctly recalled during the pretest and, as a manipulation check, the ratings of the imageability of the words used (7-point scale).

Note that it must be clear which IVs used related samples, which used unrelated samples, and the number of levels on each IV. You can find more about how to label experimental designs in Chapter 13.

Keep the DESIGN relatively brief. It should rarely need to be much longer than the above example. If it is longer than this, then check that you are not including material that should appear elsewhere in the METHOD section. (This will usually be material that should go in the MATERIALS or PROCEDURE.)

 SAQ 13   What purpose does the DESIGN serve?

Summary of Section 3.1

1 The DESIGN is a brief subsection in which you make a clear and accurate statement of the principal features of your design.

2 It is a *formal* statement using technical terms to provide a precise description of the design that you employed, and what your IV and DVs were.

3.2   The PARTICIPANTS subsection

The second part of your METHOD is the PARTICIPANTS. Here you give a brief description of the critical features of the *sample* in your study. These are the people from whom you obtained your data. The term *participants* is potentially misleading, so be clear about what is required. Concern yourself *exclusively* here with those people who were recruited to your study to provide you with scores on the DV. Do *not* mention in the PARTICIPANTS subsection any other people who played a role in the study or the analysis of the data – the experimenter, people who helped you by coding questionnaires or videotapes, or **confederates** (those who took part in the experiment as actors).

There are two aspects of your sample that interest us: in general terms, who they were and, in an experiment, how they were distributed across conditions.

Who your participants were is of importance because this contributes to the *generalizability* of your findings – the extent to which we can extrapolate your findings to other groups of human beings. This issue concerns the *external* validity of your findings (Section 10.8).

The other issue – how your participants were distributed among your experimental groups – concerns the *internal* validity of your study (Section 10.9). We would want there to be no systematic differences between the participants in your groups, other than those introduced by your manipulation of the IV. For example, we do not want disproportionately more of those who are better at the experimental task to be in one or other of the conditions.

? SAQ 14   Why not?

For this reason, therefore, it is a good idea to present a breakdown of your participants by condition. Then your reader can satisfy himself or herself that this was the case.

As a general rule, therefore, you should describe your participants in terms of those variables that are likely to have an influence on the DV. In practice, however, most of you, most of the time will need only to describe them in terms of the characteristics generally reported in this subsection: sex, age, and occupation (or courses of study, if students). Where you need to give the racial/ethnic breakdown of your sample, you should avoid describing the participants in ways that they would find negative.

Do not include *procedural* details here (see Section 3.4).

Typically, then, your PARTICIPANTS subsection should include the following:

1 Describe the number of participants per condition, including a breakdown of the sexes. However, please avoid here the "mixed-sex" joke. That is, do not say that the participants were of "mixed sex". It will only prompt your tutor to make some kind of idiotic remark in a strenuous effort to be funny.
2 Mention the age *range*, together with *mean* or *mode*, of the overall sample (break down by condition if there is a lot of variation between the groups).
3 Give some idea of the overall range of occupations or, if using students, courses of study.
4 State the means of selection (e.g., randomly, in response to a questionnaire, etc.). Do not lie about this!
5 Mention any inducements (e.g., payment, course credit) used to encourage participation. If the participants were paid, say how much.

6 Describe in principle how the participants were assigned to conditions (i.e., randomly or not). Describe the precise way in which this was done either here or in the PROCEDURE. Do not lie about this either!

This can be done quite simply:

Participants
  Overall, there were 40 participants, 20 in each condition. There were 25 women, 13 in the mnemonic condition. The participants ranged in age from 18 to 28, with a mean age of 19.8 years ($SD = 3.2$). All participants were undergraduates at the University of Sheffield. The majority, 30, were reading for science degrees. However, none were students of psychology. Participants were a convenience sample recruited personally by the experimenters from University House, the Students Union and the Octagon Centre. None of them were acquaintances of the experimenters. Participants were allocated to conditions randomly.

 SAQ 15   What information does your reader require about the participants in your study? Why?

If you do a class experiment in which you split up into groups and take it in turns to be experimenter and participant, beware here. In all probability your experiment will be based on the whole class – in which case you should treat the *class* as a whole as your participants, rather than reporting the bit of the experiment that you carried out yourself. If in doubt, check this with your tutor.

Finally, when you run your own study, make sure that you remember to ask your participants for the information that you need to describe them adequately in this subsection. It is surprisingly easy to forget this when you are so focused on your manipulation of the IV and on collecting the DVs. If, however, you do forget to record something, do *not* estimate it. Come clean and report only what you *know*; we all make mistakes!

Summary of Section 3.2

1 In the PARTICIPANTS subsection you provide a brief description of the critical features of the sample that provided the data.

2 The purpose of this account is to tell your reader *who* your participants were and *how* they were distributed across your experimental conditions, so that s/he can assess both the *generalizability* of your findings and whether there were any *confounding variables* arising from the composition of the experimental groups.

3.3   The APPARATUS or MATERIALS subsection

Studies in psychology vary a great deal in the amount of equipment used. At one extreme we might simply use a pen and paper. At the other, we might find ourselves using expensive equipment to monitor participants' performances in specially equipped rooms with online control of stimulus presentation and data collection. Be it hi-tech or ever so humble, the place to describe the equipment used in your study is here.

The first thing to decide is whether you used materials *or* apparatus – for this will dictate the title you give this subsection. Unfortunately, the difference between them is pretty vague: essentially things like pencils and paper, playing cards, and so on, come under the rubric of **materials**, whereas bulkier items, such as computers, cameras, and audio equipment, would be called **apparatus**. However, you must decide which of these types of equipment you employed in your study, and label this subsection accordingly. You should only label it "Apparatus and Materials" if you are sure that you used *both* types of equipment. Do not ignore this issue. I still get subsections wrongly entitled "Apparatus and Materials" or even "Apparatus" when the student only reports materials.

One problem that you may face here is what to do about a questionnaire or scale that you employed in your study. Advice on what to do under these circumstances can be found in Section E of the book's Web site at **http://mcgraw-hill.co.uk/openup/harris/**

If you only used materials, then this subsection will probably be little more than a description of the items you used. Make sure, however, that you write this in coherent sentences. It must not just be a *list* of the items. Write as below:

Apparatus and Materials

A computer (Gates C5 with Pentagon 3 processor) was used to present the words on an 18-inch monitor mounted immediately in front of the participant. There were 50 words used in the main experiment. Half of these words came from Clark's (1971) list of easily imaged words (e.g., garage, desk); the remaining 25 words came from Clark's list of hard-to-image words (e.g., conscience, love).

There were 20 practice words. Of these practice words, 10 came from Clark's (1971) easily imaged list and 10 from Clark's hard-to-image list. These practice words also comprised the words used in the pretest. The experimental words were matched across conditions for length and frequency using Alston and Evans's (1975) norms. (See Table 1 for examples of the words in each category; a full list of the words used can be found in Appendix 1.) Participants recorded their responses on a piece of paper.

The manipulation check consisted of a list of all 50 words from the main experiment, randomly ordered, on a single sheet of paper. The instructions requested the participants to rate each item for "how easy it is to form a mental image of each of the words." Participants used a 7-point scale to make their ratings, anchored at 0 (*impossible to image*) and 6 (*extremely easy to image*).

Note that this subsection has been labelled "Apparatus and Materials" because the computer and monitor qualify as *apparatus*, whereas response sheets, pens, and so on, are *materials*.

Describe the apparatus *precisely*. For instance, you should mention not only that you used a computer or DVD player, but also state precisely which *make* and *model* of computer or DVD player you used (as with the fictitious computer above). If you have used visual stimuli in your study, provide here an illustration of each type of stimulus. Where you use apparatus, there is scope for expansion in this subsection, especially if the layout of the equipment is either complex or theoretically important. Under these circumstances, do not hesitate to include a good, clear diagram of the layout (call this a figure; see Section 8.4). Indeed, in general do not be afraid to use figures to illustrate in your report or essay writing in psychology – they can be very helpful to both you and your reader.

? SAQ 16   What is wrong with the following subsection?
Apparatus
Computer
DVD player
Microphone
Playing cards
Response buttons
Camera
Pens and paper

Perhaps the commonest mistake made in this easiest of subsections is to describe the *function* of the equipment – how it was used. Strictly speaking, such detail is *procedural*, and therefore belongs in the PROCEDURE. So, do not describe *how* the equipment (material or apparatus) was used here. Simply outline *what* was used and, if relevant, how it was linked together. That is, this subsection should really only describe the basic *nature* and *layout* of the equipment used.

Summary of Section 3.3

1 In the APPARATUS or MATERIALS subsection you describe the equipment used in your study.

2 You should describe this thoroughly, accurately, and clearly, using diagrams (call them figures; see Section 8.4) where these might clarify the picture.

3.4   The PROCEDURE subsection

The final part of your METHOD is the PROCEDURE. In many respects, this is one of the most difficult subsections of the report, because it requires you to learn a rather subtle distinction between procedure and other aspects of methodology. Perhaps the commonest mistake made here is to include material that should have appeared at the end of the INTRODUCTION. For in the PROCEDURE we do not concern ourselves with the broad strategy of the study. We are simply interested in what *precisely* happened to participants from the moment that they arrived to the moment they left. This subsection should provide a blow-by-blow account of what you said and did to a typical participant, in the order in which you did it.

Imagine that instead of being asked to give an account of a study, you are in fact writing about an episode of a soap opera you have produced. In order to produce this episode, you have to operate at a number of levels. The episode has to fit into the storyline that has been developed before. You should have established this in the INTRODUCTION, which is essentially a brief synopsis of the story so far (the existing research) for those who have missed previous episodes (your psychologically naive reader). You need equipment to record the episode and props, scenery and locations to provide the background to the action, or even to play a role in the events that take place. This you have described in the APPARATUS or MATERIALS subsection. Similarly, you need a list of the key characters who participated in the episode – these you have described in the PARTICIPANTS subsection. So far, therefore, so good. All of this material provides the necessary *background* to your own episode. However, you have yet to talk in anything other than the barest detail about the actual *events* that took place: the key interactions between the characters, the critical props, and the crucial pieces of dialogue. That is, you have yet to give the reader any idea of how, in practice, you realized the action first mentioned in the latter part of the INTRODUCTION and summarized in the DESIGN. It is the equivalent of this sort of material – the key points of the script – that should appear in the PROCEDURE.

In principle, you should be aiming to tell your readers everything they need to know in order to replicate your study exactly. So, *precision* and *thoroughness* are the watchwords here. Everything of relevance in your procedure should be mentioned in this subsection, therefore – it can be pedantic to the point of being tortuous. However, there are techniques that enable you to lessen the burden on your reader. For instance, you usually need only to describe the procedure in detail for one of your participants. With this done, you can generally outline where the procedure in the other conditions varied in fundamental respects from the one outlined. (There should be enough commonality between the procedures in your different conditions to enable you to do this – see below.) This, of course, is where the analogy with an episode of a soap opera breaks down. If anything, in an experiment you have a number of distinctive versions of the script to report – versions that are identical in all respects other than those involving your manipulation of the IV.

? **SAQ 17**   Why should these different versions of the script be identical in all respects other than those involving your manipulation of the IV?

Where you have lengthy instructions, you can usually record the gist of them here and refer to an appendix containing the full text. However, you should always report any *critical* features of your instructions (e.g., where the instructions manipulated the IV) **verbatim** here; that is, where this happens you should report *exactly* what you said, together with what you said differently to different participants, and use inverted commas to make it clear that you are quoting exactly what you said. If in doubt about whether to paraphrase or quote here, quote. (See Section 7.6 for when and how to use appendices.)

Errors that frequently occur in this subsection are failing to state clearly whether people took part in the study individually or in groups, and describing here (instead of in the RESULTS) how the data were scored and prepared for analysis. The PROCEDURE should end with the completion of the participant's input to the study (including follow-ups, if your study had these), not with an account of what you as investigator did with the scores you obtained. (If you need to report this anywhere, do so at the start of the RESULTS.)

Finally, given the importance of randomization to *true* experiments (Section 13.8), describe clearly in this subsection *how* the randomization was done. It is not enough to say, for example, that you "randomly allocated participants to conditions". You should provide enough information to persuade your reader to accept that the process was indeed *truly* random (see Appendix 2 for more about randomization).

Procedure

Participants took part in the experiment individually. From the outset they sat in a soundproofed experimental cubicle, facing the monitor on which the words were to appear. Throughout, a closed-circuit TV link was used to monitor the procedure and observe the participants. All written instructions appeared on the monitor. Participants read the instructions in their own time, using the mouse to move between screens of instructions. The opening instructions described the experiment as an examination of "our ability to recall lists of items". They described the equipment and its function and outlined the experimental procedure. Once participants had finished reading the opening instructions, the key points of the procedure were reiterated, and any remaining questions they had were answered. (See Appendix 2 for full instructions.)

The experimental session began once it was clear that the participant understood what s/he had to do and had no further questions. The pretest words were presented on the computer in a random sequence. The words appeared singly, on the monitor, centre-screen, with a 5-second interval between each word. Participants recalled immediately after the presentation of the final word. Following the recall period (2 minutes) participants were finally assigned to condition by the experimenter who discreetly opened a sealed envelope drawn from a box in an adjacent cubicle. (The box contained envelopes placed in a sequence determined by a colleague using random number tables.)

Those in the mnemonic condition read instructions on how to use the method of loci. These participants imagined a familiar room and practised placing mental images of the presented words in various parts of this room. The practice words appeared in a random sequence, presented in the same manner as the pretest. There were two sets of 10 practice items, with no item appearing more than once. Participants recalled immediately after the presentation of the final word in both lists.

At this stage, those in the no-mnemonic condition simply practised recalling these items. These were the same items, presented in the same manner as above. In all other respects the groups received identical instructions.

At the end of the recall period, participants used the mouse to bring up the next set of instructions. These told them that the experimental session proper was about to commence. Subsequently, the 50 experimental items appeared in a random order, displayed as in the pretest.

After displaying the final word for 5 seconds, the PC presented a series of simple addition and subtraction tasks. This continued for 3 minutes, after which a fresh screen of instructions asked participants to recall as many of the experimental words as they could, using the pen and paper provided. Participants continued until they felt unable to recall any more words, whereupon they undertook the manipulation check. After this, the experiment ended. A brief post-experimental interview was used to explore whether those in the no-mnemonic condition had employed mnemonics on their own initiative (particularly ones using mental imagery) and whether those in the mnemonic condition had actually used the recommended technique during the experimental session. When participants had no further questions, they were debriefed orally and also given a sheet describing the study's aims. Those wishing to receive details of the eventual findings were sent them on completion of the analyses.

3.5 Interacting with and instructing participants

As you can see, one of the most critical features of your experiment is the instructions that you give to participants – what you tell them about your study, how you tell them what to do, and so on. Consequently, an account of your instructions is a central feature of the PROCEDURE.

In the first place, your instructions should be the *only* verbal communication that takes place between you and the participant during the experimental session. Second, in some studies you may actually find yourself manipulating the IV via the instructions you give to participants in the different conditions. Even where you are not using the instructions to manipulate the IV, you may sometimes need to give slightly different instructions to those in the different conditions. At all times, however, it is important in an experiment that you make your instructions as *similar* as you can between conditions, and *identical* within conditions.

? **SAQ 18**   Why?

For reasons such as these, therefore, you should always use **standardized instructions**. That is, you should make the instructions as consistent as you can *between* conditions in *style*, *content*, and *delivery*, and there should be *no* variation in these elements in the same condition. Thus, if you choose to give the instructions orally, you must make sure that you do so in the same manner, and with the same inflections, to all participants – you must, in effect, become an actor delivering his or her lines. If you doubt your ability to do this, then it may be a good idea to record the instructions and to play this recording to your participants instead. Equally, you might print them out and give them to your participants to read. If you are using a computer as part of the experiment, then you could display them on the screen (allowing enough time for your participant to read them, of course). I find it is generally useful to use written instructions if I can but *always* to go over the gist of what is required of the participant once they have finished reading. (Often they take in less information when reading than they realize.)

Writing good instructions is, in fact, a highly developed skill. It is one that you will acquire as you go along. The instructions should be friendly and couched in language that your participants will understand. They should contain enough material for them to be able to perform the task you give them adequately, but often without at this stage giving too much away. For this reason it is important to give participants an opportunity to ask questions *before* the start of the study. Restrict yourself, however, to answering questions about the task that confronts them, rather than addressing the wider aims of the study – there should be time set aside to discuss those at the end. Make sure that you do all this *before* you start the study in earnest. Satisfy yourself that participants understand what is expected of them before you begin – you do not want interruptions, as this will destroy the control that you have built so carefully into the design of your experiment.

Once the study has started, you should attempt to keep uncontrolled contact to a minimum. Thus you should avoid unscripted vocal contact, as well as any form of non-verbal contact such as head nodding or shaking, that might influence the participant's performance. At this stage you should be *friendly*, but *uninformative*. Of course this will make for a rather bizarre and artificial encounter – but that is the name of this particular game. Moreover, it may not be easy. Not surprisingly, participants often attempt to subvert the order you have imposed by making remarks about their performance that invite your comment. You must resist this and remain non-committal if you wish to remain loyal to your experiment. However, it is worth thinking about the extent to which this feature of experimenting in psychology influences the data that we obtain. It is another aspect of experimental psychology that has come under criticism.

As well as instructions and demeanour, you should be prepared for your participants in other respects too. Once they are with you, you should be able to devote the greater part of your attention to dealing with them. Participants are valuable! So, you should prepare everything that you can *in advance* – response sheets, random sequences of orders, and so on – so that you are free to attend to your participants. Also, as I said before, do not forget to acquire the information that you will need to compile your PARTICIPANTS subsection (gender, age, occupation, and any other information that may be relevant to your particular study, such as right- or left-handedness, quality of eyesight, ability to read English, and so on).

Summary of Sections 3.4–3.5

1 In the PROCEDURE you give a blow-by-blow account of everything that you said and did to a typical participant in your study, so that those who wish to are able to replicate it *exactly*.

2 Make sure that you *standardize* the instructions, so that they are identical within a condition and as similar as possible in style, content and delivery *between* the different conditions in your experiment.

3.6   Optional additional subsections of the METHOD

Under some circumstances, you may need to add one or more subsections to your METHOD describing some additional features of your study.

3.6.1   Pilot test

If you have run a pilot test (Section 13.9.3), then you should report the details of it in the METHOD. In most cases you can do this simply, by inserting a subsection after the DESIGN called "Pilot test". Describe in this subsection the participants and any changes that you made to the study in the light of the pilot test. Sometimes, especially with questionnaire-based studies, the pilot is more extensive and involves developing measures for the eventual study. Advice on how to report under these circumstances can be found in Section E of the book's Web site at **http://mcgraw-hill.co.uk/openup/harris/**

3.6.2   Ethical issues

When we submit our research for publication we are obliged to declare to the editor of the journal that the research has received ethical clearance and has been conducted in accordance with relevant ethical principles. Hence it is rare to see a subsection covering ethical issues in published articles. In reports of your practical work, however, it may be useful to include a subsection outlining any ethical issues that your experiment raised and describing how you dealt with these. Ask your tutor for advice on whether you need such a subsection and what to put in it.

3.6.3   Statistical power

If you have never heard of this concept, ignore this section for now. If you have heard of statistical power, you may know that it is possible to calculate in advance how many participants you need to run to achieve a given level of power. If you did not do any such calculations before running your experiment, ignore this section for now.

So, congratulations, you did some power calculations before running your experiment! That is *excellent* design work. It is important to let your reader know that your chosen sample size was based on such calculations. Provide here the details of the key assumptions you made in your calculations or when using power tables or a power-calculator on the Internet (and cite the URL of the Web site you used). Make it clear whether your effect size estimates were guesses or based on previous research or theory. If you did the calculations yourself, put the calculations in a clearly labelled appendix.

Summary of Section 3.6

Where relevant, you may need to add one or more of the following to your METHOD:

1 A subsection describing a pilot test.

2 An explanation of how you dealt with any ethical problems you faced in your study.

3 An explanation of how you calculated power to determine your sample size before the experiment.

3.7 Writing a METHOD when your study is not an experiment

You can use the four subsections that I have described for the METHOD to provide a clear and accurate account of a wide range of studies, both experimental and non-experimental. So, apart from adding some of the subsections described in Section 3.6, most of you most of the time should find yourselves being able, with some thought, to fit your study into these subsections. Of course, how much you write in each section will vary with the type of study you ran. A study involving a long questionnaire will have a longer MATERIALS section than a laboratory study that had only one or two dependent variables; an elaborate laboratory study will have a longer PROCEDURE than a study using a questionnaire handed out before a lecture. Where your study is non-experimental – such as when you have conducted a survey or have measured rather than manipulated some variables (e.g., attitudes, perceived behavioural control) to predict some outcomes (e.g., intentions, behaviour) – what you put in the DESIGN statement will be quite different from when you are describing an experiment (see Section 13.8). Nevertheless, most of the time, the above subsections should be adequate for your reporting needs and what will vary from study to study will be the content and amount you put in each subsection. However, there may be some additional things you need to include in the METHOD, particularly where you have developed or are using scales to measure a variable or have used a lengthy questionnaire. To help you think about how best to report such studies you will find a section on the book's Web site describing some things to do and watch out for (Section E) at **http://mcgraw-hill.co.uk/openup/harris/.**

Summary of Section 3.7

1 You can write up most quantitative studies using the subsections described in this chapter.

2 What will vary from study to study will be the content and amount you put in each subsection.

4 The RESULTS section

 Diagnostic questions on statistics for Chapter 4

Before reading this chapter, check that you can answer correctly the following diagnostic questions:

1 What are *inferential* statistics?

2 What is a *statistically significant* difference?

3 What does it mean to say that the *5 percent significance level* was used in an analysis?

4 What is a *type I* error?

You can find the answers at the rear of the book (p. 274). If you had difficulties answering any of these questions, turn to Chapter 11.

Of all of the sections of the report, the RESULTS is probably the one you most frequently mishandle. Yet it really is one of the more straight-forward sections of the report. All you need to do in this section is to report the *findings* of your study in the most appropriate manner, resisting in the process any temptation to *interpret* them as you go along. That is, a bit like a journalist of the old school, you must distinguish rigidly between "fact" and "comment". In this section you must not go beyond stating what you *found* ("fact") to discussing what these findings appear to you to *mean* ("comment"). That debate takes place in the DISCUSSION.

With **quantitative** data – data in the form of numbers – there will generally be *two* aspects of your findings to report. First, you must provide a description of the key features of the data you obtained. You use *descriptive* statistics to do this. Second, you must give an account of the type and outcomes of the *inferential* statistical analyses you performed on these data. I will explain the difference between these two forms of statistics next.

Summary

1 Your principal goal in the RESULTS is to report the findings of your study clearly and accurately.

2 Separate fact from comment. In the RESULTS, restrict yourself to stating what you found. Determining how best to interpret these findings takes place in the DISCUSSION.

3 Report both the descriptive statistics and the type and outcomes of the inferential statistics that you used.

4.1   Describing the data: descriptive statistics

If you reported *all* the data from your study – all the numbers you collected – it would be quite difficult for your reader to interpret what the scores of your participants had to say. Very few people are capable of grasping the essential message of a set of data from looking at the raw scores (the actual numbers you gathered from the participants themselves). We therefore need a way of conveniently and simply summarizing the main features of a set of data. **Descriptive statistics** are a way of doing this. These are statistics that describe the key characteristics of a body of data. They enable us to efficiently assess things like whether the scores of our participants tend to be similar to each or whether they vary quite a bit (measures of **variation**, such as the standard deviation or range). Likewise, we can see what score best typifies the data as a whole, or the performance of participants in each condition (measures of **central tendency**, such as the mean, median or mode). Measures like these help us to make sense of our data and of the outcomes of our inferential statistical analyses.

Table 4.1
Scores from an Experiment with One Control and One Experimental Condition

Control	Experimental
17.3	6.8
39.2	14.1
20.7	61.2
79.3	61.7
81.5	14.0
24.7	75.9
55.0	32.3
73.6	22.0
33.0	53.1
5.4	83.2
18.6	7.8
42.7	94.8
56.5	49.7
24.9	37.2
57.9	23.9

For instance, imagine that we ran an experiment and obtained the numbers in Table 4.1. In this form it is difficult to make much sense of the data. It is not easy to tell much about the comparative performance of the participants in the two groups. The scores appear to vary quite a bit from individual to individual, but is the *overall* performance of the participants in the two groups all that different? This is, of course, the question we wish to answer.

In Table 4.2, the same data are expressed in terms of two *descriptive* statistics. There is a measure of *central tendency* (in this case the

Table 4.2
The Same Data as in Table 4.1, Expressed in Terms of Two Descriptive Statistics

	Control	Experimental
M	42.0	42.5
SD	24.2	28.5

Note. M = mean; *SD* = standard deviation; *n* = 15 in each condition.

mean, which tells us the average performance in each group) and a measure of *dispersion* (in this case the **standard deviation**, which tells us about the extent to which the scores within each group vary).

Now our task is much easier. From Table 4.2 we can see, perhaps to our surprise, that the typical performance in the two groups is quite similar. In contrast, the scores of the participants *within* the two conditions vary quite a bit (the standard deviations in the two groups are high, given the mean scores). Looking at this table it would be surprising indeed if we were to find a statistically significant difference between our two groups. (If we did, we would probably want to check the analysis.)

The numbers in Table 4.1 are what we call in the trade *raw* scores. As the name implies, **raw scores** are the unprocessed scores that you obtain from your participants. Because of the difficulties inherent in grasping the essential features of raw data, we tend *not* to put such data in the RESULTS. Instead, we present an account of the principal features of the data in the form of descriptive statistics. Such material we usually display in a suitably formatted, appropriately labelled, and informatively titled *table* – like those used in the example RESULTS in this chapter.

Typically, such **tables** should contain an appropriate measure of central tendency, a measure of dispersion, an indication of the numbers of participants per condition and, once you are familiar with them, relevant confidence intervals. Occasionally you may need more than this, but generally you will not. So, just because your statistical software package pumps out every descriptive statistic under the sun, do not dump it all down into the RESULTS. Also, when reporting your descriptive statistics in tables or text, *use two decimal places* at most. Psychological measures are imprecise and do not need the false precision of lots of decimal places, whatever gets splurged out by your statistical package. Where your data are in the form of frequencies and there is only one observation per participant (as for example when you have used chi-square to analyse your data) then your table will consist of the counts in each category (as in Table 1 in Section 4.3).

Generally speaking, therefore, there will usually be at least *one* table in your RESULTS; you can find more about how to lay out your tables and how to strike the balance between tables and text in Section 8.4. However, sometimes it is still not possible to fully grasp the main features of a set of data from even a table of descriptive statistics. If you wish to enhance your reader's understanding of the data, therefore, you might go one step further and *graph* it – especially as many of those who go blank at the sight of numbers have little problem in grasping the message of a well-designed graph. Be warned, however; there are some pitfalls. Advice on the use of graphs can be found in Section 8.5.

Do not be afraid, therefore, to deploy the techniques at your disposal to aid your reader's (not to mention your own) understanding of the basic features of your data. However, do not go overboard here. This aspect of your findings is typically less interesting than the outcomes of your *inferential* statistical analyses. Think of the descriptive statistics as preparing the ground for the reporting of the inferential analyses.

Summary of Section 4.1

1 In the opening paragraph of the RESULTS reiterate briefly what data you gathered from your participants (e.g., response times, number of items recalled, number of people reporting nightmares). That is, remind your reader what the DV is (or principal DVs are if you have more than one). This both sets the scene and ensures that the reader does not have to look back at your METHOD to understand your results.

2 In general, you should not include the raw data in this section. Instead, provide a potted account of your data in the form of descriptive statistics. These should generally be presented in tables.

3 Report descriptive statistics to no more than two decimal places.

4 Feel free to graph the data as well if you feel that this will help the reader to understand the findings better. However, read Section 8.5 first.

4.2   Analysing the data: inferential statistics

After drawing attention to the descriptive statistics, tell your reader what analyses you ran on these data and the results of these analyses. These analyses involve the *inferential* statistics, such as *chi-square*, *t tests*, and *analysis of variance* (ANOVA), that you have grown to know and love. This is the part of the RESULTS that gives some of you sleepless nights. Yet, it need not be as daunting as you think. The key point is to tell your reader *clearly* and *accurately* (a) how you analysed the data; (b) what the outcome of the analysis was; and (c) what this result tells us. There are clear rules to guide you in this. These are:

1 State clearly *in what way* you analysed the data, i.e., which inferential statistical test you used. Describe this test precisely. Do not, for example, say that a "*t* test" was used. Instead, state which *type* of *t* test – for example, a "related *t* test". If you are using ANOVA, make sure you state accurately which type you used (see Section 4.6.10)

2 State the significance level that you used and (where appropriate) whether your test was one- or two-tailed.
3 State the precise value that you *obtained* for the statistic (i.e., the value printed in your output or that you calculated by hand). For example, the value of *F* or *t*. However, do this to no more than two decimal places. (Do not slavishly copy out all of the digits to the right of the decimal point on your statistical output, as this looks *very* amateurish.)
4 Provide the additional information your reader needs to look up the relevant *critical* value of your statistic should s/he want. These are usually the *degrees of freedom* or the *numbers of participants* or *observations*. Note that you are expected to provide this information, even though most of the time your statistical software package will give you an exact probability associated with your obtained statistic. (See Appendix 3 for more about critical values.) To ensure you get this right, follow the relevant examples in Section 4.6 of this chapter and on the book's Web site.
5 Wherever you can, report the *exact* probability associated with your obtained statistic regardless of whether the outcome is statistically significant or not. Do this to no more than three decimal places (e.g., $p = .002$). Where your output prints $p = .000$ or it is not possible to report the exact probability for other reasons, see Appendix 3 for what to do.
6 State whether the obtained value was statistically significant or not.
7 State explicitly what this result tells us about the data. That is, relate the outcome of your inferential statistic back to the relevant descriptive statistics.
8 Make sure, however, that you distinguish between what you have found and what you believe it means (your inferences and conclusions about your findings). In the RESULTS restrict yourself to describing the findings. Save discussion of how best to interpret these findings until the DISCUSSION.

This sounds like a lot, but in fact the above information can be conveyed surprisingly succinctly. For example: "Participants using the semantically related items were significantly quicker to reach the criterion than those using the semantically unrelated items, $t(42) = 2.23$, $p = .025$ (two-tailed test)", or "The effect of reinforced practice upon the time taken to reach criterion was not statistically significant, $t(40) = 1.30$, $p = .20$ (two-tailed test)." How to do this for some of the statistics that you are likely to use when you first start writing reports can be found in Section 4.6 of this chapter and on the book's Web site.

4.3   An example RESULTS section

Here is an example of how a basic RESULTS governed by these conventions might look. In this case, the data are frequencies and there is only one observation per participant, so the table of data contains counts, rather than measures of central tendency and dispersion.

Results

The number of participants reporting nightmares in each condition of the experiment is shown in Table 1. The data were analysed using chi-square and an alpha level of .05.

There was a statistically significant association between the consumption of cheese and the incidence of nightmares, $\chi^2(1, N = 100) = 4.89$, $p = .027$. Participants eating cheese three hours before going to bed reported a higher proportion of nightmares than did participants not eating cheese in that period.

In the post-experimental interviews, after prompting, eight participants were able to describe the experimental hypothesis in full or in part. Of these, five were in the cheese condition (of whom one reported a nightmare). Of the three in the no cheese condition, one reported a nightmare.

Table 1

The Number of Participants Reporting Nightmares and not Reporting Nightmares in the Two Conditions

	Nightmare	
Condition	Yes	No
Cheese	33	17
No cheese	22	28

On the design front, note the use here of post-experimental interviews (Section 13.9.4) to investigate the extent to which participants reported awareness of the experimental hypotheses. These are useful things to include, as you will see when we come to the DISCUSSION of this experiment.

If you have more than one set of data and attendant analyses to report, it may be necessary to include separate tables for the different data. If so, consider the data *and* their attendant analyses as two sides of the same coin. So report them as a unit, by describing the data first and then detailing the outcomes of the analyses *before* moving on to the next data/analysis set. Make sure that you work through these in order of importance, starting with the data and analyses that are central to testing the main predictions of the study and working through to material that is illuminating but essentially ancillary.

This, then, is the basic material that you should report in the RESULTS. You should aim at all times for *clarity* and *accuracy* – you must give your reader a clear idea of the type of data you gathered, describe its main features using descriptive statistics, and report appropriately the nature and outcomes of your inferential statistical analyses. Moreover, it should be clear to your reader at any given point *which* data you are talking about and *which* inferential analysis relates to that set of data, especially if you have used more than one DV or wish to test more than one set of predictions. You should also make sure that you provide enough information in this section (e.g., in labelling the conditions) for the reader to be able to make sense of your data *without* having to turn to other parts of the report for clarification.

? SAQ 19 Why should you provide your reader with a clear idea of the type of data you gathered, its main features and the nature and outcomes of the inferential statistics that you used?

? SAQ 20 If you were to come across the following in the RESULTS section of a research report, what criticisms would you have?

The data were analysed using Analysis of Variance. The results were statistically significant.

4.4 Nine tips to help you avoid common mistakes in your RESULTS section

 Here are nine tips to help you avoid some of the commoner mistakes made in this section:

1 The RESULTS should never be just a collection of tables, statistics and figures. This section must *always* have useful and informative text. To learn more about how to strike the balance between tables and text, see Section 8.4.

2 Include enough information in this section for your reader to be able to make sense of the results without having to look elsewhere in the report. For example, take care to label conditions or groups meaningfully in tables, figures and text. Avoid using **ambiguous terms** such as "Condition 1" or "Group A". You should not use meaningless or difficult-to-decipher abbreviations *anywhere* in the report (see Section 8.2).

3 It is important to look at your data and the descriptive statistics before you analyse the data inferentially (Section 13.9.5). However, do not **eyeball the data** by writing that there are "differences" between conditions, or that some means are "higher" or "smaller" than are others, *before* you have reported the outcome of the relevant inferential analysis. This is because these numerical differences may not turn out to be statistically significant and the convention in psychology is to talk about differences between conditions *only* if these have been shown to be statistically significant. For example, it is possible to describe the mean score for the experimental condition in Table 4.2 as higher than that for the control condition. However, this difference is extremely unlikely to be statistically significant. It would be misleading to talk about the data in this way and it is unnecessary to do so. Talk about differences only *after* you have reported the inferential analysis.

4 Once you have reported the outcome of your inferential statistic, you are free to comment on the presence or absence of differences among your conditions. This is no longer eyeballing the data, as now you know whether the sample differences are statistically significant or not. If you only have two conditions you can go even further and describe which condition was higher, better, faster (or whatever the DV measured) than the other. However, be careful here. One of the commonest and *most damaging* failings is to talk

about differences between conditions even though these have failed to achieve statistical significance. The purpose of testing for statistical significance is to help us to decide whether to treat the means in different conditions as equivalent or as different. If your analyses tell you that you should not reject the null hypothesis, then act on that basis and assume that there are no reliable differences between the relevant conditions. If you write about differences when the analysis has not been statistically significant, you are simply ignoring the analysis! Your marker may assume that this is because you do not understand what the analysis means.

5 You do not need to give the underlying details of the inferential statistical procedure (e.g., the rationale and workings of the *t* test) or reasoning (e.g., the principles of statistical significance testing) in this section. (Unless your tutor tells you explicitly to include such material.) One of the apparent paradoxes of the practical report is that whereas you must assume that your reader lacks knowledge of the topic that you are investigating, you *may* assume that s/he has a basic grasp of statistics and of the principles of significance testing.

6 Include sufficient information in this section to enable your reader to reach his or her own conclusions about the implications of your data. Your reader should be able to disagree with your interpretation of the data purely on the basis of the information you provide here.

7 Do not *duplicate* analyses. For example, do not report *both* a parametric test *and* its nonparametric equivalent (Section 11.4). Decide which is more appropriate for your data and report the outcomes of the one you choose.

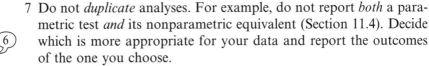

8 Include *all* of the data in this section that you wish to comment upon in the DISCUSSION, however impressionistic, **qualitative** (i.e., not involving numbers) and unamenable to statistical analysis. The inclusion of qualitative data, such as a selection of comments from your participants, can be very useful. However, in *experiments* such data should always be used as a *supplement* to the quantitative, numerical data.

9 Do not necessarily restrict yourself to reporting the obvious analyses – do not be afraid to squeeze all the relevant information from your data that you wish. Bear in mind, however, that your aim is to *communicate* your findings. So avoid overloading this section with irrelevant and unnecessary analyses (see Section 4.2). Nevertheless, there may be some way in which additional analyses of your data

can help you to clarify or choose between alternative explanations or to resolve other issues of interpretation. So, think about ways in which further analyses might be useful.

4.5   Rejecting or not rejecting the null hypothesis

Rejecting the null hypothesis entails that you accept the alternative hypothesis; this does not mean, however, that you can conclude that the psychological hypothesis underlying your study has been supported. After rejecting the null hypothesis you have, in fact, to search for the most reasonable explanation of your findings. This may well turn out to be the arguments you summarized in the INTRODUCTION, but need not be. You can only decide this after a suitable discussion in which you consider and examine closely *all* the plausible explanations of your findings. In an experiment, high on the list of issues to examine will be whether you exercised sufficient *control* to enable you to make unequivocal inferences. This is why we require the next section – the DISCUSSION.

Of course, discussion is also needed for studies in which you have *failed* to reject the null hypothesis. Under these circumstances you also have to work out what this means psychologically, as opposed to statistically. As well as examining the adequacy of the control that you exercised in an experiment another thing to consider when you have *failed* to reject the null hypothesis is whether you had enough participants (see Chapter 12).

Where your study is not experimental, you will still need to do these things – to assess rival explanations for your findings and search for the most plausible interpretation. Moreover, given that the level of control you will have been able to exercise is lower than in an experiment, it will be harder to rule out alternative explanations (see Section 5.8).

Summary of Section 4.5

1 Once you have determined whether you have to reject or not reject the null hypothesis, you begin the search for the most reasonable explanation of the findings.

2 This process takes place in the DISCUSSION.

4.6   Reporting specific statistics

Knowing what to report can be bewildering. Even when you have chosen the correct analysis and run it properly, it can be hard to detect the bits that you need to extract from the output to report in the RESULTS. This is especially so when you are a novice, but it can be bewildering even when you are more experienced. So, do not feel alone with this problem. Do *not* under any circumstances, however, cope with it simply by copying over the output from a statistical analysis package, perhaps annotating it by hand, and leaving it at that. I am amazed how often I get grubby bits of second-rate printout stapled into the report, sometimes with no supportive text, often with bits of scribble by way of annotation of the output, and am supposed to be prepared to treat that as if it were a RESULTS! In such circumstances I simply assume that the student is unable to detect the bits of the output s/he needs, cannot be bothered to do the hard work of locating the correct material and laying it out properly and neatly, and assumes that I am too stupid to realize this. As you can imagine, this does not go down well and the mark is not impressive.

The main thing, especially early on in your career, is to demonstrate to your marker that you realize what needs to be reported. The basic rule when reporting inferential statistics is that you need to provide the information that will enable someone else to check whether the outcome of a test is or is not statistically significant.

The rest of this chapter contains examples of how to report those specific statistics that you are most likely to use in the first year or so of report writing. More information about each of these statistics, together with some of the issues to watch out for when using them, can be found in Section B of the book's Web site at **http://mcgraw-hill.co.uk/openup/harris/**. The Web site also provides examples of how to report other statistics that you may meet later on in your career as a student of psychology. Before using this section or the Web site you should also be familiar with the issues involved in choosing tests. (These are discussed in Section 11.4 and Section A of the book's Web site.) Please note that, with the exception of the example results for the mnemonic experiment, the tables and figures referred to in these examples do not actually exist!

When reporting, punctuation and the use of italic are important, so pay attention to this when preparing your text. The sequencing is usually also important, as are such seemingly trivial details as whether there is a space between p and $=$ and even whether you put $p = .025$ or $p = 0.025$. This section is a joy for the anally retentive among us; for the rest, it can be a trial.

4.6.1 Chi-square, χ^2

The information you need to provide to enable someone to check the significance of your obtained value of χ^2 is the *degrees of freedom*. You should also report the total number of observations. This example has 1 degree of freedom and is based on 100 observations.

> An alpha level of .05 was used. Analysis of the data in Table 1 using chi-square revealed that breaking the speed limit was significantly associated with gender, $\chi^2(1, N = 100) = 10.83$, $p = .001$. Males tended to break the speed limit whereas females tended not to break the speed limit.

4.6.2 Spearman rank correlation coefficient (rho), r_s

The information you need to provide to enable someone to check r_s is the *number of participants*. This example has 40 participants:

> An alpha level of .05 was used. Analysis of the data displayed in the scatter plot in Figure 1 using Spearman's rho (corrected for ties) indicated that ratings of mood were significantly positively correlated with the mean ratings of the attractiveness of the photographs, $r_s(40) = .48$, $p = .002$ (two-tailed test). The ratings were thus moderately correlated, with more positive mood tending to be associated with higher ratings of attractiveness.

4.6.3 Pearson's product moment correlation coefficient, r

The information you need to provide to enable someone to check r is generally the *degrees of freedom*, given by the N of observations minus 2. In this example, there are 40 participants, so there are 38 degrees of freedom:

> An alpha level of .05 was used. Analysis of the data displayed in the scatter plot in Figure 1 using Pearson's r indicated that age was

significantly negatively correlated with the mean ratings of the attractiveness of the photographs, $r(38) = -.37$, $p = .02$ (two-tailed test). The variables were thus moderately correlated, with increases in age tending to be associated with decreases in the ratings of attractiveness.

4.6.4 Mann-Whitney U test, *U*

The information you need to provide to enable someone to check *U* is the *number of participants in group 1* and the *number of participants in group 2*. This example has 14 and 16 respectively in these groups:

> An alpha level of .05 was used. Analysis of the data in Table 1 using the Mann-Whitney U test indicated that ratings of overall satisfaction with the tutor's teaching were significantly higher among those receiving the positive comment than among those not receiving this comment, $U(14, 16) = 56$, $p = .02$ (two-tailed test).

4.6.5 Wilcoxon's Matched-Pairs Signed-Ranks Test, *T*

The information you need to provide to enable someone to check *T* is the *number of participants overall, not counting those with tied ranks* (i.e., not counting those with the same scores in each condition). This example has 18 participants without such tied ranks:

> An alpha level of .05 was used. Analysis of the data in Table 1 using the Wilcoxon test indicated that participants rated their own chances of experiencing the diseases overall as significantly lower than they did the chances of the average student, $T(18) = 27$, $p = .01$ (two-tailed test). (Six participants had tied ranks.)

4.6.6 Kruskal-Wallis one-way analysis of variance, *H*

The information you generally need to provide to enable someone to check *H* is the *degrees of freedom*, given by the *N* of groups minus 1. In this example there are 3 groups and therefore 2 degrees of freedom:

> An alpha level of .05 was used. Analysis of the data in Table 1 using the Kruskal-Wallis one-way analysis of variance indicated that

the ratings of overall satisfaction with the tutor's teaching were significantly different among the three groups, $H(2) = 7.38$, $p. = 025$.

4.6.7 Friedman's ANOVA, χ_r^2

The information you generally need to provide to enable someone to check χ_r^2 is the *degrees of freedom* given by the N of groups minus 1. In this example, there are 3 groups and therefore 2 degrees of freedom:

> An alpha level of .05 was used. Analysis of the data in Table 1 using Friedman's ANOVA indicated that ratings of the chances of experiencing the diseases were significantly different for the three targets (self, best friend and average student), $\chi_r^2(2) = 9.21$, $p = .01$.

4.6.8 The independent t test, t

The information you need to provide to enable someone to check t is the *degrees of freedom*. For the independent t test the degrees of freedom are given by the N of observations minus 2. This example has 15 participants in each condition and therefore 28 degrees of freedom:

> An alpha level of .05 was used. Analysis of the data in Table 1 using the independent t test for equal variances indicated that performance in the end-of-course examination was significantly higher among those receiving the positive comment than among those not receiving this comment, $t(28) = 2.70$, $p = .01$ (two-tailed test).

4.6.9 The related t test, t

For the related t test, the degrees of freedom are given by the N of observations minus 1. This example has 15 participants and therefore 14 degrees of freedom:

> An alpha level of .05 was used. Analysis of the data in Table 1 using the related t test indicated that performance in the end-of-course examination was significantly higher for the course in which participants received the positive comment than for the course in which they did not receive this comment, $t(14) = 2.49$, $p = .03$ (two-tailed test).

4.6.10 Analysis of variance (ANOVA), *F*

The information you need to provide to enable someone to check *F* is the *two* (NB *two*) *sets of degrees of freedom*: the degrees of freedom for the numerator of the *F* ratio *and* the degrees of freedom for the denominator of the *F* ratio. The numerator is the source under test, such as the main effect of an IV or the interaction between two or more IVs. (See Chapter 12 for a discussion of main effects and interactions.) The denominator is the bit that divides into the numerator and is also called the *error term*.

To illustrate how to go about reporting ANOVAs, here is an example RESULTS for the mnemonic experiment. This is a more advanced RESULTS than the earlier example. It is the kind of RESULTS that you will be expected to write as you become more experienced. If you have difficulty understanding any of the terminology in this, then do not hesitate to turn to Chapter 12 and your textbook of statistics for clarification.

Results

An alpha level of .05 was used for all statistical tests. The pretest data were analysed using one-way analysis of variance (ANOVA) for unrelated samples with condition (mnemonic or no mnemonic) as the independent variable. This analysis was not statistically significant, $F(1, 38) = 0.33$, $p = .57$, indicating that performance was equivalent in the two conditions (mnemonic group, $M = 10.95$ words recalled, $SD = 1.05$; no-mnemonic group, $M = 11.15$ words recalled, $SD = 1.14$). The groups thus appear to have had equivalent recall abilities for lists of words before the experimental group was taught the mnemonic.

The manipulation check on the imageability of the words used in the experiment was also satisfactory. Analysis of participants' ratings of the imageability of these words used one-way ANOVA for related samples with imageability (easily imaged or hard to image) as the independent variable. This revealed significantly higher ratings for the easily imaged words ($M = 5.21$, $SD = .77$) than for the hard-to-image words ($M = 3.39$, $SD = .95$), $F(1, 38) = 151.72$, $p < .001$.

The mean numbers of words of each type correctly recalled by those in the two conditions (excluding misspellings) are given in Table 2.

The data in Table 2 were analysed using 2 x 2 ANOVA for mixed designs, with imageability (easily imaged or hard to image) as the related samples variable and instruction (mnemonic or no mnemonic) as the unrelated samples variable. There was a statistically significant main effect of instruction, $F(1, 38) = 7.20$, $p = .01$, with those in the

Table 2

The Mean Number of Words from the Easily Imaged and The Hard-to-Image Lists Correctly Recalled in Each Condition

		Imageability	
Instruction	*n*	Easily imaged	Hard to image
Mnemonic	20		
M		18.15	13.15
SD		3.79	4.17
95% confidence interval		16.38–19.92	11.20–15.10
No mnemonic	20		
M		13.80	11.00
SD		3.25	4.62
95% confidence interval		12.28–15.32	8.84–13.16

Note. M = mean; *SD* = standard deviation.

mnemonic group recalling more items overall than did those in the no-mnemonic group (*M* = 15.65, *SD* = 3.97; *M* = 12.40, *SD* = 3.74, respectively). There was also a statistically significant main effect of imageability, $F(1, 38) = 145.22$, $p < .001$, with more items from the easily imaged list being recalled than from the hard-to-image list (*M* = 15.98, *SD* = 4.12; *M* = 12.08, *SD* = 4.48, respectively). However,

Figure 1. Mean number of easily imaged and hard-to-image words correctly recalled in each condition.

these main effects were qualified by the significant Instruction X Imageability interaction, $F(1, 38) = 11.55$, $p = .002$. Figure 1 shows this interaction.

Inspection of Figure 1 suggests that the significant interaction results from the greater number of easily imaged items recalled by the mnemonic group than by the no mnemonic group (difference = 4.35) relative to the smaller difference between the conditions in recall of the hard-to-image items (difference = 2.15). This is consistent with the experimental hypothesis. However, further analysis is required to confirm this statistically.

The majority of participants (18) in the no mnemonic condition claimed to have attempted to remember the items by rote repetition, with the remainder employing simple attempts at organizing the material into semantically related clusters. All those in the mnemonic condition reported using the method of loci, and most of these expressed their surprise at the impact that this appeared to have had on their ability to recall.

Note the use in this example of the abbreviation *M* to stand for *mean* and *SD* for *standard deviation* when reporting these descriptive statistics in text. On the design front, note the use of a pre-test to check that the groups were equivalent before being exposed to the IV and of a manipulation check to confirm that the easily imaged and hard-to-image words did differ in reported imageability. You will see the advantage of these features when we come to the DISCUSSION of this experiment (Section 5.7.2).

4.6.11 Four tips to help you avoid common mistakes when reporting ANOVA

Here are four tips to help you avoid some of the commoner mistakes students make when reporting ANOVA.

1 *Make sure that you indicate precisely which type of ANOVA you used.* The term ANOVA refers to a family of tests, not a single test. You will use different variants of ANOVA for different designs. For this reason it is important to specify *which* particular version of ANOVA you used. This is not hard: you can simply use the labelling convention that you employed in the DESIGN. For example, you can say that you analysed the data "using ANOVA

for two-way, mixed designs". Alternatively, you could say that you analysed the data "using ANOVA for a 2 × 2 mixed design". (See Section 13.3 for more on how to label designs.)

2 *Make sure that you indicate the number of levels on each IV.* Whichever way you label the design, make sure that you specify which IVs had which number of levels and what these levels were; with mixed designs, do not forget to specify which of the IVs used related samples and which used unrelated samples.

3 *Make sure that you report both sets of degrees of freedom for each F ratio.* This is an extremely common mistake and one that is both very damaging and yet easy to avoid. Remember that *every* value of *F* that you report has *two* sets of degrees of freedom. One set of degrees of freedom belongs to the *numerator* of the *F* ratio, the other set belongs to the *denominator* of the *F* ratio. Learn to identify each from your output and make sure that you include both.

4 *Do not copy over the entire ANOVA summary table and hope for the best!* This is no solution. You have to identify in text the various sources that you are testing with your ANOVA and the precise value of *F* and associated degrees of freedom in each case. In fact, researchers tend not to put ANOVA summary tables in RESULTS sections unless there are a lot of effects to report. When they do include ANOVA summary tables, they report only certain parts of the output. You can find more about this in Section B of the book's Web site at **http://mcgraw-hill.co.uk/openup/harris/**

4.6.12 Linear regression

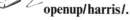 Linear regression techniques are a family of flexible and useful analytical tools based on correlation. You can find more both about regression and how to write up studies using regression in Section B of the Web site that accompanies this book at: **http://mcgraw-hill.co.uk/openup/harris/.**

In linear regression, we extend the analysis of correlation by treating one or more of the variables as predictors and one of the variables as an outcome or predicted variable. This has many advantages, but if you have used regression you should watch out in your DISCUSSION for one major disadvantage – the terminology of prediction makes it very easy to forget that you are usually dealing with correlational data. This can be exacerbated by the tendency in statistics packages and some statistics textbooks to refer to the predictor variables as IVs and the outcome variable as the DV. This is why some researchers have suggested we should use more neutral terms (see Section 13.8 for more on this). Remember, you cannot infer that the predictor *causes* any significant changes in the outcome variable unless the predictor has been experimentally manipulated (and only then after assessing the level of control in the experiment – see Chapter 5). For most of you, most of the time, when you use linear regression this will *not* be the case and you will need to be careful not to infer causality from your data.

In simple linear regression we have one predictor and one outcome variable. In multiple linear regression we have more than one predictor variable. A good set of predictors for multiple linear regression will be strongly correlated with the outcome variable but not with each other.

Linear regression tells us about the extent to which we can describe the relationship between two variables, a predictor variable and an outcome variable, using a straight line. Regression analysis provides information about how much the outcome variable changes with every unit change in the predictor variable (i.e., the *slope* of the line). This can be really useful. Regression provides two statistics to describe this:

B describes this relationship using the original units. It shows how much the outcome variable changes in whatever units it was measured for every 1 unit change in the predictor variable (in whatever units that was measured). So, for example, $B = +0.50$ between a rating of attitude (predictor) and a rating of intention (outcome) shows that for every 1 point increase in the rating of attitude, intention goes up half (.50) a rating on the intentions scale.

β (pronounced "beta") describes exactly the same relationship, but translated into a standard score rather than using the original units of measurement. It tells us how many standard deviations the outcome variable changes for 1 standard deviation change in the predictor variable. This sounds esoteric, but is actually not that hard to understand and it is really useful as it means we can compare the effects of different predictors, even though they may have different units of measurement.

Simple linear regression

Statistical packages will provide you with a range of statistics following a regression analysis. As well as *B* and β, you should find a *t* value that tests whether the slope of the line differs significantly from zero and also the correlation coefficient, Pearson's *r,* which provides information about the strength and direction of the linear relation-ship between the two variables (see Section 4.6.3). You will also find an effect-size estimate, R^2. As a minimum, you should report these. You can find out more about each of these statistics, plus some of the other statistics you will get in your output, in Section B of the book's Web site and also in the statistical textbooks that are paired with this book.

In the following study, 102 participants completed an individual difference measure of anxiety and also rated how lucky they thought they were. How much does being anxious predict how much they think of themselves as being lucky?

An alpha level of .05 was used. Analysis of the data using simple linear regression revealed that anxiety explained a small but statistically significant (5%) proportion of the variance in belief in personal luck, $R^2 = .054$, adjusted $R^2 = .044$, $F(1, 100) = 5.68$, $p = .019$. The relationship between anxiety and belief in luck was negative, $\beta = -.23$, $p = .019$, with increases in anxiety being associated with lower level of belief that one was a lucky person.

Multiple linear regression

In multiple linear regression there is more than one predictor vari-able. The output will give you an estimate of the combined predictive power of all the variables together, R, plus an estimate of the effect size of these combined predictors, R^2, which tells you the percentage variance in the outcome variable predicted (or "explained") by the combined predictors. As well as this, your output will include B and β for each predictor separately, together with a t value that tests whether the slope of the line between *that* predictor and the outcome variable differs significantly from zero. The difference between B and β here and in a simple regression is that in multiple regression these statistics control for the presence of the other predictors in the model. What this means in practice is that β tells you the relative contribution of each individual predictor to the model. So, with multiple linear regression we are able not only to assess how much variance in the outcome variable can be accounted for by the combined predictors but also how much each individual predictor contributes to the model.

In the above study, in fact, the 102 participants had completed a number of other measures, including a measure of self-esteem and a measure of how much they believed that events in the world (good or bad) happened to people at random. For theoretical reasons, the researchers were interested in whether these variables – anxiety, self-esteem and randomness – combined to predict belief in personal luck and which of them would be the most important predictor. All variables were scored so that higher values indicated more anxiety, self-esteem and belief in luck and randomness.

An alpha level of .05 was used. The means, standard deviations and intercorrelations between the variables are presented in Table 1. As can be seen in Table 1, the outcome variable, belief in personal luck, was significantly correlated with all predictor variables, with greater belief in personal luck being associated with greater belief in randomness, higher self-esteem and lower anxiety. The predictor variables had small but significant correlations with each other, the strongest being that between anxiety and self-esteem, $r(100) = -.37, p < .001$.

Analysis of the data using simultaneous multiple linear regression revealed that the combined predictors explained 25% of the variance in belief in personal luck, $R^2 = .25$, adjusted $R^2 = .22$, $F(1, 97) = 10.63$, $p < .001$. Belief in randomness was the only significant individual predictor, $\beta = .43, p < .001$; neither self-esteem, $\beta = .07, p = .50$, nor anxiety, $\beta = -.15, p = .13$, were significant individual predictors in the final model.

Where you have more than three predictors it may make it easier for your reader if you put the results from the analysis in suitably formatted and labelled table rather than in text. You can find advice on what to put in such a table in Section B of the book's Web site at **http://mcgraw-hill.co.uk/openup/harris/**

Like ANOVA, in practice, there are several different variants of multiple regression as well as different labels for the same method; for example, you may use simultaneous, hierarchical or logistic regression, and you may also encounter stepwise regression. You can find out more about these different types in Section B of the book's Web site. As ever, you should be specific and accurate when reporting which the type you have used.

4.6.13 Statistics of effect size

Once you know how to calculate statistics of effect size and understand what they mean, you should include them when reporting your inferential statistics. Effect size statistics, such as d or partial eta squared (η^2), estimate the effect your IV has on your DV. Others, such as r^2, estimate the strength of the relationship between two correlated variables. Most of the time all you need to do to report these statistics is to add them to the relevant part of the text or the table in which you report the statistic whose effect they estimate. You can find more about effect size in Chapter 12, where you can also find an example of a RESULTS section that incorporates the reporting of an effect size statistic, partial eta squared (η^2). You should only include such statistics once you have been taught about them. As ever, you should never include statistics that you do not understand or recognize, however tempting it is to try to give the impression that you are on top of things when you are not.

4.7   What you can find on the book's Web site

 As you progress you may well find yourself needing to report other statistics than those covered in this chapter or to supplement your reports with additional analyses. You can find in Section B of the Web site material on more advanced reporting, including coverage of issues such as the reporting of planned comparisons or post hoc tests, of tests designed to unpack statistically significant interactions (tests of simple effects), a discussion of when to include ANOVA tables in your report and what to put in them, and more on linear regression. You can find in Section H of the Web site a discussion of what material to put in your later RESULTS and in Section I material on preparing a final year project. You can find a full listing of the contents of the Web site at the front of this book.

4.8   What you can find in the statistics textbooks paired with this book

Σ The books paired with *Designing and Reporting Experiments* have the following coverage:

Learning to use statistical tests in psychology – Greene and D'Oliveira Greene and D'Oliveira cover all the statistical tests described in Sections 4.6.1–4.6.12 of this book.

SPSS survival manual – Pallant

Pallant discusses descriptive statistics in Chapter 6 and covers all the statistical tests described in Sections 4.6.1–4.6.13 of this book. (Note, however, that she refers to predictors and outcomes in linear regression as independent and dependent variables. See Section 4.6.12 for more on why this may pose problems for you.)

Both books have very good coverage of the issues involved in choosing statistical tests.

5 | The DISCUSSION section

 Diagnostic questions on design for Chapter 5

Before reading this chapter, check that you can answer correctly the following diagnostic questions:

1 What is the *internal validity* of an experiment?

2 What is the *external validity* of an experiment?

3 What is a *confounding variable*?

4 What is a *type II error*?

You can find the answers at the rear of the book (p. 275) If you had difficulties answering any of these questions, turn to the relevant sections of Part 2.

Researchers design experiments to test hypotheses to develop theories or to help solve practical problems. However, in psychology at least, the outcomes of experiments are *not* self-evident. That is, they require *interpretation*. It may not be apparent when you first start practical work, but we need to "discover" what we have found out. For instance, in the cheese and nightmare experiment (Section 4.3) we have been compelled by our data to reject the null hypothesis. Now, however, the real work begins. For we need to find out what *caused* the apparent link we have found between condition and the incidence of nightmares. Was it the IV (eating cheese)? Or are there *confounding* variables that could also account for this effect? The answers to such questions we can only arrive at by looking carefully at our experimental design and assessing the quality of the *control* we exercised. Only once we have done this can we decide (for it *is* a decision) which of the various options is the *likeliest* explanation for our findings. Only once we have done this will we be able to explore the *implications* of our findings for the area under consideration.

Moreover, this remains true of situations in which the data compel us *not* to reject the null hypothesis. Does this mean that the IV is *not* the causal variable after all? Or was there some aspect of the design that made it hard to detect the effect of the IV on the DV? Again, we can only decide this after a close examination of the experiment. Again, we need to sort this out before we can even begin to assess the implications of the findings for the area discussed in the INTRODUCTION.

The point is that our findings are subject to *uncertainty*. We need to interpret our results. This process is undertaken in the DISCUSSION.

There are three definable stages to the process of discussing the findings. These three stages, in sequence, provide the structure of your DISCUSSION. First, you need to say what needs to be explained. So the first task in the DISCUSSION is to state what the results of the experiment are by providing a précis (in words) of the RESULTS and describing how well they fit the original predictions. Once you have done this, you need to try to *explain* these findings. Is the IV responsible for statistically significant differences? If not, what is? Does the lack of statistical significance mean that the IV does not cause changes in the DV? The second task in the DISCUSSION, therefore, is to explore these issues, arriving if you can at a set of reasonable conclusions. Finally, you need to explore the theoretical implications of the findings, together with any practical ones they may have. For instance, if you have concluded that the IV was indeed responsible for the changes detected in the DV, what implications does this have for the material – especially the arguments and theories – that you outlined in the INTRODUCTION? This, of course, is the key issue – the reason why we design and run experiments in the first place.

We can crystallize these three phases of the DISCUSSION around three questions:

1 How well do the findings fit the predictions?
2 What do the findings mean? (What, if anything, can you conclude about the relationship between the IV(s) and DV(s)?)
3 What are their implications (especially with regard to the issues that you outlined in your INTRODUCTION)?

Of course, the balance between these three phases, and the depth to which you will be expected to follow some of the issues raised by your findings, will depend on your experience as a student of practical psychology. As a novice, considerably less will be expected of you here. Your main task will be to state your findings, outline and *assess* the more plausible explanations and, in the light of this, arrive at reasonable conclusions. If you have something sensible to say about how the experiment might have been improved, then consider also including this. In particular, remember that you should be aiming to display clarity of thought and presentation when discussing the outcomes of your experiment. Demonstrate that you understand what you have done and found.

Before we go through the phases themselves, two additional points need to be made. First, if the findings of experiments are subject to uncertainty, you can imagine that findings from studies that are not experimental are even more problematic, as these methods provide us with even less control. Second, science proceeds by argument about evidence. It is important to remember that other people may disagree with your interpretation of your findings. Your task in this section, therefore, is to argue the best case that you can, given your data, and without going beyond the data.

Summary

1 The outcomes of psychology experiments are subject to uncertainty. They require interpretation in order to find out what they have to tell us about whether or not there is a causal relationship between the IV and the DV.

2 This process of assessment and interpretation takes place in three phases in the DISCUSSION. These phases revolve around three questions: (1) What are the findings of this study? (2) What do they mean? (3) What are their implications?

5.1   How well do the findings fit the predictions?

Open the DISCUSSION by describing what you have found and how well the data fit the predictions. Doing this enables you to be clear from the outset about what needs to be explained in the DISCUSSION. All of you, therefore, regardless of your level of experience, will need to do this adequately. Where you have lots of findings to report, prioritize them in the same way as you did in the RESULTS (Section 4.3).

5.2   What do the findings mean?

Once you have decided what you found, you can set about the *process* of drawing the conclusions from the experiment. If you have *rejected* the null hypothesis, then you need to assess whether this was indeed due to the manipulation of the IV or whether something else is responsible. If you have *failed* to reject the null hypothesis, then how confidently can you conclude that this indicates the absence of a causal relationship between the IV and DV?

In order to answer these questions as well as you can, you need to sit down and re-examine the experiment. Have you become aware of a confounding variable that you failed to spot before running the experiment? How likely is this variable to account for the findings? In retrospect, was the design likely to have been able to allow you to reject the null hypothesis in the first place? It is only when you have satisfied yourself that there are no confounding variables or that your design had sufficient power (see below) that you can draw reasonable and firm conclusions.

So, how long this next bit is and how firm are your conclusions will depend on how well designed and executed your experiment was. Before starting on the DISCUSSION, therefore, take a long and hard look at your experiment, identifying its weaknesses but recognizing also its strengths. Once you have listed (to yourself) any weaknesses, then *assess* each of these. Is it a feature that undermines your capacity to attribute changes in the DV to the manipulation of the IV (*internal* validity) or does it instead compromise the extent to which you can generalize the findings (*external* validity)? Do NOT confuse these (see Sections 10.8 and 10.9); at this stage of the DISCUSSION we are concerned with things that affect internal validity. Remember that a *confounding* variable is not any old variable you failed to control by holding constant, but one that systematically co-varies with the levels of the IV. So, is the variable that you are concerned about really a confound? If not, it relates to external rather than internal validity.

Once you have done this, decide which (if any) of these features are sufficiently important to require raising and discussing explicitly in this phase of the DISCUSSION. (Your ability to judge this as well as your ability to spot important design problems is being assessed here.) Be honest, but also be sensible – novices especially. Obviously, it is important not to blind yourself to flaws and weaknesses in the design that undermine the conclusions that you can draw. You will not gain marks for pretending that all is well when it is not. However, the solution is not to assume automatically that there are problems and merely catalogue every problem you can dream up, regardless of importance. It can be tedious to read a mindless list of flaws and problems, doubly so when the experiment is in fact pretty sound and could sustain reasonable conclusions. Really watch out for this, *especially where you have failed to reject the null hypothesis*. Your marker wants to see evidence of critical engagement; you need to strike a balance between spotting and discussing important flaws and drawing reasonable conclusions from what you did and found. Look at journal articles to get a sense of how the professionals do this. A good journal discussion will contain an account of the study's limitations alongside sound (justifiable) conclusions.

With findings that are not statistically significant, are there features of the experiment that undermine your capacity to detect the influence of the IV on the DV? Failing to attain statistical significance may tell you more about the *power* of your experiment than about the existence or otherwise of an effect of the IV on the DV. If you are a novice, or otherwise not yet technically able to discuss power, you should at least consider whether you had enough participants – especially on unrelated samples IVs. Please note, however, that this is definitely *not* a licence to mindlessly trot out the old cliché that "we would have obtained significant results if we had had more participants". This is inevitably true – any effect, however trivial, will become statistically significant if you have enough participants. The question to address is whether you might reasonably have expected to obtain statistical significance given the number of participants in your study. You can find advice on this issue in Sections 12.3 and Section 13.1.1.

If you understand about power, then use any relevant confidence intervals you reported in the RESULTS to reflect on the likely power of your study where you have failed to reject the null hypothesis. Comment also on any relevant statistics of effect size that you have reported there. (Remember, it is possible to estimate effect size whether or not the results are statistically significant.) You can find advice on this in Section 12.3.1.

If your findings are unexpected, especially if they contradict established findings or ideas in the area, be careful. Under these circumstances, many of you lapse into what I call the "chemistry experiment" mentality. That is, when the results do not come out as predicted, you assume that the experiment has not "worked" and search for where you went "wrong" – just like we used to when our test-tubes of noxious substances failed to behave as anticipated in chemistry classes (which, as I recall, was most of the time). This is *not* the way to proceed. It may well be that a flaw in your experimental design has produced "anomalous" results. However, you should not automatically assume that this is the case. As a general rule, *believe* your findings until you discover a feature of your design or procedure that casts doubt upon their validity.

On the other hand, the fact that your findings fit your hypotheses should not blind you to problems. Confounding variables can be lurking anywhere. Check your design for alternative explanations for your findings, even when the explanation that you favour seems so obvious to you as to be undeniably true. (Such as when your findings fit your predictions.) Watch out for this – it is a very common and easy mistake to make.

So, it is a question of balance. Do not jump to conclusions, but do not dwell on every flaw.

If your experiment has been reasonably well designed, at the end of this process you should be in a position to say how likely it is that any difference between your conditions was caused by your manipulation of the IV, or that the absence of such a difference suggests that there is no causal relationship between the IV and DV. This is, of course, what the whole enterprise is about. This is why you spend so much time in the design phase working on such things as your controls for confounding variables. So, if at the end of this phase of your DISCUSSION you are unable to decide about the impact of your IV on your DV with *reasonable* confidence, there are obviously design lessons to be learnt. So learn them! (If at this stage your findings remain equivocal, one question that you might address is whether you adequately pilot-tested your experiment; see Section 13.9.3.)

5.3   What are the implications of these findings?

The first two phases of the DISCUSSION really are preliminaries for
what is to follow. Having decided what you have to explain, and
having drawn sensible and balanced conclusions about how best to
explain it, you can now get to the nitty-gritty – assessing the implications of the experiment for the work outlined in the INTRODUCTION.
What, if anything, have we learned about the IV from the experiment?
Does this advance our ideas in any way, or at least qualify them? To
what extent can the findings be reconciled with the theoretical ideas
discussed in the INTRODUCTION? Indeed, do they enable you to decide
between any competing theories?

A good DISCUSSION, therefore, depends upon an adequate INTRO-
DUCTION. Essentially, your task now is to return to the material that
you addressed in your INTRODUCTION with the benefit of the findings
of your study. So, what you are able to say at this crucial stage of
your report depends critically on how well you prepared the ground.
Indeed, unless something particularly unforeseeable has occurred,
you should find yourself addressing the same themes here as in your
INTRODUCTION, albeit with additional knowledge. In general, there
should be no need to introduce new evidence from the psychological
literature to this section.

Once you have done this, you should think about the direction that
future work might take. At this stage you might suggest problems
that need to be addressed next and, if possible, ways in which this
might be done. However, be sensible about this. Think about further
work that you might reasonably do yourself if you had the time –
sensible next steps in the process of exploring the causal relationships
that you have been investigating. Make positive and constructive suggestions. Never write "there is a need for further research" without
indicating something about what form this further research should
take.

This is all very well, of course, if your findings are relatively
unambiguous. However, what if it has not been possible to say much
at all about the relationship between the IV and DV? If this has
occurred because of design flaws, then you should go some way
towards improving your reputation as a designer of studies here by
indicating ways in which future experiments on the same topic might
overcome the difficulties that you encountered.

5.4 What to do when you have been unable to analyse your data properly

Sometimes, however, these problems will have arisen because you experienced considerable difficulties with your study, difficulties (such as very few participants) that render your data effectively unanalysable. This, of course, will make writing the DISCUSSION that much harder. Whenever possible, avoid such circumstances *before* running the study. However, such things can occasionally happen even when the study has been well thought out in advance. In such instances, when it comes to writing the report, the important thing is to *be seen to have made an effort*.

Do not, therefore, jump at the opportunity (as you see it) of only having to write a brief and dismissive DISCUSSION, but write as thoughtfully as you would have done in the presence of suitably analysed data. Indeed, one of the most effective ways around this problem is not only to examine *carefully* the reasons for the inadequacies in the data (together with the ways in which such occurrences might be avoided in future work), but also to explore actively the sorts of implications that your data would have held had the results turned out (a) as predicted, and (b) contrary to prediction. At least in doing this you will be able to demonstrate your reasoning skills to your reader – as well as being able to practise them.

You should regard this, however, as a last, somewhat desperate, exercise in damage limitation. It is not an alternative to spending time designing sensible studies and doing adequate pilot work. The best way of dealing with this problem is by making sure that it does not arise in the first place.

Finally, one of the aspects of the implications of your findings that you should bear in mind concerns their external validity or generalizability.

5.5 External validity: the generalizability of findings

All studies have limits on their **generalizability** – that is, on the extent to which we can extrapolate the findings to situations other than those directly assessed in the study itself (Section 10.8). In some cases these limitations are severe. In others, they are not. Yet these limitations are often among the first things to be forgotten when studies are discussed in general terms.

Many factors can affect the generalizability of a study's findings: the equipment or participants involved, the procedure used, the wording of the instructions, and so on. One particularly potent source of such limitations can come from the level at which *controlled* values were held constant. For example, if you undertake an experiment in which you control for sex by using only women, then perhaps the data are applicable only to women. Or, if you run an experiment in which you test the effects of alcohol on driving performance using participants who are only occasional drinkers, then perhaps the findings will not apply to those who drink alcohol more often.

The generalizability of findings is one of the more neglected issues in experimental psychology. It seems likely that the findings of many studies have been *over*generalized. As students, this is one issue that it will be important to think about in *all* aspects of your course, not just in your practical work. Nevertheless, in your practical work, consider this issue when assessing the studies you include in your INTRODUCTION and, of course, bear it in mind when evaluating your own findings in the DISCUSSION. However, again be sensible and balanced when raising this issue. It is easy to drone on and on about the failure to employ a random sample of the general population. Yet this is typically to miss the point. Examine whether there are likely to be any important limitations on the generalizability of your findings and whether any simple and reasonable steps could have been taken to improve the situation. Do not waffle on in a tone of self-righteous indignation about the failure to sample adequately every sentient human being within a 100-mile radius of the experimental setting.

 SAQ 21   What is the purpose of the DISCUSSION?

Summary of Sections 5.1–5.5

1 You should open the DISCUSSION by summarizing the main features of the RESULTS, so that it is clear both to you and your reader what you have to explain in the DISCUSSION. Relate your findings to the predictions.

2 Once you have done this, search for the best available explanation of the results, examining and assessing the likely candidates in

order to arrive at an overall assessment of what your findings have to say about the existence or otherwise of a causal relationship between the IV(s) and the DV(s).

3 These two stages are the necessary preliminaries for the final phase of the DISCUSSION, in which you assess the implications of your findings for the area as outlined in the INTRODUCTION. At the same time, you should think about the direction and form that future work might take.

4 Where your findings have been too ambiguous to do this, then you should examine both why this has been the case and ways in which the problems that you encountered might be avoided in future work.

5 End with a paragraph summarizing your main conclusions.

 5.6   ## Six tips to help you to avoid some common failings in the DISCUSSION

1 Do not repeat material that you covered – or *should* have covered – in the INTRODUCTION. In this section you can assume that your reader knows the relevant literature – after all, it was you who described it. Where there are gaps in their knowledge that make it difficult to conduct your argument, and where these are the result of unforeseen rather than unforeseeable factors influencing your findings, then the gaps are of your own making and reflect omissions from your INTRODUCTION.

2 Include a final paragraph summarizing your main conclusions. Be careful, however, to distinguish between conclusions and mere restatements of findings.

3 Remember: Do not confuse *statistical significance* (see Section 11.2) with *meaningfulness*. We can draw useful conclusions from data that are not statistically significant. On the other hand, statistically significant effects can be psychologically trivial. Nor should you confuse statistical significance with *proof:* statistically significant results do not *prove* that the theoretical underpinnings of your study are sound, nor do findings that are not statistically significant necessarily *disprove* your arguments. Life would be much simpler if they did, but unfortunately this is not the case; in either instance, you will have to justify your point of view in the DISCUSSION.

4 Do not simply reformulate and repeat points that you have already made. This is **waffle**. Markers are not *that* stupid. We know when

you are waffling, so do not waste your time. Each statement should add something to the picture.

5 Do not see the DISCUSSION as an opportunity to indulge in fanciful speculation. Make conjectures with caution and keep it brief.

6 Once you know how, consider the likely effect sizes of the IVs on the DVs when discussing the implications of your findings. Remember that highly statistically significant findings do not necessarily indicate large effect sizes (see Chapter 12).

5.7   Two example DISCUSSION sections

Below are two sample DISCUSSIONS, one for the cheese and nightmare experiment, and one for the mnemonic experiment. These are only suggestions as to how you might go about writing discussions for these sections, and in some respects they provide only outlines of what might be argued. (For those unfamiliar with the term, **demand characteristics** are features of an experimental setting that provide the participant with cues about the experimental hypothesis – such as asking people to eat cheese before going to bed and then questioning them about whether or not they experienced nightmares. In a culture where eating cheese is believed to cause nightmares participants may well guess what the study is about and this may influence what they report.)

5.7.1   The cheese and nightmare experiment

Discussion

The results are consistent with the experimental hypothesis: those who ate cheese 3 hours before going to bed reported a significantly greater tendency to experience nightmares than did those who did not eat cheese at this time. Participants were randomly allocated to conditions, thus lessening the likelihood of there being differences between the groups in tendency to experience nightmares to begin with.

Perhaps the most obvious explanation for this finding is that eating cheese before going to bed leads to the experience of nightmares. It may be that one or more of the ingredients in cheese affects the human nervous system and induces nightmares. However, an alternative explanation is that participants were aware of the aims of the experiment and this influenced their responses. Although the instructions concealed the purpose of the experiment, those in the cheese condition ate a measured quantity of cheese at a specified time and (among other things) subsequently recorded the number of nightmares they experienced. This may have led them by suggestion either to *experience* an increase in the number of nightmares or to *report* such an increase.

It is hard to control for this possibility. However, the questionnaire completed each morning contained three pages of questions, many of which were "filler" items designed to draw attention away from the questions on nightmares. Careful post-experimental interviewing by an investigator blind to condition revealed few participants able to state the hypothesis of the experiment, even when strongly encouraged to do so. This suggests that the participants had little or no awareness of the experimental hypothesis.

On balance, given this apparent inability of participants to state the hypothesis, it seems reasonable to assume that there may be something to the common-sense idea of a link between cheese and nightmares. Further work should attempt to replicate the current findings, controlling as much as possible for demand characteristics. These studies should move away from a complete reliance on self-reports; researchers should include less subjective measures, such as measures of rapid eye movement (REM) sleep. Although it is not possible to obtain objective measures of dream content, measures might reveal differences in the amount of REM sleep in the two conditions. In all experiments, investigators should make every attempt to conceal their hypotheses.

Once further research has established that there is a link between cheese and nightmares, work can begin to determine which of the ingredients of cheese causes the problem. Isolating such an ingredient might help to reduce such unpleasant experiences (particularly if the ingredient is common to a number of foodstuffs) and may also provide useful insights into brain chemistry.

Thus the data from this experiment raise the possibility of a link between eating cheese and experiencing nightmares. However, it is not possible to rule out an explanation of the findings in terms of demand characteristics. The next step is to replicate this study controlling as much as possible for demand characteristics.

5.7.2 The mnemonic experiment

Discussion

Participants using the mnemonic recalled significantly more of the easily imaged words than did those not using the mnemonic. However, the groups recalled similar numbers of the hard-to-image words. Thus, as predicted, the mnemonic specifically enhanced recall of the more easily imaged words.

The pre-test data suggest that, overall, the two groups had similar ability to recall lists of words prior to the experimental group being taught the mnemonic. It thus seems reasonable to conclude that the randomization to conditions was successful and that it is unlikely that the findings arose from individual differences between the groups in their abilities to recall lists of words.

The manipulation check confirmed that the participants rated the words classified as easily imaged as being easier to image than those classified as hard to image. This corroborates the classification of Clark (1971) and the manipulation of word type imageability used in the current experiment.

The findings of this study are thus consistent with those of Clark (1971). The data suggest that the method of loci does make a difference to recall and does so by enhancing the recall of easily imaged words. Earnshaw et al.'s (2007) failure to find an improvement in recall among those using the mnemonic appears to have resulted from not allowing the participants enough time to practise using the mnemonic.

The current findings have limited theoretical implications. There is some suggestion in the data that the participants recalled easily imaged words more readily than they did hard-to-image ones. (The 95% confidence intervals for the means for the easily imaged and hard-to-image words for the no-mnemonic group overlap but only by a small amount.) Of course, despite being matched for length and frequency, there may have been other ways in which the lists differed over and above their imageability that could account for any differences in recall. However, the data in both Clark (1971, Table 2) and Earnshaw et al. (2007, Table 1) show differences in the same direction and of similar size. Earnshaw et al. used different words. In combination, these data raise the possibility that easily imaged words may be intrinsically easier to recall even without the use of a mnemonic (perhaps because they typically denote more familiar, concrete objects). Given that this difference would be theoretically interesting, future research might test whether people recall easily imaged words more easily and investigate reasons for the difference if it is shown to exist.

The practical implications of the current findings are clear. Researchers must ensure that their participants have had sufficient practice in the use of the mnemonic before the start of any experiment in this area.

In conclusion, the findings suggest that the method of loci does make a difference to recall and does so by enhancing the recall of easily imaged words. Earnshaw et al.'s (2007) failure to find an improvement in recall among those using the mnemonic appears to have resulted from not giving the participants enough time to practise.

5.8 Writing a DISCUSSION when your study is not an experiment

When your study is non-experimental, the only real difference in your DISCUSSION is that you will not be attempting to interpret the causal relationship between an IV and a DV. In all other respects, however, your task will be the same and much of the advice I have offered in the rest of the chapter will also be relevant to you. You should therefore still find yourself addressing the three questions on p. 74: (1) What are the findings of this study? (2) What do they mean? (3) What are their implications?

If your data are correlational, in relation to question 1 you will be assessing the evidence that there are associations between your key variables and the magnitude of these relationships; for question 2, you should explore the extent to which the presence of third variables or other features of the data may account for your findings (see Section 9.2), and for question 3, you should consider whether your findings justify undertaking relevant experimental studies and, if possible, say something about how this might be done. You must be careful at all times not to draw any causal inferences from your data – remember, the relationship could always be the other way around. (See Section 13.8 for more on this.) This can be especially a problem when you have analysed your data using linear regression (see Section 4.6.12).

If your data are descriptive, in relation to question 1, you should summarize the key elements of your findings so that your reader knows which aspects you think are the most important. When addressing question 2, you should examine what your data have to say in relation to the goals of your study – are the findings consistent with your expectations and if not why not?; if your findings are consistent with your expectations, are there competing explanations as to why? As your research may well be descriptive because it is exploratory, question 3 is very important. What do your findings have to tell us about what research we should do next? Are they promising or discouraging? What kind of research is needed to build on your findings? In particular, can you say something about what questions this research should address and what the next study or studies should look like? What relationships between variables should be explored in future correlational research? Is there scope for any experimental research and, if so, what variables should we try to manipulate (and do you have any ideas about how?) and what should be the dependent variables (and do you have any thoughts about how these should be measured)?

If you do not understand the distinction between experimental, correlational and descriptive research, see Chapter 9.

6 The TITLE and ABSTRACT

Although the TITLE and ABSTRACT are the first items to appear in the report (see Box 1.2), I have left coverage of them until the end. This is partly because you need to understand something of the report's structure and purpose before you can begin to appreciate the nature and function of these sections. It is also because they are invariably better left until later in the writing sequence.

In order to understand the reasons for the form the TITLE and ABSTRACT take, we need to remind ourselves of the function that they serve in a *research* article (Section 1.4). They are in fact vital to its research function, for they alert potential readers to the existence of an article of interest to them. These days most of us search for articles of interest among electronic databases of titles and abstracts, such as Web of Knowledge or PsycINFO, or using Internet search engines (Section 1.5). Thus it is often on the basis of the title and abstract alone that readers will decide whether to read a research paper or ignore it. The TITLE and ABSTRACT, therefore, need to summarize the study clear, concisely, and (if possible!) engagingly. They should also be *self-contained*, being fully comprehensible without reference to any other part of the paper. These are your goals too, when writing these parts of your report.

6.1 The TITLE

The title should be as informative as you can make it within the constraints imposed by its length (no longer than one sentence, although you may include colons or semi-colons). It forms, in fact, the first step in the process of searching the literature. It is at a title that would-be readers look initially to discover whether the paper might be of interest. You should, therefore, provide sufficient information at this stage to enable readers to make this initial decision. So, never be vague in the title. Do not title your report "Memory", for example, or "The Effect of Mnemonics" but something like "The Effect of Word Imageability on Recall Using the Method of Loci Mnemonic". If it accurately describes the findings, you can even consider a directional account of them in your title (i.e., one that specifies which direction the differences went in). For example, "The Method of Loci Enhances Recall of High-Imageability Words When Participants Have Enough Practice". In experimental studies, if possible, you should mention the IV(s) and the DV in the title.

Note that you should begin the first word of the title, together with all subsequent key words (but not small connecting words, such as "on", "of", "the", and so on), with a capital letter. Avoid abbreviations and redundancy – phrases like "A Study of" or "An Experimental Investigation of" should not appear. Aim for about 10–12 words. (The directional version of the title above is therefore a bit too long.)

6.2   The ABSTRACT

The ABSTRACT constitutes the next stage in the process of searching the literature. Having gathered from the title that an article may be of interest, would-be readers will generally turn next to the ABSTRACT in order to decide whether to invest time and energy in reading the full paper. So in this section you should provide enough information to enable them to reach this decision. As well as this, however, you should attempt to be as concise as possible. The whole section, then, involves a compromise between these two aims. Unless you are told by your tutor something different, your abstracts should be an average paragraph in length, approximately 100–150 words.

Indeed, together with the DISCUSSION, the ABSTRACT is one of the most difficult sections to write; even quite experienced students (not to mention the odd member of staff, myself included) continue to encounter difficulties with this section. So do not be too dismayed if your initial attempts meet with failure. Where you experience difficulty with this section, look at some good journal articles to see

Table 6.1
What Should be Appear Where in the ABSTRACT

What to describe	Advice
1. The problem under investigation	In one sentence, if possible. Do not repeat the title.
2. The participants	Specify pertinent characteristics, such as number, type, age, sex and method of selection.
3. The empirical method	For example, experimental. You should mention also any specific apparatus, key features of the data gathering procedures, and the complete name of any published scales or testing procedures used on participants.
4. The findings	Describe succinctly your key findings. If you tested for statistical significance, mention the statistical significance level you used.
5. The conclusions	State the key message you want the reader to take from your study, plus implications or applications.

how the abstracts have been written. For there is really a "feel" to a good abstract that is perhaps best absorbed in this way.

What material should the abstract contain? The *Publication Manual of the American Psychological Association* (APA, 2001) states that the abstract of an empirical study should describe the material in column one of Table 6.1.

Address each of these features of your experiment in the above sequence. In doing so:

1 Include the bare essentials. Remember that your task is to provide the minimum amount of information necessary for someone to be able to grasp in essence what you did. In general, there is no need to include procedural details that might be expected to form part of any well-designed study, although *unusual* procedural details, or those relevant to the conclusions, should be mentioned briefly.

2 Always look for ways of condensing this section, while retaining intelligibility and informativeness. Once you have the first draft, go back through it several times, eliminating extraneous details, redundancies and phrases that contain no real information (e.g., "The implications of the findings are discussed", "It is concluded

that"). It is surprising how by doing this you can pare the text down. Whenever I start I invariably find myself with something twice the length of what I need and the task of condensing it seems impossible. Yet, after teasing away at it for a while I can suddenly find myself with a version that creeps in under the word limit. The sense of relief and achievement can be quite rewarding! (Yes, I am that sad.)

3 Make sure that the ABSTRACT is self-contained. Define any abbreviations and acronyms. Paraphrase rather than quote. The reader should not have to look elsewhere in the report to make sense of the ABSTRACT.

4 Make sure that the ABSTRACT is accurate and non-evaluative. Do *not* include information that does not appear in the body of the report. Do *not* add to or comment on what is in the body of the report.

5 In particular, make sure that the conclusions that you mention are the main ones and are those that you actually arrived at in your DISCUSSION – not ones unrelated to these or "afterthoughts". If you have a late insight, then you need to modify your DISCUSSION first. Your ABSTRACT should reflect what you argued in your DISCUSSION.

6 Despite all of this, try to make it coherent and readable! Aim for an ABSTRACT that is readable, well organized, brief, and self-contained.

As you can imagine, this is a challenging task. However, given its role, the ABSTRACT is perhaps the most important paragraph in the report, so it is worth working on. Novices should concentrate at first on the basics – providing the required information (Table 6.1, column 1) succinctly.

? SAQ 22   What functions do the TITLE and ABSTRACT serve in a research article?

Here is an example ABSTRACT for the mnemonic study. (See if you can find ways of improving it.)

Abstract
This experiment tests whether recent research failed to show an effect of word imageability on recall using the method of loci because the researchers gave participants too little time to practise. A convenience sample of 40 undergraduates (both sexes) either received instruction

in the mnemonic or did not. Experimental participants practised using the mnemonic. A computer presented participants with words that varied in imageability. Participants using the mnemonic recalled significantly more easily imaged words than did those not using the mnemonic, but similar numbers of hard-to-image words. (Overall alpha level was .05.) Thus the method of loci enhanced recall of easily imaged words. Researchers must ensure that participants have sufficient practice in using the mnemonic.

You might find that you are required to write a **structured abstract**. In this case the structure that is implicit in an ABSTRACT like the one above is made explicit by using headings – for example, Background, Aims, Methods, Results, Conclusions. Even if the ABSTRACT is not explicitly structured in this way, it is a good idea to write your drafts as if it were. For example, it would take relatively little extra work to turn the above abstract into a structured one (we would need to write an Aims section):

Abstract
Background. This experiment tests whether recent research failed to show an effect of word imageability on recall using the method of loci because the researchers gave participants too little time to practise.
Methods. A convenience sample of 40 undergraduates (both sexes) either received instruction in the mnemonic or did not. Experimental participants practised using the mnemonic. A computer presented participants with words that varied in imageability.
Results. Participants using the mnemonic recalled significantly more easily imaged words than did those not using the mnemonic, but similar numbers of hard-to-image words. (Overall alpha level was .05.) Thus the method of loci enhanced recall of easily imaged words.
Conclusions. Researchers must ensure that participants have sufficient practice in using the mnemonic.

Summary of Sections 6.1–6.2

1 The TITLE and ABSTRACT of a research article function to alert potential readers that the paper might be of interest to them.

2 The TITLE and ABSTRACT should, therefore, summarize the study clearly, concisely, and engagingly.

3 The TITLE should be at most a sentence in length, the ABSTRACT no longer than an average paragraph.

7 REFERENCES and APPENDICES

7.1 The REFERENCES section

This is one of the most neglected sections of the report. Do *not* neglect this section, as it helps to round off the report in style. When I mark essays and reports, this is in fact the first section that I look at. It tells me a lot about the student's attitude to their work, their attention to detail and their knowledge of the discipline's writing conventions.

You will be required to provide one of two types of REFERENCES. One type consists solely of a list of the sources you used in writing the report. In such a REFERENCES a book (e.g., your course textbook) or an article may appear *even though* you have not cited it in the text. Likewise, citations may occur in the text but not in the REFERENCES if you only read about them in secondary sources (see Section 1.5.1). Technically, this is a **bibliography** – a list of the sources you actually read when preparing your report or essay.

The other type of REFERENCES is the one that you see in journal articles. This is a complete and accurate list of *all* the citations that have been made in the text, *and those alone*. In such a REFERENCES a source should appear *only* if you have cited it in the text. In the UK, final-year projects are expected to have an exhaustive REFERENCES section of this sort.

Which you should use is contentious. Different tutors have different expectations and some can hold forth on this issue with vehemence. The safest bet, therefore, is to find out which your tutor expects and to provide it. Failing that, I advise you to opt for the type that you see in journal articles (i.e., the exhaustive) version and, if you get it wrong, to blame me. *In either case*, the citations in the REFERENCES should appear in the proper order and correct format.

As elsewhere in this book, the format I describe in the rest of this chapter is that used by the American Psychological Association (APA). This is the format for referencing most widely used in psychology and the one your tutors have to use if they wish to publish in many of the top psychology journals. It is therefore a good format to use as the default. However, you would be wise to check whether your department encourages you to use a different format, just in case. Whichever format you are expected to use, you will need to observe it strictly and punctiliously.

7.2   General rules for the REFERENCES section

1 Your references should be in alphabetical order, commencing with the first author's surname and taking each letter in turn.
2 Place an author's single-authored publications (those in which s/he is the sole author) *before* his or her *joint* publications. For example, Clinton, W. J., will come before Clinton, W. J., & Lewinsky, M. S. However, Clinton, W. J., & Lewinsky, M. S., will come after Clinton, W. J., & Clinton, H. R.
3 Place *multiple* publications by the same author(s) in *chronological* order. For example, Blair, A. C. L., & Bush, G. W. (2006) must appear before Blair, A. C. L., & Bush, G. W. (2007).

7.3   An example REFERENCES section

Below is an example REFERENCES. It includes illustrative examples for most of the journal articles, books and other publications that you are likely to need to reference as an undergraduate student. Note that, as is the case in *all* the example sections in this book, the precise layout is important. This is a splendidly anal section. Use italics, commas, full stops (periods), spaces and ampersands EXACTLY as in the example. Note that bold is never used. Note that each reference has a "hanging indent" – that is, the rest of the reference is further from the margin than the first line. This greatly aids reading the reference list. Note also that no spare lines are inserted between the references. This also helps in reading the reference list and saves trees. Finally, you should begin your REFERENCES section on a new page – the first new page for starting a section since the INTRODUCTION.

References

Beano, O. N. A. (2008). Workers in paradise: Working when others are having fun reduces well-being. *Journal of Pleasure Studies, 17*, 123–145.

Dull, V., & Boring, T. D. S. (2007). The effects of locus of control on attributions for performance outcomes among junior high school pupils. *The Journal of Tedious Research, 52*, 317–324.

Duller, M. (2009a). The effect of strip lighting on workers' attitudes towards their managers. *Journal of Incremental Studies in Occupational Psychology, 85*, 219–225.

Duller, M. (2009b). Strip lighting and managers' attitudes towards their workers. *The Work Psychologist, 1*, 3–15.

Fab, I. M., Smart, R. V., & Clever, B. (Eds.). (2008). *Mood, cognition and action* (Vol. 1). New York: University of New York Press.

Genius, T. (2009). Why we do what we do: Absolutely everything explained. In I. M. Fab, R. V. Smart, & B. Clever (Eds.), *Mood, cognition and action* (Vol. 2, pp. 1–110). New York: University of New York Press.

Genius, T., & Zealot, U. C. (2007). *Absolutely everything explained simply*. Cardiff, UK: The Patronizer's Press.

Gorbachov, M., & Reagan, R. (1986). Staring you in the face. In I. T. Botham & M. Argyle (Eds.), *If it had teeth: Fifteen years of research into non-verbal communication* (pp. 17–32). Moscow: Glasnost & Perestroika Press.

Harris, P. R. (2008). *Lecture 3: Boring away at another topic in social psychology* [PowerPoint slides]. University of Sheffield UK, Department of Psychology.

Heavy, B. C., Weather, A., & Grind, T. D. (2006). Twenty years later and still staring you in the face. *Annual Review of Qualitative and Quantitative Psychology, 45*, 210–275.

Nasty, B., Evil, B., Demon, C. U., & Warped, T. C. (2007). *Practical psychology for dictators* (24th ed.). Hades, TX: Pandemonium Press.

Running from home. (2008). Brighton & Hove, UK: British Exercise Society.

Tired, A., & Worne, D. A., Jr. (in press). *The psychology of aging*. London: Old, Young & Son.

Twit, A. I., & Daft, H. K. J. (in press). Holiday Preference Theory: A meta-analysis. *Psychological Reviews*.

7.4   Key to the example REFERENCES section

To help you locate which example you need to use from the above list, here is a key:

Journal articles
Single author – Beano (2008).
Two or more authors – Dull and Boring (2007); Heavy, Weather and Grind (2006).
In press (not yet appeared in print) – Twit and Daft (in press). Note that this has no volume or page numbers, as these have yet to be allocated to the paper.

Books
Edited book – Fab, Smart and Clever (2008).
Chapter in edited book – Genius (2009); Gorbachev and Reagan (1986). Note here how the editor's names now have their initials *before* their family names (don't ask me why).
Authored book – Genius and Zealot (2007); Nasty, Evil, Demon and Warped (2007).
Published by an organization with no named author *–Running from home* (2008).
In press (not yet appeared in print) – Tired and Worne (in press).

Miscellaneous
Two or more works (e.g., articles, book chapters, books) by the same author(s) in the same author order in the same year – add a lower case letter starting with "a" – Duller (2009a, 2009b).

Lecture notes
Harris (2008).

7.5   Electronic references

Nowadays, we get hold of most of our references electronically. This can create some complexities when it comes to compiling an accurate REFERENCES section, especially with material you accessed on Web sites. For the Internet is volatile – documents change, move and disappear from it altogether – and this can make it hard to relocate the material you originally cited. For this reason you should add as much retrieval information to a reference you obtained electronically as would enable your reader to locate and check it. Where the material is likely to move, be updated or otherwise altered, then you should check that the retrieval information still takes you to it the day before finally submitting your report. Indeed, you should do this for any reference where you have included a retrieval date (see below). If you find that the document is no longer available you should consider replacing it with another source or drop it from your report.

Below are some guidelines to help you with some of the issues that can arise with referencing electronic material. These are based on those in the *Publication Manual of the American Psychological Association* (APA, 2001) and the *APA Style Guide to Electronic References* (APA, 2007). If you are a graduate student using this book, you should consult these sources direct.

7.5.1 Published material obtained electronically

You should find that most of the material in your REFERENCES section has been formally published, that is, it comes in printed or electronic form from a reputable publisher. Referencing such material poses few problems – you can cite it using the same basic format as the relevant example in Section 7.3. You should then add to the end information describing accurately where you got the material. If an article has a Digit Object Identifier (DOI) then this is easy: just add the full DOI to the end of the reference. (A DOI is a unique code assigned to the document that provides a permanent link to its location on the Internet.) For example, if you had obtained Dull and Boring (2007) electronically and could find the DOI, you would format it as follows:

Dull, V., & Boring, T. D. S. (2007). The effects of locus of control on attributions for performance outcomes among junior high school pupils. *The Journal of Tedious Research, 52*(3), 317–324. doi: 10.1035/0003-9427.85.4.481

If you cannot find a DOI, you can add a **retrieval statement**. This gives the URL (which stands for "uniform resource locator" and is the technical term for a Web address) that takes your reader to the material:

Dull, V., & Boring, T. D. S. (2007). The effects of locus of control on attributions for performance outcomes among junior high school pupils. *The Journal of Tedious Research, 52*(3), 317–324. Retrieved from http://www.topicsineducation.com

The URL you give should direct your reader as closely as possible to the material you cited – the specific document rather than the home page or a menu page. Such a retrieval statement is particularly important when you have obtained the material from a source such as an author's Web site, rather than from a publisher, as authors may be less than conscientious about uploading the very final version! In this case you should also add the date of retrieval to the start of the retrieval statement and check and update it the day before you finally submit your report or essay.

Where you obtain a book or book chapter electronically, you may find it hard to find the publisher's geographical location or name. In this case you can omit it from the reference provided that your retrieval statement is dated, up-to-date, and clearly takes you to the relevant document(s).

Finally, you should, of course, make sure that all such material is legally available for you to download (see Section 1.5.4).

7.5.2 Unpublished material obtained electronically

Of course there are many other things available on the Internet that you might sometimes want to cite, such as online encyclopaedias, dictionaries, handbooks, wiki, software downloads, data sets, lecture notes, opinion pieces on Web sites, and even press releases, newspaper articles, podcasts, and blogs. There is not space here to detail how to cite all of these things, but below are some illustrative examples that you can use to base your references on; you can find many others in the *APA Style Guide to Electronic References* (APA, 2007). *All* such references must have a dated and up-to-date retrieval statement that takes your reader to the relevant material. Where you cannot find a date of publication for material from a Web site, then replace the date with (n.d.) in both text and the REFERENCES section (n.d. = "no date"). However, be wary of sites that keep such poor date records.

To reference online encyclopaedias, dictionaries, handbooks and wiki, give the home or menu page URL. For example:

Emotion. (n.d.) In *Harris's online dictionary of psychology.* Retrieved
   September 2, 2007, from http://www.harrispsycdict.com/dictionary/

For lecture notes:

Harris, P. R. (2008). *Lecture 3: Boring away at another topic in
   social psychology* [PowerPoint slides]. Retrieved October 3, 2008, from

University of Sheffield, UK, Department of Psychology
OpenCourseWare Web site: http://ocw.shef.ac.uk/psychology/harris/
lecturenotes/242/lect3

For an in press article obtained from a Web site:

Bush, G. W., Jr., & Gore, A. A., Jr. (in press). Patterns of voting behavior
by US state and region. *Machine Voting Quarterly*. Retrieved December
13, 2008, from http://www.utexas.edu/users/Bush-mvq-08.pdf

Do not describe as "in press" articles, book chapters or books that
have yet to be accepted for publication. Where the material has yet to
be accepted for publication – or you are unsure of its status – then
treat it as unpublished and cite it as follows:

Blair, E. A. (n.d.). *The personality profiles of winners of Big Brother*.
Retrieved June 3, 2008, from University of Newport, Psychology
Department Web site: http://www.unewp.ac.uk/research/papers/
bigbro.pdf

If you wish to cite an entire Web site, rather than a document or a
section of the Web site, then simply provide the address of the site in
text and omit it from the REFERENCES. For example:

The APA provides a Web site that describes different aspects of APA style:
http://www.apastyle.org/

Finally, a word of warning. Make sure that you do not rely too much on
unpublished material for your report, as it may not have been checked
for accuracy and it could be misleading. Try to restrict yourself to
using such material for illustrative purposes and use only authoritative
sources when you want to refer to more substantive content.

7.6   Appendices

Some students' reports seem to have had almost as much effort
expended on the **appendices** as on the rest of the report. This is invariably a waste of effort as few tutors look in detail at your appendices
– and when they do this is often because you have included there
something you should really have put in the body of the report. The

purpose of appendices is to enable you to expand on information that you have been able to include only in abbreviated form in the body of the report itself. *However, all vital information should appear in the report, not here!* So, include in appendices things like the verbatim instructions (when these are too long to include the full text in the PROCEDURE), a full copy of the questionnaire that you used in your study, the stimuli or lists of words that you used, and so on. However, make sure that no vital information is mentioned here for the first time! Number any appendices you do use consecutively using Arabic numerals and use these in text to refer to specific appendices. For example, "A copy of the full text of the instructions can be found in Appendix 1."

If you have a punitive word limit, then obviously more material than is usually the case has to appear in the appendices. However, think carefully and constructively about this. Do not put more material than is strictly necessary in the INTRODUCTION or write a self-indulgent DISCUSSION. Leave yourself room to put the key material in the METHOD and RESULTS. Strike a balance.

8 Producing the final version of the report

The material I have presented so far in Part 1 of this book should go a long way towards helping you to produce good reports of your practical work in psychology. In this final chapter of Part 1, I want to talk about some general aspects of report writing that you will also need to be familiar with in order to produce the final version. I also want to give some pointers to help you to produce reports that not only read well but that also *look* as if they have been produced by someone who knows what they are doing. My first piece of advice is to make sure that you allow yourself enough time to produce the report properly – it is worth taking the time to make it look professional and it takes longer to do this than you think. My second piece of advice is that what makes it look professional is likely to surprise you – it does not involve the use of bold, 3D effects, bullet points, and all the other paraphernalia of the business presentation. Read carefully the formatting rules described in this chapter and resist the temptation to think you know it all before you do.

8.1 Writing style

There is no doubt about it: psychology has more than its fair share of bad writing. The discipline's scientific aspirations have led some authors, desperate to give their writing an objective and impersonal flavour, to produce some quite tortured and turgid prose. I own up to having done my bit: there are articles of mine out there written in determinedly dull, coma-inducing prose. I have also read more than my fair share, often from students trying to find the style. It is important to recognize that scientific writing has features that set it apart from creative writing. It does not follow from this, however, that the result should be jargon-laden, stuffy or pretentious.

There are numerous guides available on writing clearly for psychology, such as Sternberg's *The Psychologist's Companion* (2003). The *Publication Manual of the American Psychological Association* (APA, 2001) also has a good chapter on principles to follow when expressing your ideas in writing. Use the most up-to-date versions of these guides.

The objective when writing is simple: to communicate clearly. The rules are pretty straightforward: present ideas in an orderly manner, express yourself smoothly, precisely and economically, avoiding jargon, wordiness and redundancy. Despite this, it can be enormously tempting to ramble about, waffle on, and obfuscate (by using words like "obfuscate"), especially when you are not quite sure what you are talking about. Resist this temptation. Above all else, learn to develop your arguments logically and to articulate them clearly. Write them down simply and clearly. Develop good habits from the outset!

In terms of writing style, there are a few rules and many guidelines. One absolute rule is that you must not use racist or sexist language. For example, only use "he" or "she" when you are actually referring to a male or female. Otherwise use alternatives (there are plenty of examples of how to do this in this book, some clumsy, some less so).

A very important guideline is to use the **active** rather than the **passive voice** as much as possible. A sentence in the active voice in English has the word order: subject – verb – object. For example: "Harris wrote this book." Sentences in the passive voice tend to be longer and duller to read. For example: "This book was written by Harris." Avoid passive phrases. So, write that someone did, found, argued, claimed, used something, rather than that something was done, argued, found, claimed, used by someone.

Another important guideline is to use references to the **first person** (*I, my*) sparingly and *only* when it is necessary for you to do so. Similarly, use the plural (*we, our*) sparingly and *only* when referring to yourself and the co-designers of your experiment. Avoid the Royal "we" – that is, referring to yourself as if you were plural. This is really only a lazy way of avoiding saying "I" and is no solution.

8.2   Definitions and abbreviations

 Always define the critical terms you use in your report and any other important terms that you use which are not part of common vocabulary or whose meaning in scientific psychology departs from ordinary language use. If you cannot decide whether or not to provide a definition, provide one – at least then you can guarantee that people know for sure how you intend to use the term. *Never* make the definition up yourself. Search for a *professional* definition rather than one from an ordinary language dictionary. This is because we often use terms (e.g., attitudes, perception, emotion) more precisely in psychology than we do in everyday life. You can obtain professional **definitions** from other papers in the area or textbooks and there are also available dictionaries of psychological terms. You must always cite the source of the definition. For definitions taken from papers or textbooks, provide also the page number (as with any quotation – Section 8.3).

If you wish to use **abbreviations**, make sure that you define these on their first appearance – by writing the term to be abbreviated out fully, together with the abbreviation in brackets. For example, "the galvanic skin response (GSR)"; "functional magnetic resonance imaging (fMRI)"; "used the Life Orientation Test – Revised (LOT-R)". After this you can simply use the abbreviated form. Use abbreviations sparingly, however. Do *not* make up your own and use abbreviations *only* where the full term would have appeared frequently in the text.

Summary of Sections 8.1–8.2

1 Get into good writing habits from the outset: develop your arguments logically and write simply, clearly, precisely, and concisely, using active sentences.

2 Define all critical terms, using a definition obtained from the literature.

3 Use abbreviations sparingly and only when the full term would have appeared frequently in the text.

8.3   References in the text

Not only is it important to reference in text, but it is also important to do so *properly*. Do *not* be slapdash about this! There are clear and detailed rules in psychology about *precisely* how you should reference in the text and you ignore these at your peril. Be warned: few things can incite the ire of a tired marker more easily than a failure to reference properly in the text. (Believe me.) Here are the basic APA rules and some specific details. Abide by these unless your tutors tell you differently.

The basic requirement is to provide the names of the authors whose work you are citing or quoting and the year of publication. These references can either be *direct* or *indirect*. In **direct references** only the year is placed in parentheses:

> Daft and Twit (2005) found that people typically prefer holidays to working.

Alternatively, you can recast the sentence and omit the parentheses:

> In 2005, Daft and Twit found that people typically prefer holidays to working.

In **indirect references** both the names and year are placed in parentheses:

> People typically prefer holidays to working (Daft & Twit, 2005).

 Note also that the "and" in the direct reference changes to "&" in the indirect reference! Watch out for this. Along with the incorrect use of "et al." (see later), getting this seemingly small detail wrong can outrage markers!

The next rule is that it must be clear to which authors and to which of their publications you are referring at all times. If there is no ambiguity – such as sometimes occurs when you are citing the same publication more than once on the same page – then you need not repeat the year. However, whenever there is potential ambiguity, include the year as well:

> Daft and Twit (2005) found that people typically prefer holidays to working. They developed *holiday preference theory* (HPT) in the light of this finding. In a review of HPT, Daft, Twit, and Total-Idiot (2008) found little or no work on the theory by authors other than themselves. They concluded the review by stating "it is time for more researchers to take up the challenges posed by HPT" (p. 32).

In the rare event that two authors of different articles share the same surname, to differentiate them put their initials before their surname each time that you cite them in the same report.

When you wish to use a number of references to support the same assertion, then put these in *alphabetical* order. The rule is that the citations appear in the same sequence as they do in the REFERENCES section (Chapter 7). Use semicolons to separate publications by different authors:

> However, others have questioned the assumptions of HPT (Prolific, 2006; Smug, 2007).

Authors may well have published more than one article in a given year. If you cite more than one publication by the same *single* author in the same year, then assign the different articles lowercase letters to distinguish them. Use these letters in the remainder of the report and in the REFERENCES section too (Section 7.3). You also need to do this for multiple authors when the same list of names appears *in the same order* on different articles in the same year.

> For example, Smug and Prolific (2007a) dismissed HPT as "having no evidential basis whatsoever" (p. 15). They based this claim in part on their own finding that people spent considerably more of their lives working than on holiday (Prolific & Smug, 2006; Smug & Prolific, 2007b).

However, beware here the mistake of copying lowercase letters over mindlessly from a reference in a published article or book and using them in your report when they are not needed. This is another tiny fault that can irritate your marker.

Talking of tiny faults that irritate out of all proportion to the offence, let's now turn to the use of "et al.".

8.3.1 Using et al. properly

The rules for using et al. are really quite simple, yet many of you fail to use it properly and, like so much to do with referencing, this can make your marker's blood boil with irrational ire. Get this right and not only avoid the risk of boiling your marker's blood, but also add that extra layer of polish to your report.

Cite *all* the author's names the first time that you cite an article *unless* there are six or more of them. Subsequently, cite only the first author followed by "et al." to indicate that there are three or more additional authors. If there are six or more authors, and only if there are six or more authors, use the et al. version even for the first citation. However, if two different publications shorten to the same form, do *not* use et al. at all.

> In further work, Prolific, Smart and Verbose (2008) used focus groups to explore the meaning of work for workers in holiday settings, such as coastal resorts. The workers were often confused by having to work when other people were on holiday. Prolific et al. found that students working on the island of Ibiza for the summer were "particularly confused" (2008, p. 27). Since then, researchers have found confused students working in coastal towns and villages throughout the Mediterranean (Beano, 2008a, 2008b, 2009; Chancer, Luck, & Happy, 2009; Happy, Luck, & Mainchance, 2008; Nicejob & Gottit, 2008, 2009, in press; Smashing, 2009).

Note also a punctuation change: when et al. is used in indirect references it becomes "et al.," with a comma added before the year, as in "Recent years have therefore seen an influx of researchers to Mediterranean coastal resorts (e.g., Prolific et al., 2008) . . .". I told you that things can get quite detailed.

 Common mistakes are to use et al. for the very first reference to fewer than six authors or to revert back to the full reference after using et al. Once you have made the first reference to all the authors, use et al. for *all* subsequent references to that paper in your report. This mistake can happen when you cut and paste text from early on in a document, so watch out for it. *Never* use et al. in the REFERENCES section.

Finally, you must make sure: (a) that the reference exists; (b) that it says what you claim it says; and (c) that you have referenced it correctly. Do not be tempted to invent references: the chances of being caught are high and the consequences serious.

8.3.2   Quotations and plagiarism

When you wish to **quote** what someone has written, you must quote *exactly* what he or she wrote (including any spelling or grammatical mistakes). You must also state on which page of which of his or her publications the quoted material appeared. (Failing to cite the page numbers is a very common mistake.) Put the quote in double inverted commas. Do this every time that you quote. The examples in the previous sections include several illustrations of how this should be done. Where the quotation or definition comes from an online source that lacks page numbers, then use the paragraph number instead, preceded by the word "para". For example, 'Prolific et al. found that students working on the island of Ibiza for the summer were "particularly confused" (2008, para 7).'

If you want to quote a sizeable chunk of an author's text (40 or more words), then put this material as a **block quotation**. This starts on a new line and forms a block of indented text that stands out from the rest of your paragraph. You can see how this has been done in journal articles and textbooks. Because the text stands out as an extract from somewhere else, you *do not use* inverted commas for block quotations. In general, however, try to avoid using long extracts if you can. Ask yourself why you feel it is necessary to use such a big chunk of someone else's words.

So, do not go overboard on quotations. It is unusual to need to quote extensively. Quote verbatim when it is essential to report the exact words used by another author (e.g., when using a definition or citing a key part of their instructions). Otherwise paraphrase rather than quote. However, when you paraphrase, it must be clear whose work or ideas you are citing. Nevertheless, there is no need to provide the page number for the paraphrased material.

Above all, make sure that you *never* wittingly or unwittingly give the impression that other people's ideas or writings are your own. To do so is to commit the heinous crime of **plagiarism**. To plagiarize is "to take something that somebody else has written or thought and try to pass it off as original" (Encarta World English Dictionary, 2007). Sensible use of the rules described here will enable you to avoid this problem. Make sure that your reader can readily identify the sources of all the ideas, arguments and findings that you include in your report. When in doubt, be explicit about the source.

? SAQ 23   Correct the following references:

> Blake, Perry & Griffith, 1994, found that performance on the experimental task improved considerably when participants were in the presence of a group of peers. This contradicted previous findings in the area. (Bennett and Bennett, 1981, 1981: Scoular, 1973, 1964: Buchanan & Livermore, 1976, Pike, 1992; Chopra et al. 2007). As Blake, Perry & Griffith put it, "it is not clear why this happened."

Summary of Section 8.3

1 There are precise rules in psychology governing the way in which you make citations in text to references.

2 The basic requirement is to provide the names of the authors whose work you are citing or quoting and the year in which the work was published.

3 The rules are designed to make it clear to which authors and to which of their publications you are referring at all times.

4 You must make sure that the reference exists, that it says what you claim it says, and that you have referenced it correctly.

8.4 Tables and figures

You will certainly need to put **tables** in your report. Tables can convey information more succinctly than text can. Likewise, a good **diagram** or **figure** can save, if not exactly a thousand words, at least quite a few. I am often struck by how reluctant students can be to include useful diagrams in their reports and essays even where the verbal descriptions that they have to use instead are convoluted and hard to follow. Diagrams are an integral part of scientific communication, so consider the use of a figure whenever you are having trouble describing something in text and if you think that including it will add to your report. Do not overdo this, of course. Too many figures can disrupt the flow of the report.

Keep the format of tables simple and clear. There are guidelines governing the production of tables for papers in journals, such as those in the *Publication Manual of the American Psychological Association* (APA, 2001). I based the tables in the example RESULTS in Chapter 4 on these. The APA guidelines produce clear and well-spaced tables that are easier to read than fussier layouts. Things to notice and emulate include the extensive use of white space rather than vertical lines to separate the elements of the table and the limited use of horizontal lines. You should *never* use vertical lines in the tables in your report. Produce tables that look like the ones in this book or those that you see in the better psychology journals. Do not be fooled by your word-processing package into producing tables that look fancy but are more appropriate for a sale's talk than for reporting scientific material. Watch out for this – the default tables in word processing packages, such as *Word* – tend to put lines around every cell in the table and you will need to remove these to get the right layout.

Make sure that your reader can readily interpret the entries in a table or a table header. Do not, for example, use terms that are hard to decipher, such as "C1" or "Group A", unless you provide the key to them in a note beneath the tables and figures in which they appear.

Where you use them, think carefully about the balance between tables and figures and what you put in the text. It is easy to get confused over what should appear in tables and what should appear in text. Tables and figures supplement but do not duplicate the text. Your task in text is to discuss their highlights. Think of yourself as somewhat like a tour guide to a new city or gallery of modern art. Your task is to help the visitor (your reader) to know where to look and something of what they should note when they do. So, you draw the reader's attention to a building or exhibit. ("The data are in Table 1"; "Figure 1 shows the interaction between . . .".) Then tell the reader something about what to note about this interesting object. ("Those receiving auditory warning signals performed significantly better on the monitoring task than those receiving visual warning signals, except when the visual displays were superimposed on the wind-shield . . ."; "Participants attributed significantly more positive traits than negative traits to themselves, but significantly fewer positive than negative traits to their randomly assigned partners . . .".) However, no guide is ever going to be able to say absolutely everything that there is to say about each and every exhibit. Similarly, you do not need to discuss every item of the table or every feature of the figure in the text. If you do, then they are redundant and should be omitted. Your goal is to draw your reader's attention to the main points of interest.

Likewise, it would be an odd guide who drew attention to one exhibit, but told the audience what to note in something else. So, put tables, figures and text together in coherent units, just as you would with exhibits in a gallery.

Where you use tables or diagrams you must observe the following rules:

1 Label all tables consecutively, using Arabic numerals, and capitalize the first letter of Table (e.g., Table 1, Table 2, etc.).

2 Call everything that is not a table a *figure*. This includes graphs.

3 Label all figures consecutively, using Arabic numerals, and capitalize the first letter of Figure (e.g., Figure 1, Figure 2, Figure 3, etc.).

4 *Always* use these labels when referring to tables or figures in the text (e.g., "Figure 1 illustrates the precise layout of the equipment"; "Figure 4 displays the interaction").

5 Give *every* Table and *every* Figure an informative title.

6 Put notes beneath the table or figure to explain any entries or features that are not self-explanatory.

Summary of Section 8.4

1 Feel free to include diagrams or other illustrations if these will help your reader to understand.

2 Keep the format of tables simple and clear. Use horizontal lines sparingly and *never* use vertical lines. Model your tables on those in the example sections of this book and in the better psychology journals.

3 Make sure that all entries in tables and figures are self-explanatory or are otherwise explained in a note beneath them.

4 Tables and figures supplement but do not duplicate the text. Your task in text is to discuss their *highlights*.

5 Where you use tables and figures, observe the rules for their use.

8.5 Graphing data

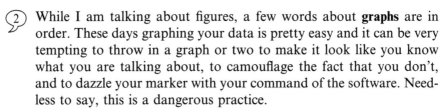

While I am talking about figures, a few words about **graphs** are in order. These days graphing your data is pretty easy and it can be very tempting to throw in a graph or two to make it look like you know what you are talking about, to camouflage the fact that you don't, and to dazzle your marker with your command of the software. Needless to say, this is a dangerous practice.

Graphs are useful things. They can display information succinctly. Used well, they enhance your report both in terms of conveying the information and the impression that you are on top of the material and good at the job. Be warned, however. In the wrong hands these useful tools can become little monsters. They can make the marker's heart sink. Avoid creating the impression that your report has been written by someone who knows how to use a graphing package, and how to cut and paste from one computer application to another, but has not really given a moment's thought to the purpose of the graph. Remember that graphs serve to convey information that is not so clear from a table of data. Bear this in mind at all times.

Before including a graph, always ask yourself what it is going to *add* to the story. Graphs should not be redundant with the text and tables. As with all figures, the best graphs enable you to reduce or eliminate lengthy bits of text. If the graph will add nothing, omit it.

Graphs can convey two aspects of experimental data that can be harder to communicate in text or glean from tables. First, they can convey information about the *pattern* of differences in summary statistics, such as a set of means. That is, a graph can make it easier to see which conditions tend to differ on the DV. Graphs are most commonly used in everyday life to display patterns of differences in this way. However, graphs can also convey information about the *shape* or *distribution* of the data. That is, they can also be used to indicate such things as how the scores were spread about the means in the different conditions. Providing this information in addition to information about the pattern of differences can be extremely useful. I will talk shortly about just such a feature that you can readily add when graphing your data – the inclusion of *error bars*.

8.5.1   One IV with two levels

Early on you can get away with graphing data from experiments with two conditions. However, recognize that this is mainly to start gaining experience of the graphing package and to illustrate to your marker that you are learning how to use it.

Use a **bar graph** (as in Figure 8.1). Keep it simple – for example, a straightforward light or dark fill for the bars. *Above all*, choose the scale wisely.

Let me explain why you should be cautious. Once your inferential analysis shows you that a difference between two groups is statistically significant, even an average buffoon can look at two numbers and work out which is higher. There is thus little to be gained from graphing such data, beyond getting valuable experience with the graphing package, and much to lose. First, you run the risk of insulting your marker, who thinks, "Hey, this person thinks I'm stupider

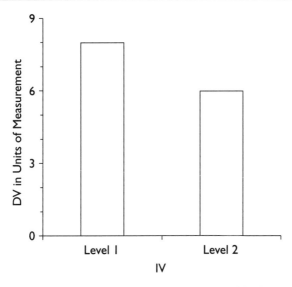

Figure 8.1.   Bar graph for a two-level independent variable.

than an average buffoon." Second, by using too small a scale you can make a small difference look huge, and by using too big a scale, make the same difference look minute. (Politicians, advertisers and other propagandists use this fact to great effect.) So, only graph two-condition effects early on in your career and when you are sure that your marker will be suitably impressed by your capacity to use the graphing package.

However, things are different if you are able to add error bars to your graphs. If you do this as well, then the graph will be conveying useful information succinctly and its inclusion is more justifiable.

8.5.2   Error bars

Once you have mastered the software, you should get into the habit of adding error bars to your graphs. **Error bars** are lines in a graph that tell us something about the margin of error in the data. There are a variety of error bars that you could use. For some purposes you might add bars that display the points that lie one standard deviation or one standard error above and below the mean. These enable us to see whether the data tend to be spread out or bunched closely around the mean. Alternatively, you might add bars that indicate confidence

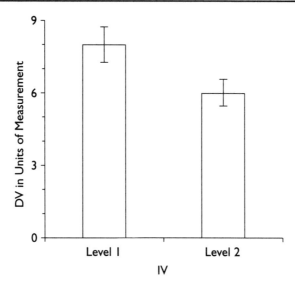

Figure 8.2.   Bar graph for a two-level independent variable.
Vertical lines depict the 95% confidence intervals about the mean in
each condition.

intervals for the mean in the population. We can then see whether
these intervals are wide or narrow and whether those for the different
conditions overlap (see Section 12.3).

For example, Figure 8.2 is the same as Figure 8.1 but includes
also error bars showing the 95% confidence intervals about the mean.
Looking at the graph we not only can see that the means in the
two conditions are quite different, but also that the 95% confidence
intervals are relatively narrow and do not overlap. We can see that
for level 1 of the IV there is a 95% probability that the mean in the
population lies between about 7.2 and 8.9; whereas for level 2, there is
a 95% probability that the mean in the population lies between about
5.4 and 6.7. The graph thus conveys a lot of information succinctly
and has the potential to add to the reader's understanding of the
findings. (You can find out more about confidence intervals in your
statistics textbook.)

Do not be daunted by this: you can certainly include graphs without error bars, especially when there are enough conditions in the
experiment to warrant a graph. However, if you know how to add
error bars as well, then this enhances the usefulness of the figure.

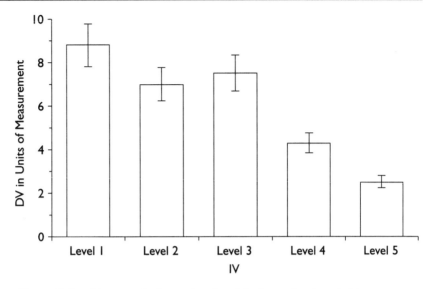

Figure 8.3. Bar graph for a five-level independent variable. Vertical lines depict the 95% confidence intervals about the mean in each condition.

8.5.3 One IV with more than two levels

The same caveats and cautions apply here as for the two condition experiment: if there are not many levels, you run the risk of insulting the reader's intelligence; if you choose the wrong scale, you run the risk of exaggerating or downplaying the size of the difference. Having said this, for IVs with four levels or beyond, a well-designed graph can provide a useful indication of the relative impact of the different levels of the IV on the DV (Figure 8.3).

8.5.4 More than one IV

Once you start to run experiments with two or more IVs, graphs of effects can become pretty much essential tools to help you and your reader to better understand what you have found. Even the effects in a **two by two** (or 2 × 2) design can be better appreciated from a well-constructed graph. You can find several examples of graphs of the effects in such designs in Section 13.7 and also in Section C of the book's Web site.

The same concerns about the size of the scale apply here as elsewhere. Do not use a scale that unduly accentuates or reduces the differences between the bars. Where the IV is categorical, use a bar graph to display the interaction. Where it is quantitative, use a line graph. (This issue is discussed in Section 13.7.) Where you have different graphs of equivalent data, use the same scale for *all* these graphs. If this is not possible, make it *very* clear in the text that the scale varies, otherwise you may mislead the reader.

You should be alert to a potential problem when using graphing packages that are attached to statistical software packages. The package may not take notice of the fact that you have more than one IV and may trot out a graph that simply represents the data as if they were from a single IV. This has happened in Figure 8.4. Here a 2×2

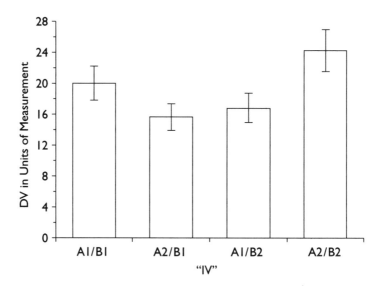

Figure 8.4. A design with two independent variables, with two levels on each, displayed erroneously as if it were a design with one independent variable with four levels. A1 = independent variable A, level 1; A2 = independent variable A, level 2; B1 = independent variable B, level 1; B2 = independent variable B, level 2. Vertical lines depict the 95% confidence intervals about the mean in each condition.

Figure 8.5. The same data as in Figure 8.4, this time correctly graphed as a design with two independent variables with two levels on each. Vertical lines depict the 95% confidence intervals about the mean in each condition.

design is displayed wrongly as a single IV with four levels. The data are graphed correctly in Figure 8.5.

8.5.5 Tips to help you produce better graphs

For all graphs in your report:

- Keep it simple. Resist the temptation to use frills, such as 3-D, background fills, colour. Your graph should make sense in black and white.
- Choose the scale appropriately. The vertical axis should be about three-quarters of the length of the horizontal axis.
- Label the axes.
- For experimental data, put the DV on the vertical axis and an IV on the horizontal axis.
- Once you know how, include error bars or graphical indices of dispersion.

Do not put too much information in one graph. Can your reader make sense of it without detailed explanation? Show it to a fellow student and see if they can explain it back to you.

Summary of Section 8.5

1 Use graphs sensibly to add to the reader's ability to understand the findings.

2 Graphs can be used to convey information about the shape or distribution of data as well as information about patterns of differences.

3 Be careful when graphing data from experiments with one IV with only two or three levels.

4 Once you have mastered the software, get into the habit of adding relevant error bars to your graphs.

5 In graphs in reports keep it simple and clear. Do not put too much information in the one graph.

8.6 Drafting the report

The next sentence is one of the most important and also perhaps the most useless in the entire book: *Allow enough time to produce the report*. It is important because it is undeniably true that many reports are written too quickly and receive poorer marks than they would have done. It is useless because nothing I say here will make any difference if you are inclined to start work on your report the day before it is due in. For those of you who *do* allow yourself enough time, here are some tips that will help you to clarify and organize your ideas and express them clearly and concisely:

- Write from an outline. Do not just bash the first draft out willy-nilly on the computer.
- Put aside the first draft and reread it after a delay. A fresh look can be a revelation.
- Read the draft out loud. You will be amazed by what this tells you about the organization and clarity of the writing.
- Get a friend or your partner to read it, preferably one who is not a psychologist. Encourage them to be frank. Get them to tell you which bits they do not understand. They will *need* encouraging – the norm

among friends is to lie and to tell you that everything is just fine when it is not. Be warned: markers do *not* adhere to this norm!

<table>
<tr><td>8.7</td></tr>
</table>

8.7 Producing the final version

In report writing, as in most things, appearance matters. Good production can enhance a good report, just as icing can enhance a good cake. However, a professional-looking layout cannot completely conceal a poor write-up any more than icing can mask a bad cake. Indeed, you can detract from a perfectly decent report by overdoing the frills. So, use the facilities of your word processor and other software packages sensibly and sensitively.

Always, *always* use the **spell-checker**. It is frankly amazing how often students fail to do this. Spell-check before you print. Also use the grammar checking facility on the word-processing package. This can reveal things that you did not even realize were mistakes.

Spell-checking does not remove the need for **proofreading**, for spell-checking software cannot detect wrong but correctly spelled versions of words – such as *there* instead of *their, casual* instead of *causal, dependant* instead of *dependent*, and so on. So, proofread for additional spelling mistakes as well as (separately) for meaning.

Make sensible use of the other features of the software packages that you are using to produce the report: lay out the report clearly and elegantly. Produce a layout that is clear and uncluttered and that helps you to get your message across. Avoid features that distract or are irrelevant and resist the temptation to show off your prowess with the software just for the sake of showing off your prowess with the software. Here are some tips:

- Choose a sensible, readable, **typeface**, such as Times, Palatino or Courier.
- Use a large enough typeface, not less than 12 point. (*Top tip*: this will go down especially well if your marker is getting on a bit.) Do not, however, try to mask a lack of material by using a big typeface or too much material by using a small one. We're not *that* stupid.
- Be consistent in your use of **headings**. Use the same style of heading for *all* the principal sections of the report. Use a different style of heading from this for the subsections of the METHOD, but the same for all subsections. I recommend that you layout your headings exactly as I have done in the example sections of this book.

- Use *italic*, **bold** or <u>underlining</u> sparingly. Again, I recommend that you do so only as I have done in the example sections of this book. Personally, I recommend not using bold anywhere in your report.
- Leave reasonable **margins** for your tutor to put comments: 1 inch or 2 cm at minimum, preferably larger.
- Do not "right adjust" your text. (**Right-adjusted text** is text as laid out in this book – where the right-hand margin is straight. Unless it is done professionally, however, it is harder to read than text that is left-adjusted only.)

If you are a graduate student writing your thesis or an article for publication, there will be precise rules about features such as those above, so find out what they are – preferably before starting. If you are considering attempting to get something published in a journal, the latest edition of the *Publication Manual of the American Psychological Association* is indispensable. For the record, I have based the example sections in this book on the 5th edition of the *APA Publication Manual* (APA, 2001). Unless your tutor tells you differently, these should suffice for you. Note that these produce quite plain-looking text. This is how those of us who try to get our ideas into print are required to produce our papers. It is a good idea to get into the habit of working with this format from the outset.

Finally, I would recommend:

- Do not use exclamation marks!!
- Think twice before trying to be funny. Does your marker have a sense of humour? Is it the same sense of humour as your own?

Summary of Sections 8.6–8.7

1 Write from an outline and allow yourself enough time to reread drafts after a delay.

2 Read the draft out loud to get a sense of the report's organization and clarity. Get a friend to read it too.

3 Use the spell-checking and grammar-checking facilities of your word-processing package. However, also proofread for spelling as well as meaning.

4 Produce a report that is clear and uncluttered. I recommend following the layout used in the examples in this guide. These will

make your reports look like the manuscripts that psychologists, such as your tutor, submit to journals for publication.

Check list for report writing

- Avoid mentioning things "in passing" – if they are worth mentioning at all, then give them the amount of space they deserve.
- Make your points *explicitly* – do not leave it to your reader to work out what you mean. Be precise *at all times*. Never assume that your reader knows something, or expect readers to work something important out for themselves.
- Do not use note form at *any* stage of the report: *prose* is always required.
- Omit extraneous details: always look for ways of condensing the information you give while keeping the meaning clear.
- *Do not waffle* – unnecessary repetition is both tedious and obvious and is unlikely to impress your marker (quite the opposite).
- Tell the truth!

What the marker is looking for

One of the most daunting things about report and essay writing is the fact that you are not always clear exactly what the marker is expecting of you. Of course, this book is an attempt to help you with this problem. In addition, here is a summary of *some* of the questions that the marker will have in mind as they read your report. Note, however, that some of these are rather more important than others.

Title
- Does this convey a clear and accurate idea of what the study was about?
- Does it mention the major variables investigated?

Abstract
- Does this convey a clear and accurate idea of what the study was about?
- Is it clear what the findings were?
- Is intelligible reference made to the contents of the DISCUSSION? Is a conclusion mentioned, and is this the one actually arrived at?
- Can you understand the ABSTRACT without referring to the report itself?
- Is it concise enough, or does it include unnecessary detail?

Introduction

Part 1

- Is the study introduced adequately, given the student's background? In particular, is there an adequate review of the relevant background literature? Is it to the point and neither too short nor too long?
- Is there a logical progression to the INTRODUCTION? Does it *build up* to an account of the study undertaken?
- Does the study have sufficient research justification? (Where applicable.)
- Does it have a good mix of classic and up-to-date material? (Where applicable.)

Part 2

- Is the study described adequately and accurately?
- Is there a clear statement of the hypotheses and predictions and has the rationale for these been clearly expressed?

Method

Design

- Is the design described clearly and accurately?
- Are the IVs described clearly and accurately, including a clear description of the levels?
- Are the DVs described thoroughly and accurately, including a clear account of the units of measurement?
- Has the design been labelled correctly using appropriate terminology?
- Is the experiment well designed?

Participants

- Are the participants described adequately?
- Are there sufficient?
- Are they appropriate for this type of study?
- Have they been allocated to groups properly?
- Were they selected reasonably?

Apparatus or Materials or Apparatus and Materials

- Is this section labelled properly?
- Is the equipment used described in the kind of detail that would enable an *exact* replication to be undertaken?
- Are figures used appropriately and do they make things clearer?

Procedure
- Is this described in enough detail to allow for an exact replication?
- Is it clear how the procedure differed for the different conditions?
- Are the instructions reported adequately, with the gist where appropriate, verbatim where necessary? Were they standardized? Were they suitable?
- Was sufficient attempt made to ensure that the participants understood the instructions?
- Is a clear account provided of the randomization procedure?
- Is the experiment free of confounding variables? Was it run well?
- Was the experiment conducted ethically? Were participants debriefed?
- Does the procedure have flaws that make interpretation of the data difficult?

Results
- Is it clear what data were analysed and how the numbers presented in the tables of data were arrived at?
- Are the data clearly presented and described using appropriate descriptive statistics? Are tables labelled appropriately and readily intelligible? Has the student resisted the temptation to dump in unedited output from a statistical software package?
- Is it clear what inferential statistics were used in any given instance? Is it clear what was found?
- Is the necessary information provided for each inferential test? Has the significance level been adhered to? Have the data been used to good effect?
- Have the data been presented intelligently and well? Are the results presented in a logical order?
- Are graphs used sensibly? Are they correctly formatted and appropriately labelled?
- Has the student resisted the temptation to *interpret* the findings at this stage?

Discussion
- Are the findings summarized intelligently and accurately? Have they been interpreted sensibly?
- Are the obvious interpretations of these findings discussed? Are any other interpretations discussed?
- Is the discussion sensible and balanced?
- Have any inconsistencies or contradictions in the findings been addressed?

- Has enough attempt been made to assess the implications of the findings for the material reviewed in the INTRODUCTION?
- Does the DISCUSSION include an account of any flaws in the design that might have affected the data?
- Have the broader implications of the findings been mentioned, and are these sensible?
- Is there any discussion of the implications for future research? Are any conclusions drawn? Are these sensible?

References
- Is this section properly laid out, and does it contain the appropriate references?

Appendices
- Is information in appendices that should have appeared in text?
- Have appendices been labelled appropriately and referred to appropriately in the text?

Miscellaneous
- Has the basis for the sample size been given? (Where applicable.)
- Have the conventions of report writing been properly observed? Does the material appear in the appropriate sections?
- Are references made for factual assertions, and is this properly done? Are any tables, figures, quotations etc., properly constructed and referenced?
- Would the report be comprehensible to someone who previously knew nothing about the study or the relevant area of psychology?

Mistakes to avoid

Some things that should NEVER appear in your report (if you are using APA format):

- bullet points;
- bold text;
- vertical lines in tables (see Section 8.4);
- the Royal "we" (see Section 8.1).

 Here is a list of things you will persist in doing even though I tell you not to!

- Leaving the DISCUSSION until last and consequently rushing it – see Section 1.2.
- Weaving every bit of reading into your INTRODUCTION to try to let your marker know how much reading you have done – see Section 2.1.
- Spelling dependent and independent variable wrongly – see Section 3.1.
- Calling it the apparatus and materials section or even the apparatus section when you have only used materials – see Section 3.3.
- Writing the materials as a list and not in sentences – see Section 3.3.
- Reporting to too many decimal places – see Section 4.2.
- Eyeballing the data – see Section 4.4.
- Duplicating analyses – see Section 4.4 and 11.4.
- Labelling your t tests and ANOVAs inadequately – see Sections 4.6.8–4.6.10.
- Confusing uncontrolled variables with confounding variables – see Section 5.2.
- Putting important material in appendices rather than in the body of the report – see Section 7.6.
- Not defining key terms – see Section 8.2.
- Using ordinary language sources when you do define key terms – see Section 8.2.
- Using & for direct references – see Section 8.3.
- Using "and" for indirect references (less common than previous mistake) – see Section 8.3.
- Using et al. for the very first reference – see Section 8.3.1.
- Not putting page numbers for quotations – see Section 8.3.2.
- Designing experiments with too many conditions for the numbers of participants you can reasonably expect to recruit – see Section 13.1.1.
- Reporting $p = .000$ – see Appendix 3.

Part 2   Design and statistics

Part 1 of this book contains advice on how to write up your studies. The issues I describe there, together with the supplementary material you can find at **http://mcgraw-hill.co.uk/openup/harris/**, is designed to help you write better practical reports.

Part 2 of this book contains material on design and statistics. It is designed to give you the background you will need in key aspects of design and statistics to help you write better reports. For some of you this part of the book will be your introduction to these issues; for others, this section provides an opportunity to assess your understanding rather than to learn new things. Chapters 9–11 contain core background material that all of you should be familiar with before you write a report. Chapters 12 and 13 contain more advanced material that you will come to as your career as a student of psychology progresses. Make sure that you understand the material in each chapter before you move on to the next one. At the end of each chapter you will find a section designed to help you assess what you know and consolidate your learning. You can test your understanding using the diagnostic questions you will find there. You will also find there references to relevant material contained in the two statistical textbooks paired with this book – Greene and D'Oliveira's *Learning to use statistical tests in psychology* and Pallant's *SPSS survival manual* – and also, where appropriate, on the Web site that accompanies this book.

Although Part 2 has experimenting as its main focus, you will also find here coverage of relevant aspects of non-experimental approaches to quantitative research.

9 Experiments, correlation and description

The practical report described in Part 1 is designed for the reporting of *quantitative* studies in psychology – that is, studies in which you have data in the form of numbers to report. As a student of psychology you are likely to use a range of such methods, from true experiments at one end to non-experimental studies involving questionnaires, interviews, diary methods or observation at the other. In this chapter, I describe the key features of the main quantitative method discussed in this book – experimenting – and also discuss two other general approaches to quantitative research, correlation and description.

9.1 Experimenting

The first term that you must learn here is the term **variable**. In the language of design we tend to use this as a noun – that is we talk of "a variable" or "the variable". To us, a variable is quite simply something – anything – that *varies*. All around us there are variables: people come in *different* shapes and sizes, belong to *different* groups and classes, have *different* abilities and tastes. As researchers we can ask the participants in our experiments to do *different* things – to learn different lists of words for a memory test, to do boring or interesting tasks, to do push-ups for 3 minutes or to spend the same amount of time relaxing. All of these things – from social class through to whether our participants did push-ups or relaxed – are variables. So, in the above example social class is a variable because there are different social classes; doing different tasks is also a variable because the task varies – it can be *either* interesting *or* boring. As our world is full of changing events, therefore, it is no surprise to find that almost anything in it is – or can be – a variable.

A variable, then, is something that can come in different forms or, as we say in design terms, that can take different *values* or *levels*. In practice, it can be anything from the number of white blood cells in a cubic centimetre of blood to whether or not someone voted in the last election. With our scientific hats on we are extremely interested in variables, especially in finding out something about relationships *between* them.

Our ultimate aim is to find out which variables are responsible for *causing* the events that take place around us. We see a world full of variables and we want to know what factors are responsible for producing or causing them. Why is it that some people react with depression to events that others take in their stride? Why is it that some public speakers are more persuasive than others? What makes some events easier to recall than others? We believe that we live in a universe of causes and effects and our adopted task is to try to determine, as far as is possible, which are the causes and what are the effects they produce. That is, ideally we want to be able to infer cause and effect relationships, to make what are known as **causal inferences**. Our principal weapon in this battle is the psychological experiment.

9.1.1 The experiment

The principles of basic experimenting are dead easy. In an **experiment** what we do – quite simply – is play around with one variable (the one we suspect to be the **causal variable**), and see what happens to another variable (the **effect variable**). That is, as experimenters we deliberately alter the values or levels of the causal variable – or, as we say in experimental design parlance, we **manipulate** this variable – and look to see if this produces corresponding changes in the other – the effect – variable. If it does, and we cannot see any other variable in the situation that may have produced this effect, we assume that the variable we manipulated has indeed produced the change we observed. That is, we infer a cause–effect relationship between the two variables (i.e., make a causal inference). This is the logic of experimental design.

For instance, if we suspected that eating foods that contained particular additives was responsible for causing changes in mood, we could *vary* the intake of these additives among our participants and see whether this produced any corresponding changes in their mood. That is, we would *manipulate* the variable food additives and *measure* the variable mood. Similarly, if we wanted to find out whether physical exercise affected mental alertness, we would *manipulate* the variable physical exercise and *measure* the variable mental alertness. In the above examples, food additives and physical exercise are the variables that we suspect to be causal; mood and mental alertness (respectively) the variables we think that they influence.

However, because they are both variables, and yet play quite distinctive roles in an experiment, we give these critical variables different names. The one we play around with – the variable we manipulate – we call the **independent variable** (IV). The IV, therefore, is the variable we suspect is the *causal* variable. The variable we look at to see if there are any changes produced by our manipulation of the causal variable – that is, the variable we *measure* – we call the **dependent variable** (DV). The DV, therefore, is the variable that shows us whether there is any effect of changing the values of the independent variable. If there is such an effect, then the values that the dependent variable takes will *depend* on the values that we, as experimenters, set *independently* on our independent variable.

It is important that you get this straight. These terms are critical and you will need to apply them properly in your report. So read back through the last paragraph carefully, and then answer the following questions.

? SAQ 24

In an experiment, what is the name of the variable we *manipulate*? What is the name of the variable we *measure*?

For each of the following experiments, write down what the *independent variable* is and what the *dependent variable* is:

(a) An experimenter is interested in the effect of word frequency upon the time taken to decide whether a stimulus is a *word* or a *non-word* (a meaningless combination of vowels and consonants). She exposes the same set of participants to three sets of words which vary in their frequency (high, medium, or low) and measures the time that it takes them to decide whether they have seen a word or a non-word in milliseconds.

(b) A researcher is interested in the effect of the sex hormone oestrogen on the feeding behaviour of female rats. He injects one group with a suitable concentration of oestrogen and another group with an equivalent volume of saline solution. After 3 days he measures the changes that have taken place in their body weights in grams.

(c) A social psychologist is interested in the role that anxiety plays in persuasion. She develops three separate public information programmes on dental care. These programmes vary in the extent to which they arouse anxiety in their viewers: one provokes a comparatively high level of anxiety, another a moderate degree of anxiety, and the third comparatively little anxiety. She exposes three separate groups of participants to these programmes and then assesses how many of those in each of the three groups subsequently take up the opportunity to make a dental appointment.

(d) An experimenter is interested in the effects of television violence upon the level of aggression it induces in its viewers. He exposes three separate groups of participants to three different kinds of television programme: one in which the violence is "realistic" (i.e., the blows cause obvious damage to the recipients), one in which the violence is "unrealistic" (i.e., the blows do not appear to damage the recipient, or hinder his ability to continue fighting), and one in which no violence is portrayed. The participants are subsequently allowed to administer electric shocks to their own victims during the course of a simulated teaching exercise (although, unbeknown to them, no actual shocks are delivered). The experimenter measures the mean level of shock (in volts) administered by those in each of the three groups.

(e) An occupational psychologist wishes to examine the impact of working with others on the productivity of a group of factory workers. She measures the number of packets of breakfast cereal this group pack into boxes in a 20-minute period when: working alone; working with one other worker; working with two others; working with four others; and working with eight others.

As experimenters we only control the values of the *independent* variable; we have no control over the precise values taken by the *dependent* variable. You will obtain these latter values from your participants – reaction times (in milliseconds), number of errors made, scores on a scale (e.g., for extraversion on a personality scale), blood glucose level (e.g., in milligrams per 100 millilitres), and so on. Note that you must *always* mention the units in which your dependent variable was measured.

Summary

1 A variable is anything that can come in different forms.

2 In experiments we manipulate variables in order to see what effects this has on other variables – in other words, which variables *cause* changes in other variables.

3 The variable we *manipulate* in an experiment is known as the *independent variable*.

4 The variable we *measure* in an experiment – to see if our manipulation of the independent variable has caused any changes – is known as the *dependent variable*.

9.1.2 Experimental and control conditions

When we manipulate an independent variable, therefore, what we do is alter the values or **levels** that it takes. We then look to see if altering these values or levels produces any corresponding changes in participants' scores on the dependent variable. Where our experiment has a single IV, the different values or levels of this variable are the *conditions* of our experiment. What we are interested in doing is *comparing* these conditions to see if there is any difference between them in the participants' scores. This, in a nutshell, is the logic of experimental design. Now let us see how it all looks in an experiment.

Suppose that you and I are interested in "folk wisdom" – and, in particular, in the old adage that eating cheese shortly before going to bed gives people nightmares. One basic way that we might test this proposition experimentally would be to take two groups of people, give one group a measured quantity of cheese (say, in proportion to their body weight) a standard time before going to bed (say, 3 hours) and ensure that those in the other group consumed no cheese during the same period. We could then count the number of nightmares reported by the two groups.

? SAQ 25   What are the independent and dependent variables in this experiment?

In this case we have manipulated our IV (cheese consumption) by forming two *conditions*: one in which the participants eat cheese

(Condition 1), and one in which they do not eat cheese (Condition 2). We are interested in the consequences of this – in the effect that this will have on the number of nightmares the participants experience in the two conditions.

This is a very basic experimental design. Our manipulation of the IV in this case involves comparing what happens when the suspected causal variable (cheese) is *present* (Condition 1) with what happens when it is *absent* (Condition 2). If cheese *does* cause nightmares, then we would expect those in Condition 1 to experience more nightmares than those in Condition 2. If cheese does *not* cause nightmares, then we should expect no such difference.

There are particular names for the conditions in an experiment where the IV is manipulated by comparing its *presence* with its *absence*. The condition in which the suspected causal variable is *present* is called the **experimental condition**. The condition in which the suspected causal variable is *absent* is called the **control condition**.

? **SAQ 26**   Which is the *control* condition in the above experiment?

Experiments in which we simply compare an experimental with a control condition can be simple and effective ways of finding things out in psychology. However, such a design does not exhaust the possibilities. We may, for instance, be more interested in comparing the effects of two different *levels* of the IV, than in comparing its presence with its absence. For instance, we might be interested in finding out whether different *types* of cheese produce different numbers of nightmares. We might therefore wish to compare a group of participants that ate Cheddar cheese with a group that ate Gorgonzola. In such an experiment, cheese would be present in *both* conditions. We would therefore have an experiment with two experimental conditions, rather than a control and experimental condition.

Such a design is perfectly acceptable in psychology. In fact, we do not even need to restrict ourselves to comparing only *two* experimental conditions – we can compare three or even more in one experiment. Moreover, one of these can be a *control* condition if we wish – that is, a condition in which the suspected causal variable is absent. So, for instance, we might expand our cheese and nightmare experiment to one in which we had a group of participants who ate Cheddar cheese, a group who ate Gorgonzola, a group who ate Brie, a group who ate Emmental, and a group who ate no cheese at all.

SAQ 27   How many conditions are there *overall* in this version of the cheese experiment? How many of these are *experimental* conditions?

 SAQ 28   Go back through the experiments described in SAQ 24, and state how many conditions each independent variable has. Do any of these have a control condition? If so, which ones?

I will discuss designs involving more than two levels of the IV in Chapter 13.

9.1.3   Control: eliminating confounding variables

What we do in an experiment, therefore, is manipulate the variable that we suspect to be causal – what we have learned to call the independent variable – and examine what impact this manipulation has upon the effect variable – what we have learned to call the dependent variable. If we subsequently find that there are indeed changes in the dependent variable, this strengthens our suspicion that there is a causal link between them.

However, in order to make this causal inference we have to ensure that the IV really is the only thing that we are changing in the experiment. Thus, in our cheese and nightmare experiment, for example, we do not want more people who are suffering life crises, or taking sleeping pills, or who are otherwise prone to having nightmares, to end up in the one condition rather than the other. If they did, we would no longer be sure that any differences we observed in our DV (incidence of nightmares) would be due to our manipulation of the cheese variable, or to these other variables. For, if our groups of participants indeed varied in their intake of sleeping pills, it might be that the variable *sleeping-pill consumption* is responsible for any differences between the groups in the extent to which they experience nightmares, rather than our IV (cheese consumption).

A variable that changes along with our IV is always an alternative possible cause of any differences we find in our DV. It represents a rival explanation for these effects, and is consequently an unwelcome intruder. We must, therefore, attempt to eliminate such variables and we do this by *controlling* them.

The most effective way of achieving **control** is to hold the other main candidates for the causal variable *constant* throughout our experiment, while changing the IV alone. Thus, in our cheese and nightmare experiment we would attempt to ensure that the only important difference between our groups of participants was whether or not they ate cheese before going to bed. Consequently, we would do our best to make sure that the groups really did not differ in their sleeping-pill consumption, or life crises, or any other variable that might make them prone to experience nightmares.

An uncontrolled variable that changes along with our independent variable is known in the trade as a **confounding variable** (to confound = to confuse), for it confounds the effects of the independent variable. Confounding variables are not just any old uncontrolled variables. Confounding variables are special – they are variables that themselves have different levels that *coincide* with the different levels of the IV – things like finding that more people with sleep problems are in the experimental than in the control condition (or vice versa). Confounding variables are spanners in the works of the experiment, fundamental flaws in the design or execution that undermine the capacity to draw causal inferences.

You will find that much of the time you spend on the design of your experiments will involve spotting and controlling potential confounding variables. Confounding variables prevent us from unequivocally attributing the changes that we find in the DV to our manipulation of the IV. This is because they provide possible alternative explanations – for example, that any difference in the occurrence of nightmares is caused by sleeping pills, rather than by cheese consumption.

To recap, then, in an experiment what we do is take a variable, the variable that might be causal (the independent variable) and manipulate this variable (e.g., by varying whether it is absent or present). We then look for associated changes on the effect or outcome variable (the dependent variable). If we find that the effect is present when the suspected cause is present, but is absent when the suspected cause is absent, *and if* we have held everything else *constant* across the two conditions of our experiment, then we can conclude that the variable is indeed causal. There can be no other explanation for the changes in the effect variable, because the only thing that differs between the two conditions is the presence or absence of the causal variable. If, however, we find that the effect occurs, even though the suspected cause is not present, then we can safely conclude that it is not the causal variable after all.

Summary of Sections 9.1.2–9.1.3

1 In order to design an effective experiment we have to isolate the variables that we are interested in and hold other variables constant across our experimental conditions. This is known as *controlling* these other variables.

2 Variables that change along with (*covary* with) our independent variable are *confounding* variables.

3 A well-designed experiment does not have confounding variables.

9.1.4 Experimental and null hypotheses

In an experiment, then, we *manipulate* an independent variable by altering the *values* that it takes. Simultaneously, we *control* other candidates for the causal variable by holding them *constant* across the conditions. We then look to see if the changes we make to the IV result in changes to the DV – that is, whether there are differences in the DV between our conditions. In particular, if our IV really is the causal variable, then we can anticipate, or *hypothesize*, what the actual outcome will be. This is a fundamental feature of experimenting. It is time to consider it in some detail.

Think back to the cheese experiment. If folk wisdom is correct, then what would we expect to happen in this experiment? Wisdom has it that eating cheese shortly before going to sleep will result in nightmares. Therefore, we should expect those in the cheese condition to experience more nightmares than those in the control condition. That is, if cheese really does cause nightmares, then we would expect more of those eating cheese before going to bed to experience nightmares than do those not eating cheese before going to bed.

 SAQ 29   However, is this the only possible outcome? What else might happen? Put the book down for a moment and think about this clearly.

In fact, our experiment can have one of *three* possible outcomes. We might find that those in the experimental condition experience *more* nightmares than do those in the control condition. On the other hand, we might find that those in the experimental condition experience *fewer* nightmares than do those in the control condition. Finally, we might find that there is essentially *no difference* between the conditions in the number of nightmares the participants experience. This will be true of *all* experiments in which we test for differences between two conditions; between them, these three options exhaust the possibilities. So – and this is important – we can specify *in advance* what the outcome of our experiment might be.

However, there is an important distinction to be made between these three potential outcomes. Two of them predict that there will be a *difference* between our conditions in the incidence of nightmares. These happen to be the outcomes we would anticipate *if* cheese affects nightmares in some way (either by stimulating or suppressing them). The third outcome, however, is that there will be no noteworthy difference between them. This is what we would expect if cheese has no influence upon nightmares.

Thus, if we assume that cheese does affect the occurrence of nightmares in some way, we would predict a different outcome to our experiment than if we assume that cheese has no effect upon the incidence of nightmares. That is, if we assume that eating cheese in some way changes the likelihood of experiencing nightmares, we would predict that there will be a difference of some sort between our groups in the frequency of nightmares they report. Of course, the assumption that cheese influences the occurrence of nightmares is the very assumption that led us to design our experiment in the first place. So, under the assumption that led to the experiment, we would predict a difference of some sort between our two groups. For this reason we call this assumption the **experimental hypothesis**. In fact:

1 *All* experiments have experimental hypotheses.
2 The experimental hypothesis leads us to predict that there will be a difference between conditions. That is, from the experimental hypothesis we derive the prediction that there will be a difference on the DV as a result of manipulating the IV.

 SAQ 30   Go back to SAQ 24 and work through the examples there, stating for each what you think the prediction might be under the experimental hypothesis.

Now, the predictions derived from the experimental hypotheses come in one of two forms. The **nondirectional prediction** states that there will be a difference somewhere between the conditions in your experiment, but says nothing about the *direction* of this difference (i.e., does not state which condition will exceed the other on the dependent variable). In contrast, the **directional prediction** not only leads us to expect a difference, but also says something about the direction that the difference will take. (Alternative names that you might come across for these are **bidirectional** for the nondirectional prediction and **unidirectional** for the directional prediction.)

Thus, in our cheese and nightmare experiment, the nondirectional prediction simply states that the experimental and control group will experience *different* numbers of nightmares. A directional prediction, on the other hand, would state, for example, that our cheese group will experience *more* nightmares than our no cheese group.

However, what of the third possible outcome – the prediction that there will be *no difference* between the two conditions? This is a very important prediction and is derived from an hypothesis called the **null hypothesis**. You will find that the null hypothesis plays a crucial role in the process by which you come to analyse your data. In fact:

1 *All* experiments have a null hypothesis.
2 The null hypothesis is that the independent variable does not affect the dependent variable. It therefore leads us to predict that there will be little or no difference on the dependent variable between the conditions in the experiment.

Under this null hypothesis we assume, therefore, that the IV does *not* cause changes in the DV. It is called the null hypothesis because it is capable of being tested and thus of being *nullified*. As you will discover in Chapter 11, we use the null hypothesis to help us to calculate the statistics that we need to make sense of our data. Despite its name, the null hypothesis is thus a very important hypothesis.

It is very important that you learn to distinguish clearly between the predictions derived from the null hypothesis and those derived from the experimental hypothesis. The experimental hypothesis leads us to predict a difference between the conditions. In contrast, the null hypothesis leads us to predict that there will be no such difference. Do not confuse these! Design your experiments so that the *experimental* hypothesis leads to predictions of a difference *somewhere* between your conditions. Otherwise you will actually be failing to test your theoretical ideas (because you will be confusing the predictions derived from the experimental hypothesis with those derived from the null hypothesis – see Appendix 1).

This is why it is important not to think of the experimental hypothesis as the *experimenter's* own personal hypothesis. It is perfectly conceivable that you might design and run an experiment in which you do not really expect there to be a difference between your conditions (e.g., if you are testing a theory that you do not agree with). Nevertheless, the experimental hypothesis would still lead you to predict a difference, even if this was not the hypothesis that you favoured or expected. For instance, you might be sceptical about the validity of folk wisdom and thus expect (privately) to find no difference in the incidence of nightmares in the two conditions (eating or not eating cheese). Nevertheless, the *experimental* hypothesis will still lead you to predict such a difference. For this is the proposition under test in the experiment.

Summary of Section 9.1.4

1 All experiments have a null hypothesis and at least one experimental hypothesis.

2 The experimental hypothesis involves the assumption that the IV affects the DV. It leads to the prediction that there will be a *difference* on the DV somewhere among the conditions in the experiment.

3 The prediction derived from the experimental hypothesis can either lead us to expect a difference between conditions in one direction (*directional*) or in either direction (*nondirectional*).

4 The null hypothesis involves the assumption that the IV does *not* affect the DV. It therefore leads to the prediction that there will be *no difference* among the conditions in the experiment.

9.1.5 **More on controlling variables**

As budding experimenters, you will come to appreciate not only that the world is full of variables, but that when you have on your experimenter's hat, most of them, most of the time, are at best irrelevant and at worst a downright nuisance. When we are interested in whether cheese causes nightmares, as well as consuming or not consuming our measured amount of Cheddar at a standard time before retiring for the night, our experimental and control participants will also vary in what they had for their evening meal, how long they take to drop off to sleep, what they wear in bed, what colour the bedroom wallpaper is, what TV programme they watched and for how long that evening, whether they drank any alcohol, how many in-laws they have, whether and how they voted in the last election, how recently they last went swimming and whether they believe in God. Some of these variables may be obviously relevant to the issue at hand, the relationship between the IV and the DV, and others will not. For example, drinking alcohol will influence a person's quality and depth of sleep and may, therefore, influence whether or not they experience nightmares. For this reason we would not want to discover that too many more of our participants in one of the conditions drank alcohol over the course of the experiment than did participants in the other condition.

 SAQ 31   Why not?

Indeed, we may well be concerned enough about the possibility that alcohol would nullify or otherwise distort the relationship between our IV and DV that we would want to make this one of the variables that we held constant across our experimental conditions. Unpopular though it might make us, we might therefore outlaw alcohol consumption for our participants during the period in which they took part in the experiment.

However, what about everything else? Should we attempt to control for the number of in-laws? The colour of the bedroom wallpaper? Whether our participants believe in God? Well, whereas in theory we would control absolutely everything if we could, so that the *only* difference between our conditions was the IV, in reality – in human work at least – this is not possible. Instead, we use our judgement and discretion to decide which of the millions of irrelevant or **extraneous variables** (extraneous = not belonging to the matter in hand) swishing around in the psychological universe we need to control by holding them constant. Other variables we control for, not by holding them at a constant level, but by attempting to ensure that they will vary equally enough across the conditions of our experiment to not be confounding variables. We will talk more about this in the next chapter, when we consider *randomization*. For now, however, you need to recognize that you cannot control for absolutely everything. Instead, you have to decide on the priorities for control. That is, you have to decide which of the variables in the situation you will be able to control by holding them constant across conditions.

Although this may sound pretty confusing, it is in fact relatively straightforward. With the cheese and nightmare experiment, we have already sketched a basic design: One group of people will consume a measured amount of cheese a standard time before going to bed. The control group will not eat cheese before going to bed.

 SAQ 32   It would be even better if the control group ate a standard amount of something that looked like cheese, but contained none of the ingredients of cheese, an equivalent time before going to bed. Why?

We have already mentioned some of the other key variables that we would wish to control by holding them constant: we would probably exclude from the study anyone on medication likely to influence sleep quality (thus holding this variable at the level *no relevant medication* across both conditions). We would also probably not allow alcohol consumption (thus holding this variable at the level *no alcohol* across both conditions). We might also investigate the sleep history of our participants and exclude from the study anyone with a history of sleep problems (thus holding this variable at the level *no sleep problem history* across both conditions). In doing this you can see that, if we do find more nightmares in our experimental condition, we can rule out explanations that these are caused by more people in the experimental group having their sleep disturbed by medication, alcohol, or just being more prone to sleep problems in the first place.

There may be other variables that we would control for in this way, but we would have to stop somewhere. For instance, our participants will sleep in rooms with different coloured walls. We would be unlikely to demand that for the purposes of our experiment they all had their rooms painted a standard shade of a restful pastel colour. Thus, participants in both conditions will sleep in rooms of different colours and the variable *colour of bedroom walls* will be left to vary rather than being held constant. However, we would hope that there was no consistent or *systematic* difference in the colours in the bedrooms of the experimental group when compared with the control group.

Of course, if we were very concerned that an environmental factor like the colour of the bedroom walls was likely to make a difference, then we might well take active steps to control for it. One way in which we could rule out such environmental factors would be to have the experiment take place not at home but in a sleep laboratory. There we could ensure that a whole range of additional factors was held constant across our experimental and control conditions. Laboratories offer opportunities for controlling a whole range of extraneous variables, which is one of the reasons for their appeal in psychology.

Summary of Section 9.1.5

1 In reality, there are usually too many irrelevant or *extraneous* variables in the situation for us to hold all of them constant.

2 We thus select the more important of these to be controlled by holding them constant, so that each participant has the same value or score on this variable.

3 The remaining variables we allow to vary among the participants *within* our conditions, but try to ensure that the overall or average scores or values for this variable do not differ *systematically* between conditions (i.e., that if calculated, the average score would be roughly equal for each of the conditions).

4 However, this control at the level of the group or condition, rather than at the level of the individual participant, does not *guarantee* that there will be no systematic differences between the conditions.

9.2   Correlation

I have more to say about designing experiments in Chapters 10 and 13. However, it is not always possible to conduct experiments. There may, for instance, be practical or ethical factors that prevent us from actually *manipulating* variables in the way we need for our studies to qualify as true experiments. Under such circumstances we can turn to a rather less powerful, but still informative, technique – **correlation**.

The critical difference between the experiment and correlation is that, with correlation, we are unable to distinguish between *independent* and *dependent* variables. This is because we do not *manipulate* variables when we undertake correlational work. Instead, we rely on *natural* changes or differences to tell us something about which variables are related in some way to each other.

To illustrate this, imagine that you and I are interested in whether living close to the transmitters that relay messages to and from mobile (cell) phones is a cause of behavioural problems in children. An experimental approach to this question would involve assigning people from birth randomly to live either close to or far away from such transmitters and then comparing the numbers in each group that eventually developed behavioural problems. This is not only profoundly unethical but clearly also impractical. Under these circumstances, if we wish to gather data on humans, then we are restricted to *correlational* data. In this instance we rely on differences that exist already in the population. That is, we would look to see if there was any correspondence between the distance existing groups of people lived from the transmitters and the incidence of behavioural problems. However, this has significant implications for our ability to say whether there is a *causal* relationship between the variables "distance from transmitter" and "behavioural problems".

For instance, suppose that we find that there is a relationship between these variables and that this is indeed the one we suspect: that, as the transmitters get closer, so there is an increase in the incidence of behavioural problems. This would be an example of what we call a **positive correlation** (because *increases* in proximity to the transmitters are accompanied by *increases* in the incidence of behavioural problems). Such a relationship is depicted graphically in Figure 9.1.

Now, at first glance it may seem obvious to conclude that the transmitters are responsible for *causing* the behavioural problems. However, we actually have no grounds for drawing this conclusion. For, with correlational data, all we know is that there is an *association* between these variables – that as one varies (goes up, goes down), so does the other. It could be that the transmitters do indeed cause the problems. On the other hand, it could be that people with behavioural problems end up living close to transmitters (perhaps because they have less control over where they live). It could also be that something else is responsible for the relationship. Perhaps the transmitters are placed in poorer areas of towns and cities, where people need the money from the telephone companies or feel too powerless to object to them placing transmitters in their communities. In which case the association may not be between the transmitters and the behavioural problems, but a **third variable**, such as poor diet or unsatisfactory schooling, may be responsible for the behavioural problems and the relationship between transmitters and behavioural problems is more apparent than real. Such a relationship is described in the trade as **spurious** (spurious = not genuine).

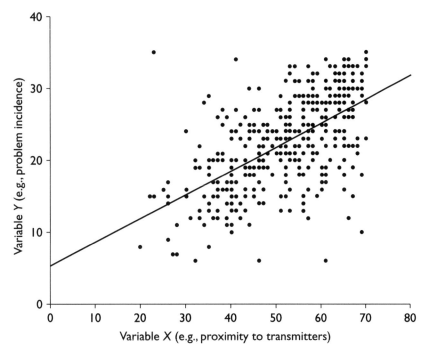

Figure 9.1. A scatter plot showing a positive correlation between variables X and Y.

An illustration might reveal this more clearly. There is, in fact, a positive correlation between the consumption of ice cream and the incidence of deaths by drowning. That is, as people tend to eat more ice cream, so more people tend to die in drowning accidents.

 SAQ 33   Does this mean that there must be some kind of causal relationship between them (even if we cannot say which way it goes)?

Now the relationship between ice cream consumption and deaths by drowning is sufficiently bizarre for us to suspect that something strange is going on. Nevertheless, *even where the direction of causality seems obvious* it is still not permissible to assume that one of the variables is responsible for producing changes in the other. For, in relying upon natural changes, rather than manipulating variables, we are unable to control variables that *covary* with (i.e., vary along with) the ones that we are interested in. That is, we are unable to control for *confounding* variables (for, as you know, a confounding variable is an extraneous variable that covaries with the variable we are investigating).

Correlational data are thus *inevitably* confounded. So, be aware of this problem – it applies to many issues within and outside psychology, even those – such as smoking and lung cancer, or the consumption of saturated fats and heart disease – in which the direction of causality seems "obvious". With such data we cannot rule out the possibility that the causal relationship is the reverse of the one we believe or even spurious. (Thus, although the experimental data on animals and other data suggest it is highly probable that smoking causes lung cancer and excessive consumption of saturated fat contributes to heart disease, it remains possible that those who are prone to lung cancer are those who for some reason choose to smoke, or that those who are prone to heart disease are those who for some reason tend also to like eating saturated fat.)

As you can see, it is no surprise that the biggest debates in our scientific and public lives often centre around issues for which the data, concerning humans at least, are *correlational*. Moreover, as you can see from the above examples, this is certainly not an issue that is restricted to psychology.

9.3 Description

Rather than concerning ourselves with relationships between variables, we may be content simply to describe particular variables. For instance, we might wish to examine the nature of people's attitudes towards genetically modified crops, or to find out what they can tell us about some aspect of their social behaviour. Such studies are neither experimental nor correlational. They are *descriptive*.

A classic example of such an approach is the public opinion poll. Opinion polls tell us things like the percentage of the sample questioned who stated that they would be prepared to vote for particular parties if an election were held immediately, or who they think would make the best prime minister or president. This is **description**. It is simply an attempt to make a statement about the characteristics of the variable "the voting public". However, there is no attempt to *explain* these findings. That is, the data themselves are not used to explain *why* the individuals sampled intend to vote the way they do. Data of this nature are usually generated by *questionnaire* or *interview*, take the form of what is called a *survey*, and are described solely in terms of *descriptive statistics*, such as percentages and means (Section 4.1). It is highly unlikely that as a student of psychology you will generate numerical data that are simply descriptive. If not experimental, your quantitative data are likely to be correlational.

Summary of Sections 9.2–9.3

1 The critical difference between the correlation and the experiment is that in the correlation we are unable to distinguish between *independent* and *dependent* variables. This is because we do not *manipulate* any variables in a correlation. Instead, we rely upon differences that already exist to discover which variables are related to each other.

2 The consequence of this is that we are unable to draw *causal inferences* from correlational data. That is, correlations reveal *associations* between variables, rather than causes and effects.

Consolidating your learning

This closing section is designed to help you check your understanding and determine what you might need to study further. You can use the list of methodological and statistical concepts to check which ones you are happy with and which you may need to double-check. You can use this list to find the relevant terms in the chapter and also in other textbooks of design or statistics. The diagnostic questions provide a further test of your understanding. Finally, there is a description of what is covered in the two statistics textbooks paired with this book plus a list of relevant further material that you can find on the book's Web site.

Methodological and statistical concepts covered in this chapter

In this chapter we discussed the following issues. You should now understand what is meant by the following terms:

Causal inference
Causal variable
Confounding variable
Control condition
Controlling extraneous variables
Correlation (positive, negative)
Dependent variable
Description
Directional (bidirectional, unidirectional) hypothesis
Effect variable
Experiment
Experimental condition
Experimental hypothesis
Extraneous variables
Independent variable
Levels of a manipulated variable
Manipulating variable
Non-directional hypothesis
Null hypothesis
Placebo
Self-fulfilling beliefs
Spurious correlation
Third variable
Variable

Diagnostic questions – check your understanding

1 What is a *variable*?
2 What is the name of the variable we *manipulate* in an experiment?
3 What is the name of the variable we *measure* in an experiment to assess the effects of our manipulation?
4 From which hypothesis can we predict that there will be *no difference* between the conditions in an experiment? Is it (a) the experimental hypothesis or (b) the null hypothesis?
5 What is a *nondirectional* prediction?

You can find the answers at the rear of the book (p. 275).

Statistics textbooks

Σ The books paired with *Designing and Reporting Experiments* have the following coverage:

Learning to use statistical tests in psychology – Greene and D'Oliveira
Greene and D'Oliveira cover variability in Chapter 1, and independent and dependent variables, experimental and null hypotheses, and experimental and control conditions in Chapter 2. They also cover different tests for correlation in Part IV. As an undergraduate student you will only need to look in Part IV if you need to find out about a particular test and you are likely at first to need the earlier chapters in this section (on Chi-square, Pearson's *r*, and simple regression) rather than the later ones, (which cover more advanced tests and issues (e.g., multiple regression and the General Linear Model).

SPSS survival manual – Pallant
Part four of Pallant covers correlation. You need turn to these chapters only once you have some data to analyse. For more advanced students, the chapter on correlation contains a useful account of how to test whether two correlation coefficients differ significantly (Chapter 11). Pallant also covers partial correlation (Chapter 12), multiple regression (Chapters 13 and 14), and factor analysis (Chapter 15). The latter are again more relevant to more advanced undergraduates and graduate students.

 ### The *Designing and Reporting Experiments* Web site

In Section B of the Web site at **http://mcgraw-hill.co.uk/openup/ harris/** you will find a discussion of how to report a wide range of statistical tests that you might use to analyse experimental or correlational data, including particular things to watch out for when you do.

10 Basic experimental design

Although experiments have a universal *basic* logic, they vary in design and complexity. For instance, they may have one or more than one independent variable, any or all of which may employ *unrelated* or *related* samples. It is time to find out what this means.

10.1 Unrelated and related samples independent variables

Suppose that you and I have been approached to undertake some research into the effect of listening to music in the car on driving performance. There are lots of ways that we could go about doing this. For instance, we might examine actual driving performance on the road, or on a test track, or perhaps we could gain access to a driving simulator and test people's performance on that. We might decide to focus on particular aspects of driving performance, such as maintaining control of the car or average speed. Or we could assess the number of mistakes made over a standard course, or monitor the participants' eye movements as they drive to discover whether there are any differences in the way that they monitor the situation unfolding outside as a consequence of having music on or off.

On the other hand, we might wish to refine the question that we address – examine whether different materials (e.g., different types of music or different types of radio programme) affect performance in different ways or to a different extent. Similarly, we might examine whether the volume at which people listen is important and whether this differs with the material being listened to. Or we might want to find out whether teenagers are affected more than older drivers, or men more than women.

All of these possibilities hold different implications for the experiment we would eventually design and the conclusions we would ultimately draw. Essentially, we have here a whole series of decisions that we have to make about the IV(s) and DV(s) in our experiment. However, there is one fundamental feature of our design that we would still have to decide upon, even after we have determined the precise question we wish to examine, chosen our IV and DV, and set the levels on the IV. This is how we will *distribute the participants* in our experiment.

For instance, suppose we decided to run the above experiment on a driving simulator, using a computer to display a standard set of hazards and problems in a random sequence. We could then measure driving performance on a range of *relevant* measures from average speed through manual control to number of (virtual!) pedestrians knocked over. Participants would be free to choose their own listening material and to set the volume and adjust it whenever they desired.

So far, so good. However, we have yet to decide how we are going to distribute our participants across the different conditions (music on or music off). We could, for example, have one group of participants performing in the music on condition and another (different) group in the music off condition. If we did this, we would have different groups of people performing in the two conditions. The scores on our DV would therefore be from *different* samples and be *unrelated* to each other. Our IV would thus be an **unrelated samples** IV.

However, instead of assessing the driving performance of different participants, we could compare the driving performance of the *same* participants. That is, we could measure each participant's performance when driving with music off and his or her performance when driving with music on. In this experiment we have the same group of participants performing in the two conditions. The scores on our DV would therefore be from the *same* sample and would be *related* to each other. Our IV would thus be a **related samples** IV.

? SAQ 34 What type of IV did we have in our original, two-condition cheese experiment (Chapter 9)? How else could we have run this experiment, and what type of IV would we have then employed?

These, then, are the two basic IVs used by psychologists: the *unrelated* samples IV, in which we take a different batch of participants for each of the conditions or levels on the IV and the *related* samples IV, in which we use the same batch of participants for the conditions or levels on that IV.

 SAQ 35   Now go back through the experiments outlined in SAQ 24 and state what type of IVs the experimenters employed in each.

Designs involving these IVs are illustrated in Tables 10.1 and 10.2. You can see that for our experiment involving unrelated samples we need 32 participants to have 16 participants per condition. For the related samples version, however, we need only 16 participants to achieve this.

Table 10.1
An Unrelated Samples IV with Two Conditions: Allocation of Participants

Condition 1	Condition 2
p02	p01
p04	p03
p09	p05
p10	p06
p11	p07
p13	p08
p14	p12
p19	p15
p21	p16
p24	p17
p25	p18
p26	p20
p28	p22
p29	p23
p30	p27
p32	p31

Note. Participants have been allocated to conditions randomly. p = participant. Note that you would probably want to use more participants than 16 per condition (see Section 10.6).

Table 10.2
A Related Samples IV with Two Conditions

Participant	Condition 1	Condition 2
p01	2nd	1st
p02	1st	2nd
p03	1st	2nd
p04	2nd	1st
p05	2nd	1st
p06	1st	2nd
p07	2nd	1st
p08	1st	2nd
p09	2nd	1st
p10	1st	2nd
p11	2nd	1st
p12	2nd	1st
p13	1st	2nd
p14	2nd	1st
p15	1st	2nd
p16	1st	2nd

Note. Orders have been counterbalanced and allocated randomly. p = participant.

Those of you who are not expected to contribute to the design of your experiment will still need to be able to state which type of IV(s) you employed. So you must learn to make the above distinction. However, those of you who are expected to contribute at the design stage will also need to be able to decide which type to employ. So let us turn to a consideration of the factors to bear in mind when deciding which types of IV to use in your experiment. First, however, we need a brief word about terminology.

Summary of Section 10.1

1 Two basic independent variables employed in psychology are the *unrelated* samples IV and the *related* samples IV.

2 In the unrelated samples IV, a *different* set of participants is assigned to the conditions or levels of the IV.

3 In the related samples IV, the *same* set of participants appears in the conditions or levels of the IV.

10.2 Other names for unrelated and related samples independent variables

Sometimes when you are learning about methodology and statistics in psychology you can feel that you are spending almost as much time learning terminology as you are learning concepts. Moreover, just when you get to grips with one term for something you find that there is another term for the same thing (perhaps more than one additional term, which is about the last thing that you need). Sadly, this is especially true of names for this basic distinction between types of IV.

Some time ago psychologists referred to the participants in their experiments as *subjects*. These days this term is considered unacceptable, as our participants are above all our fellow human beings and not simply "subjects" of experimental enquiry. However, some important terms in statistics and methodology retain the old-fashioned language and you may well come across this terminology in some other textbooks or certain statistical software packages.

A traditional term for unrelated samples IVs is **between subjects**. This is because, when we use *unrelated* samples, our comparisons are *between* different participants. Other terms that you may come across for the same thing are **independent** or **uncorrelated samples**, **independent** or **uncorrelated measures** or **between participants** or **between groups**.

A traditional term for related samples IVs is **within subjects**. This is because, when we use *related* samples, our comparisons are *within* the same participants. (That is, we are comparing the performance of the same person across the different conditions and thus making comparisons *within* the person.) Other terms that you may come across for the same thing are **dependent** or **correlated samples**, **dependent** or **correlated measures**, **repeated measures** or **within participants**.

Unfortunately, the problem is compounded by the fact that people can become surprisingly worked up about which label should be used. Throughout this book I use "unrelated samples" to denote IVs where the data in the different levels come from different participants. I use "related samples" to denote IVs where the data in the different levels come from the same participants. Given the strength of feeling that this issue can evoke, however, it is a good idea to find out whether your tutor favours other labels for these IVs and, if so, to use these instead. The important thing (of course) is to make sure that you can recognize these different types of IV and understand the distinction between them. What you choose to call them is secondary. However, you *must* be consistent in your use of terminology in a report.

Summary of Section 10.2

1 There are a number of different terms available to make the same basic distinction between IVs where the data in the different levels come from different participants and IVs where the data in the different levels come from the same participants.

2 The important thing is to understand the distinction underlying these types of IV and to be able to recognize which is which.

3 Do not chop and change terminology in a report: decide which terms you are going to use and stick to them throughout.

10.3   Deciding whether to use related or unrelated samples

In order to consider how you might choose between these types of IV, we must think back to the logic of experimental design discussed in Chapter 9. The aim is to manipulate the variable we suspect to be causal (the IV) and examine what impact this manipulation has upon the effect variable (the DV). If we find that, when we alter the IV, there are changes in the DV as well, this strengthens our suspicion that there is a causal link between them.

However, as we pointed out earlier, in order to make this causal inference we have to ensure that the IV really is the only thing we are changing in the situation – that is, we do not want any *confounding* variables. One source of confounding can be our particular sample of participants. Thus, in our driving and music experiment, for example, we do not want too many more of the better drivers to end up in one condition than the other. For, if they did, we could no longer be sure that any differences that we observed in our DV (e.g., number of errors made over a standard course) would be due to our manipulation of the music variable or to basic differences in driving ability. Confounding variables, remember, prevent us from unequivocally attributing the changes we find in the DV to our manipulation of the IV. This is because they provide possible rival explanations for any effects we find (e.g., that any difference in driving performance between the conditions is due to basic differences in ability to drive rather than to the effect of having music on or off). Essentially, related and unrelated samples IVs differ in the nature and extent of their potentially confounding variables.

Let's illustrate this with an example. Suppose we ran our driving and music experiment using *unrelated* samples and found that those who drove without music performed better than those who drove with music on. This could of course be because listening to music affects concentration and impairs ability to drive. However, it could also be simply because more of the better drivers were put into the "music off" condition. For there are pronounced *individual differences* in driving ability. Any differences in driving performance between groups of different people, therefore, might well stem from this basic fact of life, rather than from any manipulation of the independent variable. When we use *unrelated* samples, of course, we are inevitably comparing the performances of different people.

There are ways in which we can attempt to minimize the impact of individual differences upon our experiment. However, there is only one way in which we can actually eliminate this source of extraneous variation. This is by employing *related* samples.

When we use related samples, we do not compare the performances of different people. Instead, we compare the performances of the *same* people on different occasions. So, in the case of our music experiment, we would assess the driving performances of any given individual both when driving with music on and when driving with music off. We can safely assume that any differences in performance under the two conditions cannot stem from individual differences in driving ability because it is the same person in both conditions.

If you are still confused by this, imagine that we developed a revolutionary kind of running shoe that we suspected would improve the running performance of those who wore it. Using *unrelated* samples would be like giving the shoes to half of the runners in a race and comparing their finishing positions with the runners who did not have the new shoes. Using *related* samples would be like getting the runners to run at least once with the new shoes and at least once with their normal running shoes. In the first race it is possible that our runners with the new shoes might find themselves up against people who were simply much better than them anyway. In the latter race, however, you can see that this would not matter, because we are not interested in where our runners came in *absolute* terms, but simply in how well they fared in comparison with their performance without the new shoes (e.g., in time taken to complete the course). That is, in the first instance it would make a great deal of difference if they found themselves running against a team of Olympic athletes; in the latter case it would not matter at all (provided, of course, that they ran against the same athletes on both occasions and that they were not too demoralized by the first drubbing).

Using related samples, therefore, eliminates from the experimental equation permanent or chronic **individual differences** in ability at the experimental task – the things that make people *generally* better or worse at the task regardless of the IV. We know that some people will simply be better than others on the driving simulator regardless of whether they are listening to music or not. Using unrelated samples, we trust that the variation due to such individual differences in ability will be spread roughly equally between the two conditions. With related samples, however, differences in performance arising from such individual differences in ability are constant across the two conditions and can be removed from the equation.

In eliminating chronic individual differences from our experiment, related samples IVs reduce the amount of background or **extraneous variation** that we have to cope with – variation *other than* that arising from our manipulation of the IV. From our point of view, this is a good thing. For this reason, using related samples is, at least in principle, to be preferred to using unrelated samples. As you have to start somewhere, therefore, a good rule of thumb when designing experiments is to start by exploring the possibility of using related samples IVs, and only turn to the alternatives when you discover obstacles that prevent you from doing so.

Summary of Section 10.3

1 In all experiments the effects of the IV on the DV are assessed against a background of *inherent* or *extraneous* variation.

2 Permanent or chronic *individual differences* in ability at the experimental task are a considerable source of such extraneous variation.

3 Related samples IVs eliminate such *individual differences* and thereby remove a large part of this extraneous variation. Related samples IVs should, therefore, be used in preference to unrelated samples IVs when there are no insurmountable obstacles to using them.

10.4   Related samples

Related samples are preferable *in principle* to unrelated samples. However, this does not mean that using related samples is without problems.

10.4.1   Advantages

The major advantage of using related samples is that doing so reduces the background variation against which we have to assess the impact of the IV on the DV. It does this by *eliminating permanent* or *chronic individual differences*. There is also a practical advantage that, as students, you will probably find extremely useful – you need fewer participants.

10.4.2   Disadvantages

If using related samples eliminates one source of variation, it unfortunately introduces another – *order* effects. When we run an experiment using related samples, by definition, we will obtain more than one score from our participant (see Table 10.2). This means, of course, that we will have to present our conditions one after the other. This produces problems of its own – problems that do not exist when we use unrelated samples.

For example, suppose that we ran our music experiment using related samples, testing all of our participants first with the music off and then with the music on. Suppose that we found that driving actually improved when the drivers had the music on. Can you think of an alternative explanation for this finding, other than the suggestion that listening to music led to the improvement in performance?

Well, the improvement in driving performance might simply be due to the fact that the participants in our experiment got better at the task as they became more familiar with the driving simulator. That is, they might have got better because they became more *practised* and, because they all did the music on condition second, this **practice effect** contributed more to performance with the music on than to performance with the music off. In other words, we have here a *confounding* variable arising from the *order* in which we ran the conditions.

Moreover, the same argument would apply even if we had found the opposite: that is, if we had found that the performance of our drivers had *deteriorated* from the first condition to the second. In this case, it could simply be that our participants had become *bored* with the task or were *fatigued* and started to make more mistakes because of this.

Order effects are the price we pay for eliminating individual differences with related samples. Order effects come in two forms. There are those that lead to an *improvement* in the participant's performance – things like practice, increasing familiarity with the experimental task and equipment, increasing awareness of the task demands. In contrast, there are those that lead to a *deterioration* in performance – things like loss of concentration, due to fatigue or boredom. Both types of effect occur simultaneously, but have opposite effects on the DV. Both types of effect need to be controlled for.

10.4.3 Controlling for order effects

The best way of controlling for order effects is to **counterbalance**. When we counterbalance we ensure that each condition in our experiment follows and is preceded by every other condition an equal number of times. Thus, for each participant who does one particular sequence of conditions, there are other participants who perform the conditions in all the other possible combinations of orders. Although in the abstract this sounds horrendously complicated, generally it can be achieved comparatively easily. So, for instance, in our driving experiment a very simple control for order effects would be to ensure that half of the participants drove with the music on *before* they drove with the music off, whereas the other half drove with the music on *after* they had driven with the music off (see Table 10.3). This way, although we would not have *eliminated* order effects – our participants are still likely to get better or worse as time goes by – we will have rendered these effects *unsystematic*. That is, practice, fatigue and boredom should affect the music on condition about as much as they affect the music off condition.

We will talk more about counterbalancing when we consider extending the number of levels on an IV (Section 13.1.2). Sometimes, however, there are too many conditions to counterbalance. Under these circumstances there are a number of alternatives. One of these is to **randomize** the order of the conditions.

Table 10.3

A Counterbalanced Design Using Related Samples to Examine the Effects of Having Music Off or On upon Driving Performance

Participant	Music on	Music off
p02	1st	2nd
p03	1st	2nd
p06	1st	2nd
p08	1st	2nd
p10	1st	2nd
p13	1st	2nd
p15	1st	2nd
p16	1st	2nd
p01	2nd	1st
p04	2nd	1st
p05	2nd	1st
p07	2nd	1st
p09	2nd	1st
p11	2nd	1st
p12	2nd	1st
p14	2nd	1st

Note. Participants have been randomly allocated to orders. p = participant.

For example, if we had an experiment with six conditions, this would give us 720 different orders. If we wished to counterbalance these orders, we would need a minimum of 720 participants (one for each different sequence of the six conditions). Although there are alternatives that you may come across later on in your statistics course (e.g., the *Latin square*), under these circumstances you will most probably find yourselves *randomizing* the orders undertaken by your participants.

When we randomize the order of our conditions we do not actually ensure that all the conditions are followed by and preceded by every other condition an equal number of times. Instead, we trust that a *random sequence* will spread the order effects more or less equally around the various conditions. So, for instance, if we randomized the orders in which our participants performed in an experiment with six experimental conditions, we would hope that each of the conditions would appear in each of the ordinal positions (first, second, third, etc.) just about as often as the others. The more participants we have, the likelier it is that this will be the case.

This is because the critical feature of a random sequence is that the items in the sequence all have an equal chance of being selected for any of the positions in that sequence. In the case of orders, what this means is that any of the conditions can appear first, second, third, etc., for any of the participants. So, for example, in a six-condition experiment, Condition A has the same chance as Conditions B, C, D, E, and F, of being the first condition undertaken by Participant 1. If Condition C is the one actually chosen by the random process, then Conditions A, B, D, E, and F, all have an equal chance of being the second condition undertaken by Participant 1. (See Appendix 2 for the details of how to go about making such random allocations.) If Condition D is chosen as the second condition, then Conditions A, B, E, and F, all have an equal chance of being the third condition undertaken by Participant 1, and so on until all the conditions have been assigned to this participant by the random process. Moreover, the same applies to Participant 2, and indeed to *all* of the participants in the experiment (Table 10.4). (For the record, this is randomization *without* replacement – see Appendix 2.)

When used to control for order effects, however, both counterbalancing and randomization have one thing in common. They are based upon the assumption that our participants are *not much more* fatigued or bored or practised when the music off condition

Table 10.4

Randomized Orders of Conditions for the First 10 Participants in a Six-Condition Experiment Employing Related Samples

Participant	Sequence
p01	C D A E F B
p02	B D F A C E
p03	F D B A E C
p04	A C B F D E
p05	F A D E B C
p06	A B F C E D
p07	E D B F A C
p08	C D B F E A
p09	D A E B F C
p10	E F C D B A

Note. Each sequence of conditions has been created randomly and separately for each participant. p = participant.

comes after the music on condition, than they are when the music off condition comes first. If they are, then we have what we call a significant **carry-over effect** among the conditions in our experiment. Neither counterbalancing nor randomization can control for such carry-over effects.

When you suspect that the conditions of your experiment will have a carry-over effect, therefore, you should not use a related samples design. An extreme example of such a case would be, for instance, if we were attempting to compare two different techniques of teaching a particular task. Once participants have learned the task once, it is not possible to make them unlearn it in order to learn it once again by the different method. Similarly, if we were undertaking research into the effects of alcohol upon risk perception, it would be a mistake to have our no alcohol condition immediately following our alcohol condition. So you must watch out for treatment conditions in your experiments that tend to markedly alter the state of your participant. Such conditions will have a lingering effect and will consequently influence performance in subsequent conditions, thus having a carry-over effect.

If these effects are only temporary, one way around them is to introduce a longer than usual time delay between conditions (e.g., hours, days, or even weeks). However, if the effects are more or less permanent (e.g., teaching methods) or if this strategy is not feasible (e.g., lack of time, lack of co-operation on the part of your participants), then it would be better to employ one of the alternative designs.

So, when designing any experiment involving related samples IVs, think sensibly and carefully about whether there are likely to be any significant carry-over effects between conditions and, if there are, about whether it is possible to modify your design to cope with them. If not, then you need to abandon the idea of using related samples on the offending IV.

Another problem that arises with related samples is the need to duplicate and *match* materials. For example, suppose that you and I were interested in establishing whether scores on a test of reasoning are influenced by the ways in which the questions are phrased – in particular, whether the problems are couched in *abstract* terms (e.g., using algebraic expressions like $A > R$) or in *concrete* terms (e.g., by using examples drawn from everyday life to express the same relationships – things like "Antony is older than Richard"). There are profound individual differences in people's ability to reason, so ideally we would like to run this experiment using related samples. We could do this by giving participants *both* concrete and abstract

Table 10.5
A Design Using Related Samples with Matched Materials to Examine the Effects of the Phrasing of the Questions (Concrete or Abstract) on Reasoning Performance

Group	Test A	Test B
1	Concrete	Abstract
2	Abstract	Concrete

problems and comparing their performances on the two types of item. However, we would need to make sure that any differences in performance between the two conditions arose from the ways in which the problems were expressed and not from the fact that one set of problems was simply easier to solve. That is, we would need to *match* our materials so that they were equivalent in all respects other than the IV (concrete or abstract problems). In this case, this is not all that difficult to do. If you imagine two sets of problems, Test A and Test B, we can give one group of participants Test A expressed in concrete terms and Test B expressed in abstract terms, and the other group of participants Test A expressed in abstract terms and Test B expressed in concrete terms (Table 10.5). Thus, any differences we find in overall performance on the concrete and abstract items cannot be due to differences in the ease of the items themselves – because the two sets of items have appeared equally as often under the concrete and the abstract conditions.

Summary of Section 10.4

1 The cost of eliminating individual differences when we use related samples is the introduction of another source of extraneous variation – *order effects*.

2 Order effects are of two kinds: those that lead to an *improvement* and those that lead to a *deterioration* in the participant's performance on the experimental task.

3 These order effects must be *controlled* for – for example by *counterbalancing* or by *randomizing* the order of the conditions.

4 These methods do not *eliminate* the variation introduced by order. They *transform* it into unsystematic variation.

5 These methods will not work when there are significant *carry-over* effects. Under these circumstances, you should not use related samples.

6 With related samples you are likely to need to duplicate and *match* the materials.

10.5   Principal alternatives to related samples

Where there are insurmountable order effects, or it is difficult to match materials, or when the participants *have* to be different (e.g. in personality research, studies involving differences in intelligence, culture, gender, etc.), then related samples are not suitable. Under these circumstances, you should turn to one of the alternatives. The principal alternative is to use unrelated samples. However, you might also consider matching your participants in some ways (Section 10.7). If you have more than one IV, then you may be able to use a combination of related and unrelated samples IVs (see Chapter 13).

10.6   Unrelated samples

The principal alternative to the use of related samples is to use unrelated samples on your IV. As pointed out earlier, however, the biggest disadvantage of unrelated samples is the presence of *individual differences*. However, there are ways in which we can attempt to minimize their impact on our experiment.

10.6.1 Advantages

It just so happens that the advantages of unrelated samples correspond to the weaknesses of related samples. That is, there are no problems with order effects and we do not need to duplicate and match our materials.

10.6.2 Disadvantages

However, the reverse is also true. If there are no problems with order effects, this is more than offset by the intrusion of individual differences. Likewise, if we do not have problems with materials, we have to find a lot more participants.

10.6.3 Ways around these disadvantages

With respect to the bigger disadvantage, individual differences, we must attempt to rule out any *systematic bias* stemming from such differences between participants. We cannot eliminate individual differences; we can, however, try to ensure that they are equally distributed across conditions (e.g., that as many good drivers are assigned to the music on as to the music off groups). One possibility would be to try to *match* our participants, assessing them on driving performance and making sure that equal numbers of good and bad drivers are assigned to each group (Section 10.7). In order to do this we would need to assess the performances of our participants *prior* to running the experiment (i.e., run a *pretest*).

Often, however, we have neither the resources nor the time to collect and act upon this information. Under these circumstances, the alternative we turn to is again *randomization* – in this case the *random assignment* of participants to their conditions (see Appendix 2). To do this, we go to our pool of participants and assign them randomly to conditions, trusting the random sequence to spread individuals who differ in basic ability at the experimental task more or less equally among the conditions. So, for instance, in our music and driving experiment we might assign our participants to either the music on or the music off condition using random number tables (Appendix 2). We would hope that this procedure would give us a reasonably even split of good, poor, and average drivers between the conditions. The more participants we use, the more effective this procedure is likely to be.

Random assignment of participants to the conditions of an unrelated samples IV (or to the different orders of conditions on a related samples IV) is the critical feature that makes an experiment a true experiment. Random *assignment* of participants to conditions should not, however, be confused with the random *selection* of participants from a population. Ideally you should do both. In practice, as students, you will probably only do the former (see Sections 10.8 and 10.9). Moreover, unless you check, you can never really be sure that your randomization has been effective. That is, you will be unable to state categorically that differences in ability among your participants did *not* lead to the differences that you observed on your DV. The same is true of randomizing to control for order effects. It may be that there were systematic differences in the orders in which your conditions appeared, even though allocation of orders was randomized. So, you should bear this in mind when you come to interpret your findings. (Once you have become experienced enough, you should consider checking the effectiveness of your randomization. You can find advice on this in Section G of the book's Web site at **http:// mcgraw-hill.co.uk/openup/harris/**)

With regard to the problem of having to obtain larger numbers of participants with unrelated samples than with the related samples equivalent, like the problems with materials in related samples designs, this is simply something that you have to live with. However, where you have more than one IV you may be able to reduce the number of these that require different participants by employing what we call a *mixed* design (Section 13.3) and thereby reduce the number of participants that you need overall.

Summary of Sections 10.5–10.6

1 Using *unrelated* samples eliminates order effects and the need to duplicate materials.

2 It introduces individual differences and requires larger numbers of participants than the equivalent related samples design.

3 We can attempt to control for individual differences by assigning our participants to conditions randomly.

4 This does not eliminate the variation introduced by individual differences; it is simply an attempt to render it *unsystematic*.

5 Assigning participants randomly to conditions is no guarantee that systematic differences between conditions will be eliminated. You should bear this in mind when interpreting your findings (and check the randomization if you know how – see the Web site accompanying this book for more on how to do this).

10.7   Matching participants

If you have the time and the resources to collect the relevant information, then **matching** your participants can give you a good halfway house between the unrelated and related samples designs. Matching involves finding groups or even pairs of participants who are similar on some variable that you think is related to the IV. With the music and driving experiment, for instance, we might assess each participant's driving ability *before* assigning them to experimental conditions and then attempt to make sure that equal numbers of good and poor drivers are allocated to each group. Similarly, we might run the reasoning experiment by allocating equal numbers of good, poor, and indifferent reasoners to the concrete and abstract conditions. This way we do not trust to a random sequence to spread individual differences equally between conditions – instead we ensure that this happens.

Where possible, therefore, it is a good idea to match the participants in an experiment in which you have different participants in conditions, as this will reduce the possibility of individual differences confounding the effects of your independent variable. However, you will of course still have to assign matched participants to the experimental conditions *randomly*. That is, which particular condition any one of the better drivers or reasoners or any one of the less able drivers or reasoners is allocated to must be decided at random in exactly the same way as you would do with a sample of unmatched participants.

 SAQ 36   Why?

Where you have *matched* participants, therefore, you will still need to assign them to experimental conditions randomly. You do this by randomly assigning the members of each group of matched participants separately. So, for instance, you would assign the *better* drivers to their conditions using the sort of methods described in Appendix 2. Separately, you would do the equivalent with the *less* able drivers. This way you would end up with the same spread of ability in each condition but within any level of ability participants would have been assigned randomly to their conditions.

In effect, in doing this, you will have introduced an additional IV into your experiment – an unrelated samples IV comprising the better and poorer drivers. This is not a problem (in fact, usually quite the reverse): I will talk in Chapter 13 about such designs.

When you have matched *pairs* of participants, it is sometimes argued that the data can be analysed statistically as if it were from a *related* sample. As a student, however, it is extremely unlikely that in human work you will achieve the necessary level of matching for this, so usually you should consider data from matched pairs of participants to be *unrelated* when analysing them.

Summary of Section 10.7

1 A good halfway house between the related and the unrelated samples design is to use unrelated samples in which the participants have been matched and assigned to conditions so that there is an equal spread of ability on the experimental task between the conditions.

2 Such designs reduce the possibility of individual differences confounding the effects of the independent variable.

10.8   External validity

With this knowledge about unrelated and related samples IVs and about matching participants you are already well on the way towards being able to design interesting experiments in psychology. In theory, there is no limit either to the number of levels that you can have on an IV or to the number of IVs that you can have in an experiment. In practice, however, there are important issues that you need to consider when using IVs with many levels or more than one IV. I will introduce you to these in the final chapter, once you have learnt about significance testing and have been introduced to the important issue of the power of your experiments. Next, however, I want us to turn to two other issues that you need to be aware of when experimenting: validity (the subject of this section and the next) and ethics (the subject of Section 10.10).

In the previous chapter we considered how the capacity of the experiment to allow causal inferences stems from the *control* that is achieved. Control involves holding other factors constant across the conditions so that they cannot account for any changes observed in the DV. Remember, we can make unequivocal causal inferences – that the IV causes the changes we see in the DV – only if we have held everything else constant.

Of course, this is a condition that can never be realistically achieved. There are just too many variables in the world. In practice, we aspire to holding constant those variables that plausibly may be rival explanations for the observed changes in the effect variable and others that can be held constant without too much effort or too much distortion of the situation. Others we allow to vary in the hope that they will not turn out to differ systematically across the conditions. Yet others – the vast majority – we assume are irrelevant (perhaps wrongly) and disregard. Often we take it one step at a time, controlling for different variables across a series of separate experimental studies.

There is, however, an inevitable tension between experimental control and **generalizability**. Generalizability is the extent to which the findings generated by your experiment can be extrapolated. For example, are they relevant to everybody, regardless of race, class, gender, age? Or are they circumscribed in some way – for example, relevant only to middle-class, white, youngsters of above average intelligence?

The worst state of affairs is that the findings cannot be generalized to any people or circumstances beyond those used in the particular experiment that you ran. This is very unusual. However, it can be the case that the findings are of limited applicability because of some of the variables that you had to hold constant for control purposes. An obvious example would be if you choose to use only male participants (i.e., hold the variable *gender* constant across conditions); then there would be question marks over the extent to which the findings could be generalized to females.

The generalizability of the findings is also called the **external validity** of your study: *external* validity because it concerns the relevance of your findings to situations beyond or external to those used in the study. Experiments high in external validity have highly generalizable findings – that is, the findings apply to a range of people, times and situations not directly assessed in the experiment.

One threat to external validity comes from the conditions that you imposed on the time, setting and task for the purposes of control.

 SAQ 37

For instance, for some years I helped to run a class experiment at a summer school to test whether people can taste the difference between mineral water and tap water. We found that most people cannot. In this experiment, we controlled the variable *temperature* by keeping the water at room temperature. Does this mean that we can conclude that people in general cannot taste the difference between mineral water and tap water?

Another potential limit to external validity stems from your participants. Are they representative of the group from which you took them (e.g., students)? Are they representative of a wider range of people? Many studies in psychology, for example, use undergraduate psychology students as participants. Yet students, of course, tend to come from a restricted sector of the population. They are almost invariably young, supposedly intelligent, and predominantly middle-class. Add to this the probability that those interested in psychology may also have peculiarities of their own, and it could be that the findings of studies based on samples of undergraduate psychologists cannot be generalized to other populations.

However, the validity of this criticism depends on the variables in question. If the variables that *differentiate* such participants from the general public (e.g., age, intelligence, class) are thought to have some impact on the DV (e.g., reasoning, attitudes), then the criticism may be valid. However, other variables may not be so influenced (e.g., motor skills, visual perception). So, do not *automatically* assume that having a student sample seriously limits the extent to which you can generalize your findings. Always bear in mind that – if your study is in other respects well designed – the results should be generalizable to at least some subgroup in the population. After all, in some respects at least, students are still members of the human race and, of course, there are young, middle-class, intelligent people who are not students.

At first, many of you are concerned that you should always have a random sample of people from the general population in your experiments and doubt the usefulness of experiments lacking such samples. For now, remember that this is a concern with **random selection** and it relates to the *external* validity of the experiment. We will consider this issue further in a later section. But next I want to introduce you to *internal* validity.

Summary of Section 10.8

1 There is often a tension between the demands of experimental control and the extent to which you can generalize your findings to people, times, and situations not directly assessed in the experiment.

2 Experiments with highly generalizable findings are high in *external* validity.

3 Threats to external validity can come from constraints on the time, setting, task, and the participants used.

4 Concerns about the failure to randomly select a sample from a population relate to the external validity of the experiment.

10.9   Internal validity

For practical reasons, most of the experiments that you run as a student are unlikely to be very high in external validity. They must, however, be high in *internal* validity. **Internal validity** refers to the extent to which we can relate changes in the DV to the manipulation of the IV. That is, a well-designed experiment with no confounding variables is an experiment very high in internal validity. This is an experiment in which we can make the unequivocal causal inferences we desire.

However, to achieve high internal validity, we often need to hold many extraneous variables constant, thus compromising external validity. For example, in our cheese and nightmare experiment, the more we introduce controls for variables that might also produce nightmares, the more we run the risk that the generalizability of our findings will be limited by the values at which we hold those variables constant. For example, if we require people to eat cheese 3 hours before they go to bed, the findings may not apply to cheese eaten 10 minutes before going to bed. Likewise, if we restrict ourselves to one type of cheese (say, Cheddar), the findings may be limited to that type of cheese, or only to hard cheeses, or only to cheeses made with milk from British cattle, and so on.

Internal validity represents the degree of control that we exercise in the experiment. One of the key elements in achieving high internal validity (but by no means the sole one) is that we randomly assign participants to conditions (or orders of conditions to participants) in order to maximize our chances of rendering the variation on extraneous variables unsystematic between conditions. This is the issue of **random assignment** and it relates to the internal validity of the experiment.

Thus, random assignment of participants to conditions should not be confused with *random sampling* of participants from a population. At the start of your careers in psychology most of you tend to be much more concerned about the latter than you are about the former, whereas at this stage the reverse should be the case! This is because, although both of the types of validity described above are important, internal validity is the more important. It is of little consolation to be able to generalize a set of equivocal findings to a lot of people and many situations, when you run an experiment high in external but low in internal validity. In contrast, an experiment high in internal validity usually has at least a modicum of generalizability. Of course, ideally in our studies we should aim for both. However, as students, most of the time you should concentrate your time and energies on ensuring that your experiments are at least high in internal validity. You now know how to do this: by selecting carefully the variables to hold constant across conditions, standardizing your procedures and materials, and using *truly* random procedures to attempt to ensure that other important sources of variation do not differ systematically between the conditions. Random assignment of participants to conditions (or orders of conditions to participants) is a key element in striving to achieve this.

Summary of Section 10.9

1 The experiments that you run as a student are unlikely to be very high in external validity.

2 They must, however, be high in *internal* validity.

3 In an experiment high in internal validity, we can relate changes in the DV unequivocally to the manipulation of the IV.

4 One of the key elements in achieving high internal validity is to randomly assign participants to conditions or orders of conditions to participants.

5 You should not confuse random assignment of participants to conditions with random sampling of participants from a population. The former relates to the internal validity of the experiment, the latter to the external validity of the experiment.

10.10   Ethics: The self-esteem and well-being of your participants

A concern with variables and control is not the only element of experimental design in psychology. Regard for the welfare, rights, and dignity of your participants is as essential to good experimental practice as is the pursuit of experimental rigour and elegance. Never underestimate the impact that being in a psychological experiment can have on your participant. We live in a competitive society and the experiment has all the trappings of a test. Those of you who have participated in a psychological experiment will probably have been struck by just how difficult it can be to shake off the feeling that somehow you are under scrutiny. You can feel that you have to do your best, even though you know that an experimenter's interest is rarely in particular individuals, but invariably in making statements about the influence of the IV on *groups* of people. Those of you who have not participated in one should try to if possible. It gives you an invaluable insight into the sorts of factors that can influence a participant's performance in an experiment.

When designing any study it is important to have clearly in mind the participants' welfare, self-respect and dignity. You must not put people through an experience that undermines their welfare or self-regard. So, think about the impact that your study will have on your participant when you think about designs that you might employ, measures that you might use, and issues that you might address. For example, look closely at your procedures, the wording of your instructions, the items on any questionnaires or other measures that you are thinking about using. Is it really appropriate and sensitive to use the depression inventory that you are considering? Could some of the questions on the anxiety scale that you are thinking of using cause embarrassment or distress? If so, are there better alternatives? If not, is your use of these measures really justified and ethically acceptable? (While we are on the topic of published measures, such as scales and tests, make sure that you have permission to copy and use any published measures that you want to use in your study, including any you have downloaded from the Internet. See your tutor for advice on this.)

Even as students, your conduct is expected to adhere to ethical principles. In your early work in practical classes the tutors running the course will have primary responsibility for ensuring that the things they ask you to do are ethically acceptable. However, when you undertake your own project work (e.g., in the UK in the final year of an undergraduate degree), the likelihood is that you will be expected to submit details of your proposed study to an ethics committee for prior assessment. You will be allowed to run your study only once you have received approval from that ethics committee.

It is important, therefore, that you get hold of a copy of the ethical code that is used in your department or school. You must familiarize yourself with these from the outset. When the time comes, you should also make sure that you know when and how to submit your studies to the relevant ethics committee and that you do not undertake work that needs prior ethical approval without having that approval. If in any doubt, check with your tutor.

In the unlikely event that your department or school does not have a set of **ethical principles** then you can obtain some from the professional body that oversees the conduct of properly qualified psychologists in your country. These are organizations such as the British Psychological Society, the Australian Psychological Society and the American Psychological Association. You can usually download these principles from the organization's Web site. Failing that, you can ask them to send you a copy.

The principles deal with a number of aspects of conducting yourself ethically with participants. These include:

- approaching people and encouraging them to take part in your study;
- what you do to them and how you interact with them during the study;
- how you respond if they decline to take part or wish to withdraw once they have started;
- what you say to them after they have finished;
- how you safeguard and report the data that you obtain from them.

You must make sure that you have read the most recent and relevant set of principles and that you abide by them.

10.10.1   Informed consent

A key feature of all ethical principles is that of **informed consent**. Informed consent is what it sounds like – telling people enough about your study to enable them to make an *informed* decision about whether or not to take part. For example, the *Publication Manual of the American Psychological Association* (APA, 2001, p. 391) states that psychologists should "use language that is reasonably understandable to research participants" to do the following:

- inform them of the nature of the research;
- inform them that they are free to participate or to decline to participate or to withdraw from the research;
- explain the foreseeable consequences of declining or withdrawing;
- inform participants of significant factors that may be expected to influence their willingness to participate (such as risks, discomfort, adverse effects);
- explain other aspects about which the prospective participants inquire.

Standard 8.02 of the APA's new ethics code (APA, 2002) is similar, as is principle 3.3 of the British Psychological Society's *Ethical Principles* (BPS, 2006).

The principle of informed consent is very important. However, respond to it sensibly. It is not a directive to spell out *everything* about the study to prospective participants. Given that people would respond very differently in many studies if they knew *precisely* what it was about, you must think carefully about what you need to tell them about your study. It is important to give your participants a general idea about what you will ask them to do, how long it will take (honestly!), and so on. It is *essential* that you tell them about risks, discomfort, or any other aspects that might affect their willingness to take part. (Indeed, the ethics committee will insist on this as a condition of approval.) However, think carefully about what you tell potential recruits about what the study is *about*. Tell them the things that they need to know in order to make an informed decision. Do not jeopardize the study unnecessarily by telling them things that are important to interpreting the experiment and yet *not* key to whether or not they will agree to take part. (As ever, take your tutor's advice on this.)

Do not confuse *masking* or *concealing* or *withholding* the hypothesis with *deception*. **Withholding the hypothesis** involves encouraging participants to suspend judgement about what you are investigating until after the study has finished and you are ready to debrief them. **Deception** involves deliberately misleading participants into believing that the study is about something it is not about. Participants generally are quite willing to do the former and can be pretty aggrieved by the latter. As a student, you must not run a study involving deception without prior ethical approval and *extremely* close supervision by a tutor.

10.10.2 Debriefing your participants

You must make time available for those who want it at the end of your study to discuss any questions that they may have regarding what you have asked them to do. This is known in the trade as **debriefing** your participant, and it is an integral part of good research practice. At this stage, answer their questions informatively, honestly, and willingly, discussing the thinking behind your ideas, and the purpose of the study if that interests them. If you cannot tell them precisely what the study is about, for fear that word will get about and future participants will no longer be naive about the study, then see if they are prepared to wait for full debriefing until all the participants have taken part. If so, you should take contact details and send them an account of the study and the findings as soon as these are available. Debriefing is for the *participant's* benefit, not yours.

10.10.3 Studies on the Internet

You may be tempted to run a study on the Internet. If so, then you will need to work very closely with your tutor to ensure that the study is ethical. This is because the Internet presents a number of significant problems for the principles we considered above. For example, it can be difficult to get genuinely informed consent and to debrief all participants properly, especially those who quit your study before the end. Because you do not have face-to-face contact with the participant, you cannot monitor, support or terminate the study if it upsets them. Likewise, you have no control over the conditions under which they view and interact with your stimulus materials, and – as you now appreciate – rigorous control is key to good experimenting. For these and other reasons, you should think very carefully before deciding to run your study on the Internet, make sure that you familiarize yourself with ethical guidelines for running Internet studies before you do, and make sure that you work closely with a tutor at all stages.

10.10.4 Data confidentiality

Ethical considerations do not finish with the completion of the study. Most countries now have regulations regarding how data on human beings are stored and professional guidelines also cover this aspect of conduct. You must keep the data safe, secure, and confidential, no matter how dull, boring and uninteresting they may seem to you to be. This includes both the original measures (such as a set of questionnaires or response sheets) and the data that you have on computer. Consult the relevant guidelines to learn more.

Summary of Section 10.10

1 Regard for the welfare and comfort of the participants in your study is an integral part of good design. You must not put your participants through an experience that undermines their welfare, self-respect or dignity, and you must bear this in mind when thinking about procedures that you might employ and issues that you might address in your studies.

2 You should be aware of the contents of the most relevant set of ethical principles before you start designing and running your own studies. Even as students, your conduct must adhere to ethical principles.

3 If you go on to do project work, you may need to submit your proposed study to an ethics committee for approval. If so, you must not start the study before receiving ethical approval.

4 A key feature of all ethical principles for research with human beings is the principle of informed consent. Make sure that you understand this principle and abide by it.

5 Make time available at the end of your experiments to discuss any questions that your participants have regarding what you asked them to do. You should answer their questions honestly, openly, and willingly. This is known in the trade as debriefing your participant, and it is an essential feature of any well-run experiment.

6 Exercise care if you wish to run a study on the Internet, as Internet studies raise a number of significant ethical issues.

7 Keep all data you collect safe, secure, and confidential and in accordance with the laws governing the storage of information about humans.

Consolidating your learning

This closing section is designed to help you check your understanding and determine what you might need to study further. You can use the list of methodological and statistical concepts to check which ones you are happy with and which you may need to double-check. You can use this list to find the relevant terms in the chapter and also in other textbooks of design or statistics. In this chapter we also discussed ethical issues and below you will find key ethical terms. The diagnostic questions provide a further test of your understanding. Finally, there is a description of what is covered in the two statistics textbooks paired with this book.

Methodological and statistical concepts covered in this chapter

Carry-over effect
Counterbalancing
External validity
Extraneous variation
Generalizability
Individual differences
Internal validity
Matching participants
Order effect
Practice effect
Random assignment
Random selection
Randomizing
Related samples (within subjects, within participants, dependent/correlated samples, dependent/correlated/repeated measures) IV
Unrelated samples (between subjects/groups, between participants, independent/uncorrelated samples, independent/uncorrelated measures) IV

Ethical concepts covered in this chapter

Data confidentiality
Debriefing
Deception
Informed consent
Withholding the hypothesis

Diagnostic questions – check your understanding

1 What is a *related* samples IV?
2 What is an *unrelated* samples IV?
3 What is *random assignment* to conditions?
4 What is the *internal validity* of an experiment?
5 What is the *external validity* of an experiment?

You can find the answers at the rear of the book (p. 276).

Statistics textbooks

Σ The books paired with *Designing and Reporting Experiments* have the following coverage:

Learning to use statistical tests in psychology – Greene and D'Oliveira
Greene and D'Oliveira discuss issues involved in using the same or different participants in the conditions of the experiment in Chapter 2.

SPSS survival manual – Pallant
Note that Pallant uses "independent samples" or "between groups" to describe unrelated samples IVs and "paired samples", "repeated measures" and "within subjects" to describe related samples IVs. She describes in Part Five a wide range of statistical methods suitable for analyzing data from studies like those I have described in this chapter; however, you should not consider using any of these until you are familiar with the material in Chapter 11.

11 Statistics: significance testing

So far in this book I have talked rather glibly about *differences* between conditions and *correlations* between variables. However, what I have really meant here is what you will come to understand as differences and correlations that are **reliable**. For there is something special about the differences and correlations that interest us. We are not interested simply in, say, a difference in the numbers between two conditions; we are interested in those differences (and correlations) that would usually be repeated if we were to run the study again.

Thinking back to our driving and music experiment in Chapter 10, if we were to measure the performance of any given participant on the driving simulator on a number of occasions, we would not expect him or her to obtain an *identical* number of errors on each occasion. We would not even expect this when s/he was fully accustomed to the apparatus. Similarly, I have already pointed out that one of the problems with *unrelated* samples is that there are generally differences between people in their basic abilities on experimental tasks. This means, of course, that even when we assign participants to experimental conditions randomly, we would hardly expect our different groups to obtain identical mean values on the dependent variable.

If you have any doubts about this, then try the following exercise. Try balancing a book on your head. (Make sure that it is not too heavy, and keep away from breakable objects!) See how long you can keep it there (a) in silence and (b) with the radio on. Do it five times under each condition. (Make sure that you set up a *random* sequence *in advance*.) Record your times, and then work out the *mean* time for balancing under both conditions. Are they identical? I bet they are not! Does this mean that having the radio on has affected your ability to balance a book on your head? (I trust that you have controlled adequately for the effects of practice and fatigue.)

The point of this is that you will more or less inevitably find differences between conditions on the DV in an experiment, *even when the IV does not in fact cause changes in the DV*. So, for example, even if listening to music has absolutely no impact whatsoever on the ability to drive, we would still expect to find our participants driving at least slightly better in one of the conditions of our experiment than another. That is, we will always have to assess the effects of our independent variable against a background of *inherent* variation.

We need, therefore, to find a way of being able to discriminate a difference that *has* been influenced by our IV (a *reliable* difference) from one that has *not* been so influenced – a difference that would be there anyway. That is, we need to be able to detect the sort of difference that would occur simply if we took a group of participants and measured their performances on repeated occasions *without* exposing them to the IV. This is why we turn to *inferential statistics*.

Summary

1 We will invariably find that there are differences on the DV between the conditions even when the IV does not cause changes in the DV.

2 We therefore have to find some way of distinguishing a difference that has been caused by the IV (a *reliable* difference) from one that is simply the product of chance variation.

3 We employ *inferential* statistics to assist us with this task.

11.1 Inferential statistics

Think back to our cheese and nightmare experiment (Chapter 9). Imagine that we actually ran this experiment one night and obtained the data in Table 11.1. (There are 50 participants in each condition.) You can see from Table 11.1 that 11 more of those in the cheese condition reported nightmares than did those in the no cheese condition. Thus, *more* people reported nightmares in the cheese condition than in the no cheese condition. This is a difference, but as yet we do

Table 11.1
The Number of Participants Reporting Nightmares and not Reporting Nightmares in the Cheese and No Cheese Conditions

	Nightmare	
Condition	Yes	No
Cheese	33	17
No cheese	22	28

not know whether it is the sort of difference that we would be likely to find anyway. The question is, if eating cheese actually has *no effect* upon the incidence of nightmares, how likely would we be to obtain a difference of 11 between our conditions?

To understand this, imagine that we took 100 table tennis balls and stamped "nightmare" on half of them and "no nightmare" on the remainder. We then placed these in a large black plastic bag, shook them up, and drew them out one by one. Imagine also that we simply decided to assign the first 50 table tennis balls we drew out to a hypothetical *cheese* condition and the remainder to a hypothetical *no cheese* condition. The question is, doing this, how likely would we be to get the sorts of values that we have in Table 11.1?

Ideally we need some way of assessing this. This is precisely where **inferential statistics** come in. These statistics enable us to assess the likelihood that we would obtain results like ours *if* we assume that our IV did *not* cause changes in our DV. That is, using such statistics we can assess whether we would have been likely to get data like ours *if* we assume that there is not a genuine effect of eating cheese on the incidence of nightmares.

You may have spotted that the assumption that the IV does *not* cause changes in the DV is one that we have met before. It is, of course, the *null hypothesis* (Section 9.1.4). Essentially, therefore, inferential statistics tell us the probability that we would obtain results like ours *if we assume that the null hypothesis is true*. This is what we call the probability *under the null hypothesis*.

There are inferential statistical tests available to assess this probability for all kinds of data. For all of these tests, however, at the end of the calculations you should end up with a single score. This score is the value of the statistic that "belongs" to your data. Associated with

Table 11.2
Probabilities Under the Null Hypothesis Associated with Particular Values of Chi-Square with One Degree of Freedom

Chi-square	Probability
0.016	.90
0.15	.70
0.46	.50
1.64	.20
3.84	.05
5.02	.025
10.83	.001

this statistic is a *probability*. This is the probability we are interested in. It tells us how likely we would be to obtain our value – and, by implication, these data – if we assume the null hypothesis to be true. Statistical software packages usually display this probability for you, along with the statistic. If you have calculated the statistic by hand, however, you can look up the probability associated with your calculated statistic in the appropriate tables of *critical values* (to be found at the rear of most textbooks of statistics – see Appendix 3).

For instance, as we have only one observation from each participant (nightmare or no nightmare), an appropriate statistic for the above example is chi-square (Section 4.6.1). Chi-square tests for an *association* between two variables – in this case whether there is any association between eating cheese and the numbers of nightmares reported. So, you can see that it is eminently suited for the question that we wish to ask of our data.

Table 11.2 contains a range of values of chi-square, together with their associated probability if we assume the null hypothesis to be true. You can see that, under this assumption, a value of $\chi^2 = 0.15$ has a probability of occurring of $p = .7$, which is quite high. A value of $\chi^2 = 3.84$ however, has an associated probability of only $p = .05$, which is quite low.

For those new to the idea of **probability**, it is measured conventionally from one to zero. An event with a probability of one is *inevitable*. An event with a probability of zero is *impossible*. Most events in our universe tend to lie somewhere between these two extremes.

If you enter the data in Table 11.1 into your statistics package it will calculate for you the value of chi-square that belongs to these data. Alternatively, you can find details of how to calculate chi-square

Σ by hand in textbooks of statistics (see, for example, Greene & D'Oliveira, Chapter 20). Either way, you should obtain a value of $\chi^2 = 4.89$. What you need to establish next is whether this value is *likely* or *unlikely* to have occurred under the null hypothesis – that is, even if cheese does not cause nightmares.

If you calculated chi-square using a statistical software package, the package will give you the *exact* probability associated with the statistic. This value is $p = .03$. Those of you who worked out the value of chi-square by hand can establish from Table 11.2 that the value of $\chi^2 = 4.89$, with 1 degree of freedom, has a probability under the null hypothesis of somewhere between $p = .05$ and $p = .025$. For, the value of chi-square that has a probability of $p = .05$ is 3.84 which is *less* than our obtained value of chi-square. However, the value of chi-square that has a probability of $p = .025$ is 5.02 which is *greater* than our obtained value. So, our value lies somewhere in between these and consequently the probability associated with it must lie somewhere between $p = .05$ and $p = .025$. This agrees with the $p = .03$ that we obtained from our statistics package but is less exact. (See Appendix 3 for more on how to work out the probability associated with your statistic when you do not use a statistics package.)

The probability of obtaining a value of chi-square as *large* as 4.89 under the null hypothesis, therefore, is 3 times in 100 (this is just another way of expressing $p = .03$). Essentially, therefore, if we were to draw our table tennis balls randomly from our big black plastic bag we would expect, *on average*, to obtain data like ours 3 times for every 100 times that we did it.

? SAQ 38   Our obtained value of chi-square has an associated probability of $p = .03$. Is this nearer the inevitable or the impossible end of the continuum? (That is, is it nearer one or zero?)

Let's recap. We've run our experiment and generated the data in Table 11.1. We then realized that in order to make any sense of it – in order to find out what it tells us about the relationship between eating cheese and experiencing nightmares – we needed to discover how likely we would be to have obtained results like these anyway, even if eating cheese did not cause nightmares. So, we employed a statistical test appropriate for our data (chi-square) and we discovered that the value of chi-square that we obtained (4.89) has a low probability of having occurred *if* we assume that eating cheese *does not* induce nightmares. Does this mean, therefore, that we can safely conclude that eating cheese *does* induce nightmares?

Well, the simple and rather unsettling answer to that question is – no. For the problem is that we still do not know whether the IV does or does not affect the DV. All we know is that the probability of getting data like ours is relatively low *if* we assume that the IV does *not* affect the DV. Thus, under the null hypothesis, data like ours are *unlikely*. However, they are still *possible*. We know, therefore, that on any given occasion we would be unlikely to draw a similar distribution of values to those in Table 11.1 from our big black plastic bag of table tennis balls. Nevertheless, we might actually do so. We have, in fact, about a 33-1 chance of doing so. Moreover, as some of us know to our (very!) occasional benefit, long shots, though infrequently, still win races.

In fact, we will *never* know whether the null hypothesis is true or false. Inferential statistics do not provide us with sudden insights into the laws of the universe. They simply tell us the probability that we would get values like those we obtained on our DV *if* the null hypothesis *were* true.

So how do we get around this problem? Well, all is not lost. The procedure that we traditionally adopt to resolve this dilemma is described next.

11.2 Testing for statistical significance

In this procedure, what we do is set up a criterion probability for our statistic. We do this before we even begin collecting the data. We decide subsequently to obey a simple rule. The rule is as follows. If we find that the *probability* associated with our obtained statistic falls *at* or *below* this criterion (i.e., is the same value as the criterion probability, or nearer zero), then we will *reject* the assumption that the null hypothesis is true (see Figure 11.1). If, however, we find that the probability associated with the statistic falls *above* this criterion (i.e., is nearer one) then we will *not* reject the assumption that the null hypothesis is true.

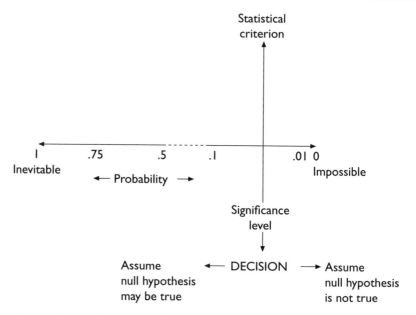

Figure 11.1. Statistical inference. If the probability associated with
the obtained statistic falls to the left of the statistical criterion (i.e.,
nearer $p = 1$), then assume that the null hypothesis may be true.
If it is the same as the criterion probability or falls to the right
(i.e., nearer $p = 0$), then assume that the null hypothesis is not true.

This is the principle of **statistical significance** testing. Using this
approach, we *always* do this when we test our data for differences
between conditions. The criterion is referred to as the **significance
level** or **alpha level**. Although we are free to vary it, this level is often
set at a probability of less than or equal to .05 (in other words 5 times
in a 100 or 1 in 20). This is known as the **5 percent significance level**
(Figure 11.2).

What we do, therefore, is compare the probability associated with
the obtained value of the statistic with our chosen significance level.
If this probability *equals* or is *less* than the significance level (i.e., is
nearer zero, a less probable event), then we decide that we have sufficient evidence to **reject the null hypothesis**. Such data we describe
as **statistically significant**. Under these circumstances we would talk
of a "statistically significant difference" between our conditions. If,
however, the obtained statistic has a probability *greater* than our

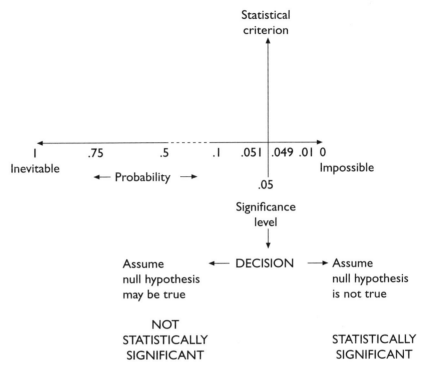

Figure 11.2. The 5 percent significance level. If the probability associated with the obtained statistic is greater than $p = .05$, do not reject the null hypothesis. The data are not statistically significant. If this probability is equal to or less than $p = .05$, then reject the null hypothesis. The data are statistically significant.

significance level (i.e., is nearer one, a more probable event) then we decide that we have insufficient evidence to reject the null hypothesis. We thus **fail to reject the null hypothesis**. Findings such as these we describe as **not statistically significant**.

This terminology, though widely used, is nevertheless unfortunate. To call our results *statistically* significant does not necessarily mean that they have much *psychological* importance. Likewise, results that are not statistically significant may yet be psychologically informative. Significance, in this context, is a statistical concept. It tells us something about the statistical nature of our data. The psychological importance of a set of findings, whether statistically significant or not, remains to be established. When working with inferential statistics it is important, therefore, to differentiate in your mind the concepts of statistical significance and psychological importance. Do not assume that the former implies the latter. I have more to say about this in Chapter 12.

In the strict application of this procedure, once you have set up the significance level, you are compelled to abide by the outcome. So, if the probability associated with your obtained statistic turns out to be *greater* than the significance level (even if only by a minute amount), then you must assume there is not enough evidence to reject the null hypothesis. I will have more to say about this in the next section.

In the case of our cheese and nightmare experiment, we calculated a value of $\chi^2 = 4.89$. We now need to find out whether this is statistically significant at the 5 percent significance level. (This is the significance level that I chose on our behalf before collecting the data.) This means that we need to work out whether the probability associated with $\chi^2 = 4.89$ is less than or equal to $p = .05$.

? SAQ 39

Earlier we established that the probability associated with $\chi^2 = 4.89$ with 1 degree of freedom is $p = .03$. Is our value of χ^2, therefore, statistically significant at the 5 percent significance level?

In effect, therefore, at the end of our experiment, having analysed the data, we find ourselves in a position to make a decision regarding the null hypothesis – that is, whether to reject it or not to reject it. We do this on the basis of whether or not the probability associated with our obtained statistic is less than or equal to the significance level we set prior to running the experiment.

Summary of Section 11.1–11.2

1 *Inferential* statistics tell us how likely we would be to obtain data like ours *if* the IV did *not* cause changes in the DV. That is, they tell us this probability *assuming the null hypothesis is true*. Such statistics do not, however, tell us whether or not the null hypothesis really *is* true.

2 In fact, we can never know for certain whether the null hypothesis is true or not true.

3 One way around this problem is to adopt a criterion probability. We call this the *significance level* or *alpha level*.

4 Although we are at liberty to alter the significance level, it is set conventionally at $p = .05$. This is known as the "5 percent significance level".

5 If the *probability* associated with our obtained statistic is *less than* or *equal to* our significance level, we decide to reject the assumption that the null hypothesis is true. Such results we describe as *statistically significant*.

6 If the probability associated with our obtained statistic is *greater than* our significance level, we decide *not to reject* the assumption that the null hypothesis is true. Such results we describe as *not statistically significant*.

7 In this context, significance is a statistical concept. To say that a difference is *statistically* significant does not mean that *psychologically* the difference has much theoretical or practical importance. Likewise, the absence of a statistically significant difference may nevertheless be of theoretical or practical importance.

11.3   Type I and type II errors

At the end of our experiment, therefore, we will have decided whether or not to reject the null hypothesis. However, the simple fact is – *we could always be wrong*. That is, we may find ourselves rejecting the null hypothesis when – had we seen the tablets of stone on which are written the Laws of the Universe – we would find that the null hypothesis should *not* have been rejected. For instance, in the case of our cheese and nightmare experiment, our obtained value of chi-square is 4.89, which has an associated probability that is less than the conventional significance level of $p = .05$. Using this significance level, therefore, we would have to reject the null hypothesis. However, suppose that you receive a visitation from the powers that run the universe, who reveal to you that actually the null hypothesis is in this case correct. Under these circumstances we would have *rejected* the null hypothesis when we should not have done. This is known as a **type I error**. Moreover, not only is it an integral feature of the process of statistical inference – of acting as if we know something for certain when we do not – but, in this world at least, we never know whether we have made it (visitations from the powers that run the universe aside). However, we do know the *probability* that we have.

What is the probability of making a type I error (i.e., of incorrectly rejecting the null hypothesis)? The probability of making a type I error (if the null hypothesis is true) is, in fact, the significance level. We decide to reject the null hypothesis when the probability associated with our obtained statistic reaches the significance level. Under these circumstances we *always* reject the null hypothesis. On some of these occasions, however, unbeknown to us the null hypothesis will be true. With the 5 percent significance level, therefore, because we reject the null hypothesis *every* time that our data reaches this level, we will make a mistake, on average, once in every 20 times that we do it.

So, what can we do about this? After all, we would like to minimize our mistakes. We do not want *too* many of the factual assertions that we make about the psychological universe to be wrong. Well, if our significance level is a measure of our type I error rate, then one thing that we might do is to reduce the probability of making this error by *making our significance level more stringent* (Figure 11.3). We make our significance level more stringent by choosing to use a *lower* probability under the null hypothesis to be the significance level – such as $p = .01$. A significance level of $p = .01$ has a type I error rate of only 1 in 100, rather than the 5 in 100 (or 1 in 20) of the $p = .05$ significance level.

Now, doing this is not necessarily wrong. However, although we can get the probability of making a type I error *closer* to zero, the only way that we can actually *make* it zero is by saying nothing at all about the existence or non-existence of a reliable difference between the conditions in our experiment. If we wish to say anything at all, therefore, we have to accept some probability of making a type I error.

Making the significance level more stringent is a cautious or, as we say in the trade, a *conservative* thing to do. Sometimes it may be the appropriate step to take. For example, those who undertake research into extrasensory perception tend routinely to employ more stringent significance levels in order to reduce their chances of making a type I error. However, our job as scientists is essentially to make the best guesses we can about the existence of causal relationships. Making the significance level more stringent may well reduce our tendency to make mistakes, but it does so at the cost of reducing our ability to say anything. Take it too far and we are in danger of throwing the scientific baby out with the statistical bath water.

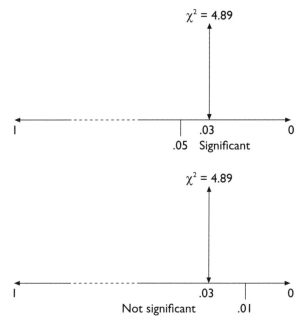

Figure 11.3. The effects of making the significance level more stringent. A $\chi^2 = 4.89$ with 1 degree of freedom is statistically significant at the 5 per cent significance level but is not statistically significant at the 1 per cent significance level.

To put it another way, in making the significance level more stringent, we are indeed reducing the probability of making a type I error. That is, we reduce our chances of thinking there is a reliable difference when there is not one. However, at the same time, we *increase* the probability of making another type of error – that is, of *not rejecting* the null hypothesis when we should have done. This is known as a **type II error**. When we make a type II error, we *fail* to detect a reliable difference that *is* there.

For instance, suppose that we had adopted the $p = .01$ level of significance for our cheese and nightmare experiment. With $\chi^2 = 4.89$ (our obtained value), we would not have achieved statistical significance, and so would have been compelled not to reject the null hypothesis (Figure 11.3). However, suppose that on the tablets of stone containing the Laws of the Universe was written that eating cheese will induce nightmares in humans. By making our criterion too stringent, we would therefore have missed the opportunity to make a correct statement about the universe in which we live. I will have more to say about type II errors in Chapter 12.

Summary of Section 11.3

1 Sometimes we will reject the null hypothesis when it is in fact true. This is known as a *type I error*. We cannot avoid making such errors if we wish to say anything positive about the psychological universe.

2 If the null hypothesis is true, then the probability of making a *type I error* is the *significance level*.

3 We can, therefore, reduce the likelihood of making a type I error by using a more stringent significance level. However, this *increases* the probability of making a *type II error* – the error of *not* rejecting the null hypothesis when it is in fact false.

4 The conventional significance levels ($p = .05$ and $p = .01$) are compromises between the rates for these two types of error.

11.4   Choosing a statistical test

This, then, is the procedure in principle. It is the same for all tests of statistical significance. However, how you realize the procedure for testing for statistical significance in practice depends on the precise test that you need to employ to analyse your data. You will have to employ different tests of significance under different circumstances if you wish to arrive at a meaningful answer to the same question: should I reject the null hypothesis in my experiment? Even if you are not using the test for the purposes of significance testing (see Chapter 12), you still need to know the most appropriate procedure for obtaining the statistics you require.

  Choosing the appropriate statistical test is the key to the whole process of finding out exactly what your data have to tell you. However, it is nowhere near as daunting a process as it may seem. (I know, we all say this, but believe me it *is* true.) If you keep a clear head and take things *step by step*, most of the time you should have few problems in arriving at an appropriate test for your data. Indeed, your problems will be reduced in this respect if you get into the habit of thinking about how you are going to analyse your data *before* you start running your study. You can then modify the design if you foresee any problems.

In order to decide which test to employ, you need to be able to answer a number of questions about the *type of study* you conducted, the *nature of the data* you obtained, and the *precise questions that you wish to ask* of these data. Below is a list of the key questions that you need to answer:

1 Do you want to (a) compare conditions or (b) correlate variables?
 2 What type of data do you have? Are they (a) nominal, (b) ordinal or (c) at least interval?
 3 If at least interval, can you assume that the data come from a population of scores that is normally distributed?
4 If you wish to compare conditions, did you manipulate more than one IV in your study?
5 If you wish to compare conditions, how many do you wish to compare at any one time?
6 Do you have the *same* or *different* participants in these conditions?

You can find more about each of these questions in Section A of the book's Web site at **http://mcgraw-hill.co.uk/openup/harris/**. They are also discussed in the statistics textbooks paired with this book (see the end of this chapter).

One problem to watch out for when writing your report is that there can sometimes be more than one way of analysing the same set of data. That is, it is not uncommon to find that you can test the *same* prediction using the *same* dependent variable but with *different* statistical tests. For example, the independent *t* test and the Mann-Whitney U test are alternative tests for data from an unrelated samples IV with two conditions. For the purposes of your report, however, you should not duplicate tests. That is, under these circumstances you should use and report only one of the comparable tests. (For example, either the independent *t* test or the Mann Whitney U test.)

Summary of Section 11.4

1 Choosing the appropriate statistical test is the key to the whole process of arriving at a meaningful answer to the question: should I *reject* or *not reject* the null hypothesis in my experiment?

2 In order to decide which test to employ, you will need to address a number of questions about the type of study, the nature of the data, and the precise questions that you wish to ask.

3 Often there may be more than one way of testing statistically the same prediction using the same dependent variable. Under these circumstances, however, you should report the outcome of only one of the tests.

11.5   Two-tailed and one-tailed tests

With some statistics you need to decide whether to use a **two-tailed** or a **one-tailed test** of significance. This relates to whether or not you consider the predictions derived from your experimental hypothesis to be directional or nondirectional and it introduces us to another controversy.

Earlier I said that you should consider your predictions to be directional if you were able (for sound theoretical reasons) to specify the *direction* in which the difference between your conditions should occur. Some authors argue that this translates directly into whether or not you should employ a one- or a two-tailed test of significance.

The difference between a one- and a two-tailed test of significance has to do with the way in which you use the tails of the distributions of the statistic you are employing. What it means in practice is that you can obtain significance with data using a one-tailed test that would fail to reach significance with a two-tailed test. This is the reward for specifying the direction in which the postulated difference will occur.

Now, you may read elsewhere that whether or not you choose to employ a one-tailed or a two-tailed test depends on whether the predictions are directional or nondirectional. That is, on whether or not you have reasonable grounds for specifying in advance that one of the conditions will exceed another on the DV. Unfortunately, however, it is not quite as simple as that.

I recommend that you employ the one-tailed test *only* when you have asked a "whether or not" question of the data. That is, a question of the form, "whether or not" a particular teaching method improves the rate at which people learn a particular task, or "whether or not" a particular set of work conditions improves output. Under these circumstances, if you find a difference between the conditions *opposite to the one you are testing* this would mean the same to you as if you had found *no difference* between the conditions. That is, if you found that the teaching method actually *impairs* the rate at which people learn the task, or the work conditions actually *decrease* output, this would be the same to you as finding that the new teaching method was no quicker than the old one, or that production was similar under the usual working conditions.

In practice, such questions generally concern those attempting to solve an *applied* problem. As students, however, most of the time you will be running studies in which findings that contradict the predictions will be every bit as important as findings that are consistent with the predictions. So, most of the time you will also be interested in findings that go in the opposite direction to the one you specified and your test should therefore be two-tailed. Only when your experimental question can simply be either confirmed or refuted – when it is open to a simple yes or no answer – should you employ the one-tailed test of significance.

If you are using tables of statistics, most contain the probability values for two-tailed comparisons. For many of the tests that you are likely to use as a student, you can derive the one-tailed value simply by halving the significance level. So, if the value that you obtain is significant at the 5 percent level (two-tailed), then the significance for a one-tailed test is actually 2.5 percent. Check in your textbook of statistics whether this is the case for the statistic that you are using.

 SAQ 40   The value of $t = 1.73$ is the critical value of t with 20 degrees of freedom at the 5 percent significance level for a one-tailed test. What is its associated probability for a two-tailed test?

One final thing to bear in mind about your analyses is that statistics only deal with the numbers fed into them. A statistical package will churn around any set of numbers that you feed into it in a suitable format. Just because the data were analysed does not mean either that the analysis itself or its outcome was necessarily meaningful. For instance, the value of chi-square for the cheese and nightmare experiment is perfectly reasonable, given the numbers that I fed into the analysis. Nevertheless, this does not tell us *anything* about the relationship between eating cheese and experiencing nightmares – I made the numbers up! Bear in mind also that rejecting the null hypothesis does not automatically entail that the results went in the direction you predicted. I am constantly amazed how few students actually *look at* their data once they have analysed them, or think much at all about what the results really mean. Get into the habit of going back to your data and thinking about what the outcome of your analyses might mean. (This is particularly a problem when you reject the null hypothesis but fail to spot that the difference is actually *opposite* in direction to the one you predicted with a directional hypothesis. You would be surprised how often this happens.)

Summary of Section 11.5

1 Tests of significance can be one-tailed or two-tailed. The difference in practice between these versions of the same test is that you can obtain statistical significance using the one-tailed version, with data that would fail to reach statistical significance using the two-tailed version.

2 You should only use one-tailed tests when you are able to *ignore* differences *opposite* in direction to those predicted by the experimental hypothesis. When you must not ignore such differences, the test is two-tailed. Most of you, most of the time, will therefore be undertaking two-tailed tests.

3 Just because the data have been analysed statistically does not mean that the analysis or its outcome is necessarily meaningful. Get into the habit of going back to the data to interpret the outcomes of the analyses and to ensure that these outcomes appear to make sense. In particular, watch out for occasions when you have been compelled to *reject* the null hypothesis and yet the differences between the conditions are in fact *opposite* in direction to the ones that you predicted.

11.6   Testing for statistical significance: summary of the procedure

1 Decide whether the *inferential* question involves *comparing* conditions or *correlating* variables.

2 Choose a test that asks this question and that is appropriate for the type of data you will collect.

3 Before starting, set your significance level and decide whether the test will be one- or two-tailed.

4 Calculate the *obtained* value of the above statistic, whether using a statistical package or by hand.

5 With statistical packages the software will print out for you the exact probability associated with the obtained value. Check whether this probability is equal to or less than the significance level you decided to use before the experiment (commonly $p = .05$). If it is, then the data are statistically significant. If it is not, then the data are not statistically significant.

6 If calculating by hand, look in the appropriate set of tables for the statistic used, at the significance level you have adopted, to find the relevant *critical* value of the statistic (Appendix 3). If the *obtained* value of the statistic is *equal* to the critical value or differs from it in the direction required for statistical significance, then the data are statistically significant. Under these circumstances, *reject* the null hypothesis. If not, then the data are not statistically significant. Under these circumstances, *do not reject* the null hypothesis.

 7 Look again at the descriptive statistics and think about why the data have compelled you to reject or not reject the null hypothesis. What, if anything, does this tell you about the relationship between the IVs and DVs?

Consolidating your learning

This closing section is designed to help you check your understanding and determine what you might need to study further. You can use the list of methodological and statistical concepts to check which ones you are happy with and which you may need to double-check. You can use this list to find the relevant terms in the chapter and also in other textbooks of design or statistics. The diagnostic questions provide a further test of your understanding. Finally, there is a description of what is covered in the two statistics textbooks paired with this book plus a list of relevant further material that you can find on the book's Web site.

Methodological and statistical concepts covered in this chapter

> 5 percent significance level
> Failing to reject the null hypothesis
> Findings that are not statistically significant
> Inferential statistics
> One-tailed test of significance
> Probability
> Rejecting the null hypothesis
> Reliability
> Significance level (alpha level)
> Statistical significance
> Statistically significant findings
> Two-tailed test of significance
> Type I error
> Type II error

We also discussed how to go about choosing a statistical test.

Diagnostic questions – check your understanding

1 What are *inferential statistics*?
2 What is a *statistically significant* difference?
3 What does it mean to say that the *5 percent significance level* was used in an analysis?
4 What is a *type I* error?
5 What is a *type II* error?

You can find the answers at the rear of the book (p. 276).

Statistics textbooks

Σ The books paired with *Designing and Reporting Experiments* have the following coverage:

Learning to use statistical tests in psychology – Greene and D'Oliveira
Greene and D'Oliveira have helpful coverage of how to choose a statistical test, which is a core theme of their book, with a section on this in each chapter. There is a handy decision tree inside the rear cover of the book and Chapter 3 describes how to use this. You will also find coverage of probability and statistical significance, including coverage of significance levels (pp. 16–17) and of two-tailed and one-tailed tests (p. 19). They discuss the assumptions of non-parametric tests in Chapter 5 and of parametric tests in Chapter 13 and compare them in Chapter 8.

SPSS survival manual – Pallant
Chapter 10 of Pallant gives excellent step-by-step coverage of how to go about choosing a statistical test, with a handy summary table at the end. She also repeats the key relevant points from this when covering which statistical technique to choose when comparing groups in the opening section to Part Five (pp. 201–5), where she also discusses type I and type II errors.

The *Designing and Reporting Experiments* Web site

In Section A of the book's Web site at **http://mcgraw-hill.co.uk/ openup/harris/** you will find expanded coverage of Section 11.4 of this book on how to choose a statistical test.

12 Statistics: effect size and power

When we test for statistical significance, therefore, we end up either rejecting the null hypothesis or not rejecting it. Following this, we critically examine our experiment, looking for any flaws that might be rival explanations for our findings (see Chapter 5). The ultimate goal of this procedure is to be able to determine whether or not the IV has a causal effect on the DV. This is the traditional procedure by which psychological experimentation has worked.

However, some people argue that we should be asking a subtly different question of the data. That is, instead of asking whether there is or is not a causal effect of the IV on the DV, why not ask *how big* an effect there is? Does the evidence suggest that the IV affects the DV not at all, a small amount, a medium amount, or a large amount? For example, in our driving and music experiment, it would be useful to know that listening to music makes a big difference to driving performance rather than a small one.

The difference between the questions is subtle, but the implications are quite profound. For example, some of those who promote asking the "how big" question also advocate abandoning significance testing altogether. Some of the reasons for this may become clearer as you work through this chapter. For now, however, I want you to focus on two issues that arise from the "how big" question that are important to think about even when you are testing for statistical significance: the *effect size* of your IVs and the *power* of your experiments.

12.1   Effect size

There are statistics available to help us to answer the "how big" question. These statistics use the data to form estimates of the difference that the IV makes to scores on the DV. They are called statistics of **effect size**. For many years psychologists tended to ignore the issue of effect size and concentrated on whether or not an effect or a relationship was statistically significant. One psychologist in particular – Jacob Cohen – has been especially influential in making psychologists think more about the size of the effects that we report.

Put loosely, effect size is the magnitude of the difference between the conditions in an experiment. (With correlations the issue concerns the strength of the relationship between the variables.) In a well-designed experiment effect size is the difference that the IV makes to the scores on the DV. So, for example, in a well-designed, two-condition experiment of the sort discussed in Chapter 10, it is the difference between the scores when not exposed to the IV (the control condition) and when exposed to the IV (the experimental condition). Thus, everything else being equal, the bigger the impact that the IV has, the bigger will be the difference between the scores and the bigger will be the effect size.

Effect size can be measured in standard deviations. One of the advantages of this is that we can then compare effect sizes across different experiments. In order to help us to describe and compare effect sizes, Cohen (1988) suggested some guidelines for determining whether an effect is large, medium or small. He suggested that we consider an effect of at least 0.8 standard deviations to be a large effect size and one of around 0.5 standard deviations to be a medium effect size. An effect of 0.2 standard deviations, he suggested we regard as a small effect size.

You will learn more about effect size in your statistics course. The important thing to note for now, however, is that Cohen argued that in psychology effect sizes are typically small or medium, rather than large. This has important implications for the way that we should design our experiments and other studies. For, if many of the effects that we are interested in are likely to be small or at best medium, then we need to make sure that our studies have the *power* to detect them.

Summary of Section 12.1

1 Instead of asking whether there is or is not a causal effect of the IV on the DV, some authors suggest we should ask how big an effect there is.

2 There are statistics available to help us to answer the "how big" question. These are called statistics of effect size.

3 In an experiment, effect size is the relative magnitude of the difference between the conditions. It is often expressed in standard deviations.

4 Cohen has argued that in psychology effect sizes are typically small or medium, rather than large.

5 If the effects that we are interested in are likely to be small or medium, then we need to make sure that our studies have the power to detect small or medium effects.

12.2   Power

Let's imagine for a moment that we have had the privilege of seeing some of the tablets of stone on which are written the Laws of the Psychological Universe. These state that our IV – say, listening to music – has a particular size of effect – say medium – on driving performance. In this context, **power** is the capacity of our study to detect this. That is, power is the probability of *not* making a type II error, of *not* failing to find a difference that is actually out there in the psychological universe. The power of a statistical test is its capacity to *correctly* reject the null hypothesis.

Experiments vary in power. The more powerful the experiment is, the smaller are the effects it can detect. In this way, experiments to psychologists are like telescopes to astronomers. Very powerful telescopes can see even dim and distant stars. Likewise, very powerful experiments can detect even tiny effects of the IV on the DV. Low-power experiments are like low-power telescopes. Telescopes lacking in power may be unable to detect even fairly close and bright stars. Similarly, experiments lacking in power may be unable to detect even quite strong and important effects of the IV on the DV.

Power is measured on a scale from zero to one. With a power of zero, there is no chance of detecting an effect of the IV on the DV, even if one exists. With a power of .25, there is a 25 percent chance of detecting a particular effect of the IV on the DV. This is not very likely and thus not very powerful. With a power of .80, there is an 80 percent chance of detecting such an effect of the IV on the DV and we are beginning to be in business. We need our designs to have at least this level of power if they are going to be worth running. So, how do we go about assessing and improving the power of our experiments?

12.2.1 Estimating power

Fortunately, we can estimate the power of our studies – including our experiments – before we run them. This enables us to check whether they will be powerful enough to detect the effects we are interested in. If they look like they will not be powerful enough we can then take steps to increase their power.

Power is influenced by a number of factors:

- the effect size;
- the significance level;
- whether the test is one- or two-tailed;
- the type of statistical test;
- the number of participants;
- whether the IV uses related or unrelated measures.

Perhaps you can see that the only one of these factors that we do not know for sure *before* running the experiment is the *effect size*. If we can make a reasonable guess about the likely effect size in our experiment, therefore, we can estimate the power of our experiment before running it. If necessary, we can then think about ways of increasing power.

There are two basic ways of estimating the likely effect size before running the experiment. The best way is to base the calculations on other experiments that have investigated the effects of this particular IV. This enables us to estimate the *likely* effect size of our IV. If such research is not available, however, we can still estimate how powerful our experiment would be if the IV had a given effect size. That is, we can assume that the effect size will be small or medium or large and calculate how likely our experiment would be to detect the effect under each of these circumstances. Again, we can then think about ways of increasing power if we find that the current design will be unlikely to detect a small or medium effect. On the other hand, if we find that it has the power to detect a small effect, we know that it will also be able to detect a medium or a large effect.

These calculations, not surprisingly, are called **power calculations**. Typically, we use them to help us to estimate how many participants we will need for our experiments to have enough power (say, .80) to stand a reasonable chance of detecting the effect we are interested in. Alternatively, we can save some effort by looking up power in relevant *power tables* or by using one of the many Web sites that are available to calculate power for us. You may learn more about power and even about how to calculate it in your statistics course. If so, you will find that the results are salutary: it can be surprising to find out quite how many participants you will need to stand, say, an 80 percent chance of rejecting a false null hypothesis with an unrelated samples IV.

This leads us to the next question. How can we go about *increasing* the power of our experiments if we need to?

12.2.2 Increasing the power of our experiments

In theory, we could increase power in any of the following ways: by increasing the effect size, making the significance level less stringent, using a one-tailed test, employing a parametric test, increasing the number of participants, and using a related samples IV. In practice, however, some of these are more practical and desirable ways of increasing power than others.

Changing the effect size is, of course, beyond the powers of us mere mortals. As we saw in Chapter 11, making the significance level less extreme (e.g., using the 10 percent significance level instead of the 5 percent significance level) means that there is greater chance of rejecting the null hypothesis. However, it increases our chances of doing so when we should not (i.e., of making a type I error). We should therefore be cautious about altering this. Likewise, you should be cautious about using one-tailed tests as these limit the inferences that you can draw from your experiment (Section 11.5). You should use the most powerful statistical technique that your data allow (e.g., parametric rather than nonparametric tests where appropriate). The remaining routes of increasing the power of our experiments, therefore, are to run enough participants and to use related samples IVs whenever possible. Let us consider these.

One relatively straightforward way of increasing power is to run more participants, especially with unrelated samples IVs. You need as many as will enable you to detect an effect of the size that you suspect that the IV may have on the DV. For example, if listening to music has only a small effect on driving performance, you will need more participants to detect this small causal effect than if listening to music has a medium effect on driving performance. With too few participants you would fail to detect the effect and conclude (erroneously) that listening to music makes no difference to driving performance.

? SAQ 41   What type of error would you have made?

So, with unrelated samples in particular, increasing the number of participants can be an effective way of increasing the power of your experiment to the level you need. The larger the sample size, the greater the power (other things being equal). We will discuss this further in Section 13.1.1.

Using related samples increases power by reducing the background variation against which we have to assess the effect of the IV on the DV (Section 10.4). This is a very efficient way of increasing power. It is a bit like using a radio telescope that has a filter that cuts out a lot of the background "noise" – the irrelevant signals that can mask the signals from the less powerful stars. Filter this out and you can "see" the signals from these weaker stars more clearly. This is one of the reasons why I suggested earlier that you should try to use related samples IVs whenever possible. However, as you know, it is not always possible to use related samples for an IV (Section 10.4).

Summary of Section 12.2

1 Power, in this context, is the capacity of an experiment to detect a particular effect of the IV on the DV. It is thus the capacity to *correctly* reject the null hypothesis.

2 Experiments vary in power. The more powerful the experiment is, the smaller are the effects it can detect.

3 Experiments that lack power may be unable to detect even strong and important effects of the IV on the DV.

4 Power is measured on a scale from zero to one. The closer to one, the greater the power of the design and the better its chance of correctly rejecting the null hypothesis.

5 We can estimate the power of our studies before we run them. If we need to, we can then take steps to adjust their power. Doing this in advance helps us to avoid wasting time by, for example, running an experiment that has too little power to detect the effects we are interested in.

6 The principal ways in which we increase power are to run enough participants and to use related samples IVs whenever possible.

12.3 Effect size and power: reporting and interpreting findings

Let's recap. The more powerful the experiment, the smaller the effect sizes it can detect. If the design lacks power, however, we may not be able to detect even quite large effects. Therefore, our experimental designs can be insufficiently powerful to detect effects of our IV on our DV, even if such effects exist and even if the effect size is quite large. This is just like using a weak telescope to look for stars: if the telescope is weak, we will not be able to see even quite bright stars.

Of course, we would not conclude that the only stars that exist are those we can we see through a weak telescope! Likewise, it is important to make sure that our experiments are powerful enough to detect the effects we are searching for. Using our data to estimate effect size *as well as* testing for statistical significance assists us with this problem. Doing so helps us to assess whether the lack of statistical significance is a result of the IV having little or no effect on the DV (the question the experiment was designed to answer) or because the experiment lacked sufficient power.

As you can see, these issues have important implications for the studies we run and the ways in which we report and interpret our findings. In terms of design, it obviously helps to consider power from the outset, to think carefully about the size of the effect we are expecting and to adjust the design accordingly. However, what about the implications of effect size and power for reporting and interpreting our findings? The rest of this chapter has advice on this. (If you already know how to calculate power or effect size statistics, you can go straight to Section 12.3.2.)

Reporting for those who do not know how to calculate power or effect size statistics

Courses vary greatly in when they teach you about these issues. Some of you will be introduced to them from the very start of your careers as students of psychology. Others may find that you are taught about power and effect size only quite late on in your studies. Some of you will be taught how to calculate effect size statistics and even power. Others of you will be taught about these things conceptually but not taught the calculations. Nevertheless, most of you should have at least some awareness of these issues by the time you come to undertake project work (e.g., in the final year of a UK degree course). If you have not been taught how to calculate power or to obtain effect size statistics by that stage, you should at least be aware of how these issues affect the inferences that you can draw from and about statistically significant and statistically nonsignificant findings.

Here is some advice about what you can do in your reports if you have been taught about these things conceptually but not taught how to calculate effect size statistics or power.

In the RESULTS you can do the following, as I advised in Chapter 4:

1 Whenever possible, report the exact probabilities associated with the obtained values of your statistic, whether these are statistically significant or not.
2 Where appropriate, report standard deviations as well as means in tables of descriptive statistics.
3 If you know how, report appropriate confidence intervals such as the 95 percent confidence intervals around the mean, or for a difference between two means. You can do this regardless of whether or not the effects are statistically significant.

Reporting relevant confidence intervals is increasingly being encouraged in psychological research. There are a variety of reasons for this. Among them is the insight that such confidence intervals offer about the power of your experiment. To put it simply, the more powerful the study (other things being equal), the narrower will be the confidence interval. This will help you to interpret results in which the null hypothesis has not been rejected. With a low-power study, the confidence interval will be wide and will encompass everything from zero effects to quite large effects of the IV. With a high-power study, the same confidence interval will be narrow and will encompass zero to very small effects only.

Those of you using and reporting the correlation coefficient Pearson's r might also consider reporting and commenting on an easily computed statistic of effect size. If you *square* the value of r (i.e., calculate the statistic called r^2), this will tell you how much of the variance is shared between the two variables in the correlation. This is a measure of effect size. It is useful to do this, as it will help you to avoid giving precedence to the statistical significance of the coefficient rather than to the size of the relationship. For, with enough participants, even correlations as small as $r = .2$ or even $r = .1$, can become statistically significant at the 5 percent significance level. Yet these are very small relationships. An $r = .2$, for instance, gives $r^2 = .04$, which indicates that only 4 percent of the variance is shared. So, think about calculating r^2 when you use Pearson's r.

One thing to avoid at all costs – especially in the DISCUSSION – is to confuse statistical significance with the size of the effect. If you have been able to follow the drift of the discussion in this chapter, you will perhaps see how the problem arises. If the experiment or study is powerful enough, *any* difference between your conditions will be statistically significant, no matter how small it is numerically and trivial it is psychologically. (Many of you realize this intuitively when you write in your reports that "our findings would have been significant if we had had more participants". It is precisely because this is *inevitably* true that – unless you defend it sensibly – this remark tends to evoke the scorn and wrath of your marker.) A very powerful experiment may well tell you that an effect is statistically significant even if the IV has only a relatively trivial effect on the DV. Thinking about effect size *in addition* to statistical significance helps you to avoid this problem. Doing so helps you to assess whether the effect is large enough to be potentially interesting psychologically. Remember that with a very powerful experiment it is possible for an effect to be highly significant *statistically* but for the effect size to be so small that the effect of the IV on the DV is trivial, both numerically and psychologically.

Don't panic if you don't yet know how to produce or calculate confidence intervals or statistics of effect size! Even without them you can still make some efforts to address effect size in your report. *Look at the sample size.* If the experiment has been well designed in other respects, the sample size is small and yet the effect is statistically significant (especially on an unrelated samples IV), then this suggests that the IV has a pretty large effect size. However, if the sample is large, then the results are ambiguous, for even trivial effects may be statistically significant with large samples. If the experiment has been well designed in other respects, the sample size is small and the effect is not statistically significant (especially on an unrelated samples IV), then the results are ambiguous, for even large effects may not be statistically significant with small samples. However, if the sample is large, then the failure to reject the null hypothesis suggests the absence of an effect of much size or psychological importance. (Of course, this depends on just how large the sample size is.)

It is very easy to confuse statistical significance and effect size, and people often do. So, do not worry if this discussion doesn't fall into place at once. These issues require thought and effort before they become clear. You may need to reread this chapter and also your statistics textbook several times before the penny even begins to drop.

12.3.2 Reporting for those who have been taught how to calculate power or effect size statistics

Obviously, if you are taught how to do even rudimentary power calculations or to use power tables or Web sites, then you should include these in the METHOD of your report. Advice on how to do this is in Section 3.6.3.

If you know how to calculate confidence intervals or how to get a statistical software package to produce these, then include them in the RESULTS (see Section 4.6.10). Likewise, once you know how to calculate or produce effect size statistics and understand what they mean, you will be able to report relevant statistics of effect size *as well as* the obtained value of your statistic and its associated probability. To give you an idea of how you might do this, here is the paragraph describing the principal findings from the mnemonic experiment, this time with an effect size statistic added. This statistic is known as *partial eta squared* (η^2) and is one of the effect size statistics available when using ANOVA.

The data in Table 1 were analysed using 2 × 2 ANOVA for mixed designs, with imageability (easily imaged or hard to image) as the related samples variable and instruction (mnemonic or no mnemonic) as the unrelated samples variable. There was a statistically significant main effect of instruction, $F(1, 38) = 7.20$, $p = .01$, with those in the mnemonic group recalling more items overall than did those in the no mnemonic group ($M = 15.65$, $SD = 3.97$; $M = 12.40$, $SD = 3.74$, respectively). Partial $\eta^2 = .16$, indicating that 16% of the overall variance was attributable to this manipulation. There was also a statistically significant main effect of imageability, $F(1, 38) = 145.22$, $p < .001$, with more items from the easily imaged list being recalled than from the hard-to-image list ($M = 15.98$, $SD = 4.12$; $M = 12.08$, $SD = 4.48$, respectively). Partial $\eta^2 = .79$, indicating that 79% of the over-all variance was attributable to this manipulation. However, these main effects were qualified by the significant Instruction X Imageability interaction, $F(1, 38) = 11.55$, $p = .002$. Partial $\eta^2 = .23$, indicating that 23% of the overall variance was attributable to the interaction between the variables. Figure 1 displays this interaction.

You should use these statistics in the DISCUSSION to help you to answer the following questions:

1 If an effect is statistically significant, what do the effect size statistics tell us about the likely size of the effect? Is the effect big enough to be of psychological interest and importance?
2 If an effect is not statistically significant, what do the confidence intervals tell us about power? Are the 95 percent confidence intervals broad (suggesting that the analysis lacked power) or narrow (suggesting that it did not)? What do the effect size statistics indicate about the likely size of the effect? If these indicate that the effect is not small, this suggests that the analysis lacked power. If you conclude that the experiment lacked the power to detect the effects, suggest what steps might be taken in future to run studies with sufficient power.

Perhaps now you can see why some researchers have called for the abandonment of significance testing altogether. If we report statistics of effect size together with the exact probability associated with the obtained value of our statistic, so the argument runs, then at best statistical significance is redundant and at worst it is downright misleading. Pursuing this debate is beyond the scope of this book. However, you may well discuss these issues further in your statistics course.

Summary of Section 12.3

1 There are some things that you can do about these issues in your reports even if you have not been taught how to calculate power or to obtain effect size statistics.

2 These include reporting the exact probability associated with your obtained statistic and, once you know how, reporting appropriate confidence intervals.

3 Whatever you do, make sure that you do not confuse statistical significance with effect size. A very powerful experiment may well tell you that an effect is statistically significant even if the IV has only a relatively trivial effect on the DV. On the other hand, a large effect may not be found to be statistically significant if the design lacks power.

4 Even without statistics of effect size, looking at the sample size can help you to make some inferences about effect size.

5 If you do any power calculations, report this in the METHOD. You may also be taught to generate other statistics indicative of effect size and power. If so, report these statistics in the RESULTS and use them to help you to interpret your findings in the DISCUSSION.

Consolidating your learning

This closing section is designed to help you check your understanding and determine what you might need to study further. You can use the list of methodological and statistical concepts to check which ones you are happy with and which you may need to double-check. You can use this list to find the relevant terms in the chapter and also in other textbooks of design or statistics. The diagnostic questions provide a further test of your understanding. Finally, there is a description of what is covered in the two statistics textbooks paired with this book plus a list of relevant further material that you can find on the book's Web site.

Methodological and statistical concepts covered in this chapter

Effect size
Power calculations
Statistical power

Diagnostic questions – check your understanding

1 What do we mean by *effect size*?
2 What is the *power* of an experiment?
3 What does it mean to say that an experiment has a power of .80?
4 What are *power calculations*?
5 How practically might we *increase* the power of an experiment if we did not want to change the significance level and could not use a one-tailed test of significance?
6 What percentage of the variance is shared by two variables where $r = .50$?

You can find the answers at the rear of the book (p. 277).

Statistics textbooks

Σ The books paired with *Designing and Reporting Experiments* have the following coverage:

SPSS survival manual – Pallant
Pallant covers power and effect size in the introduction to Part 5. Helpfully, she also describes how to obtain effect size statistics from SPSS for most of the tests included in the book. For example, partial eta squared (the effect size statistic referred to in this chapter) is described in the introduction to Part 5 and in Chapters 18 and 19.

 ### The *Designing and Reporting Experiments* Web site

In Section B of the book's Web site at **http://mcgraw-hill.co.uk/ openup/harris/** you will find coverage of some issues to consider when reporting statistics of effect size.

13 More advanced experimental design

Once you have mastered the basics, you can start to think about designing more complex experiments. This will enable you to ask more subtle questions of the psychological universe, such as whether variables *interact* with each other. There are two basic ways of extending experiments:

1 You can use an IV with more than two levels.
2 You can manipulate more than one IV simultaneously.

You can do either of these things or both at the same time.

13.1 Extending the number of levels on the independent variable

As you know, we need not restrict ourselves simply to manipulating the *presence* versus the *absence* of the suspected causal variable. Experiments using IVs with three or more levels are very common in psychology and are not hard to design. As with any IV, these can employ either unrelated or related samples. The principal design issues that arise have to do with using enough participants with unrelated samples to ensure sufficient power or being able to adequately control for order effects with related samples.

13.1.1 Unrelated samples IVs

Having adequate numbers of participants to ensure sufficient power is an issue for *all* experimental designs, but it is an especially pressing issue with unrelated samples because it is so easy to design a study that lacks power. As discussed in Section 12.2, power in this context refers to the capacity of your experiment to detect an effect of the IV on the DV where one exists. The *more* participants you use, all things being equal, the *more* likely you will be to detect any impact of the IV on the DV. Indeed, unless the IV has a pretty dramatic impact on the DV (e.g., listening to music *massively* impairs or improves driving performance), designs using unrelated samples with small numbers of participants will be useless.

How many participants do you need? The number of participants you need depends on a number of factors, including how strong you estimate the effect of the IV on the DV will be (Section 12.2.2). Sadly, therefore, there is no simple answer to this question. (It really is just like asking how long is a piece of string.) Obviously, the ideal way of estimating this number is through *power calculations* (Section 12.2.1). However, this is of little help to those of you who have no idea how to obtain such calculations. For you, the only sensible answer I can offer is that this number is almost certainly going to be much larger than the one you first thought of! Thinking in terms of 10–15 participants *per condition* is unlikely to give you much chance of rejecting a false null hypothesis. Even double these numbers may be insufficient. As an incredibly rough rule of thumb, with a number plucked out of the sky, look to use no fewer than 20 per condition and try to use substantially more than this if you can. You therefore need to think very carefully when considering extending the number of levels on an IV with unrelated samples. Make sure that you have the time and the resources to get reasonable numbers of participants in each condition. When in doubt, keep it simple!

Particularly early on in your career, you may *have* to use fewer participants than this (e.g., for reasons of time or problems with access to people who can take part in the experiment). Under these circumstances, remember two things. First, if you are playing a role in the design of the experiment (as opposed to having it designed for you by a tutor) then make sure that the IV *has* to use unrelated samples. Moreover, think carefully *before* extending the levels on this unrelated samples IV beyond two or three. Second, if your findings are not statistically significant, bear in mind that a potential explanation for this is that the design was not powerful enough to detect the effect, rather than that there was no effect to detect.

 Later on (for example, in final-year projects in the UK), this is likely to be one of the issues on which you are assessed. When using IVs with unrelated samples you need to have sufficient numbers of participants in each of the conditions, so bear in mind when designing the experiment the number of participants likely to be available. However, do not overreact to this problem by using *too many* participants. The number of participants you run should be optimum, as determined by power calculations or, failing that, reasonable guesswork.

Summary of Section 13.1.1

1 With unrelated samples the principal design issue arising from IVs with more than two levels is to use enough participants in each condition to ensure sufficient power.

2 This means that you will have to think carefully when considering extending the number of levels on an unrelated samples IV. Will you have the time and resources to get enough participants in each condition?

3 Do not overreact to this issue by using too many participants. The number of participants should be optimum – either as determined by power calculations (preferably) or by reasonable guesswork if you cannot do the calculations.

4 With findings that are not statistically significant, examine whether this is because the experiment lacked sufficient power to detect an effect.

13.1.2 Related samples IVs

As we discussed in Chapter 10, numbers of participants is much less of a problem when using *related* samples. This is because of the greater power of related samples (Section 12.2.2). Here, instead, the principal problem is usually *order effects*. Exactly the same issues arise as we considered in Section 10.4.3. You cannot eliminate order effects; you therefore need to ensure that the effects due to order contribute approximately equally to each of the experimental conditions. As

Table 13.1
All Possible Combinations of Four Conditions (A, B, C and D)

ABCD	BACD	CBAD	DBCA	ACDB	BCDA
CADB	DCAB	ACBD	BCAD	CABD	ABDC
DCBA	BADC	CBDA	DBAC	ADBC	CBDA
BDAC	DABC	ADCB	BDCA	CDAB	DACB

Note. Use this table to help you to counterbalance any experiment in which you have a four-level, related samples IV.

before, the ideal way of achieving this is to *counterbalance* the design. With three conditions, there are six different combinations (given by three factorial, $3! = 3 \times 2 \times 1 = 6$). With four conditions, there are 24 different combinations ($4! = 4 \times 3 \times 2 \times 1 = 24$), as you can see in Table 13.1. You can use this table to help you to counterbalance any experiment in which you have a four-level, related samples IV – it lists for you *all* of the possible combinations.

With five conditions there are actually 120 different combinations. This means, in effect, that counterbalancing is possible for most of us only up to IVs with *four* levels. After that we need too many participants and will have to use alternative controls for order.

? SAQ 42   Suppose that you wanted to run an experiment with three conditions using related samples.

(a) Which, if any, of the following numbers of participants would you need to run to ensure the design was counterbalanced?

　　3 5 6 10 12 15 18 20 22 25

(b) Which, if any, of the numbers you have chosen would it be better to use?
(c) What is the next highest number you could use to ensure that the design was counterbalanced?

? SAQ 43   Suppose that you wanted to run an experiment with *four* conditions using related samples.

(a) What would be the minimum number of participants you could run to ensure that this experiment was counterbalanced and why?

(b) If you considered that this minimum number was unlikely to be sufficient to detect the impact of the IV on the DV, what would be the next highest number of participants that you could run to ensure that it was counterbalanced?

If for some reason you cannot counterbalance to control for the effects of order, then you might try partially controlling for these effects instead. For example, the first column in Table 13.1 contains four orders in which every condition appears in each ordinal position (first, second, third, fourth) and is followed by and preceded by every other condition once only. You could use this to partially control for order in an experiment involving fewer than 24 participants. (For example, if you had 12 participants you could randomly assign each of the 4 orders to groups of 3 participants using randomization without replacement – see Appendix 2.)

When even this solution is not possible, then turn to that good old standby, *randomization*. Just as before, however, remember that randomization does *not* guarantee that the order effects will be spread around equally, and also that it is likely to be more successful in achieving this (though again not inevitably so) the more participants you have.

Finally, remember that controls for order are *only* useful where there are no *carry-over* effects. Just as before, if you suspect that doing one of the conditions before another will have a permanent or disproportionate effect on performance, then do not use related samples for that IV.

? SAQ 44   Those of you who relish a challenge might now like to go back to SAQ 24 and work out how you could control for order effects in the two designs using related samples, (a) and (e). State what the minimum number of participants would be for these experiments, given the controls you have chosen to employ.

Summary of Section 13.1.2

1 With related samples IVs with more than two levels the principal design issue is controlling for order effects.

2 With IVs with three or four levels it may be possible to control for order by counterbalancing. (Table 13.1 lists all the possible

combinations of a four-level IV to help you counterbalance such a design.)

3 With more than four levels you are more likely to control for order partially or by randomizing.

4 Controls for order are only useful when there are no carry-over effects. If doing one of the conditions before another will have a lingering, permanent or disproportionate effect on participants' responses, then related samples should not be used for that IV.

13.2 Experimental designs with two or more independent variables

Experiments involving more than one IV are very common in psychology. Such experiments enable us to test more sophisticated ideas about the variables in the psychological universe, such as whether the variables *interact* with each other.

For example, rather than simply concerning ourselves with the effects of having the music on or off on driving performance, we might want to find out whether this affects those who have been drinking alcohol more than those who have not been drinking alcohol. In order to do this we could design an experiment in which we simultaneously manipulated *both* the IV *music* and the IV *alcohol*. How would we do this? Well, we could turn to our pool of participants and assign half of them randomly to a music on condition, and half to a music off condition. Of those in the music on condition, we could assign half randomly to drink a standard amount of alcohol, with the remainder remaining sober. Likewise with the music off condition, we could ask half of our participants to drink the standard amount of alcohol, with the other half remaining sober (Table 13.2). We would thus have manipulated *two* independent variables, (music and alcohol) with two levels on each (music on or music off, and alcohol or no alcohol). This is quite a common design in psychology. It is sometimes referred to as a **two by two** or **2 × 2** design.

Of course, we need not restrict ourselves to manipulating the *presence* versus the *absence* of the suspected causal variables. We could, for instance, vary the *amount* of alcohol that our participants consumed, so that one group drank no alcohol, another drank the equivalent of one glass of wine, another the equivalent of two glasses of wine, and another the equivalent of three glasses of wine. At the

Table 13.2
An Experimental Design with Two Independent Variables, Two Levels on Each

	IV: music	
IV: alcohol	Level 1: off	Level 2: on
Level 1: no	Condition 1	Condition 2
Level 2: yes	Condition 3	Condition 4

same time we would have half of the participants driving with the music on, the other half with the music off. Such a design appears in Table 13.3. On the other hand, we could simultaneously vary the *volume* at which the music was played – with one group listening to the music at low volume, another at medium volume, and a third at high volume. Such a design appears in Table 13.4.

In principle, there is no limit to the number of independent variables you can manipulate simultaneously in an experiment. Neither is there any restriction over whether these variables employ related or unrelated samples. For example, in the first version of the above experiment the variables could *both* be unrelated (with different participants in conditions 1–4) or *both* related (with the same participants in conditions 1–4, albeit with a suitable time lag between the alcohol and the no alcohol conditions). Or we could have a *combination* of related and unrelated samples (for instance, the music variable could employ *related* samples, the alcohol variable, *unrelated* samples).

Table 13.3
An Experimental Design with Two Independent Variables, One with Two Levels, the Other with Four Levels

	IV: music	
IV: alcohol[a]	Level 1: off	Level 2: on
Level 1: 0 glass	Condition 1	Condition 2
Level 2: 1 glass	Condition 3	Condition 4
Level 3: 2 glasses	Condition 5	Condition 6
Level 4: 3 glasses	Condition 7	Condition 8

Note. [a] Glasses of wine, where each glass contains 1 standard unit of alcohol.

Table 13.4
An Experimental Design with Two Independent Variables, Four Levels on Each

	IV: music			
IV: alcohol[a]	Level 1: off	Level 2: low volume	Level 3: medium volume	Level 4: high volume
Level 1: 0 glass	Cond 1	Cond 2	Cond 3	Cond 4
Level 2: 1 glass	Cond 5	Cond 6	Cond 7	Cond 8
Level 3: 2 glasses	Cond 9	Cond 10	Cond 11	Cond 12
Level 4: 3 glasses	Cond 13	Cond 14	Cond 15	Cond 16

Note. Cond = Condition.
[a] Glasses of wine, where each glass contains 1 standard unit of alcohol.

Given this flexibility, it is important to know how to design and run studies involving more than one IV. It is also important to know how to refer to such designs in the DESIGN and RESULTS. The next section describes two ways of labelling such designs.

Summary of Section 13.2

1 It is perfectly possible to design experiments in which we manipulate more than one IV at the same time.

2 In experiments involving more than one IV, each can have two or more levels. The IVs can be exclusively unrelated samples or exclusively related samples IVs or any combination of unrelated and related samples IVs.

13.3 Labelling designs that have two or more independent variables

One way of labelling these designs is to describe them in terms of a combination of the *number* and *nature* of their IVs. So, for instance, the experiment in Table 13.2 would be called a "two-way" experiment, because it has two IVs. If both IVs used unrelated samples, the experiment would have a "two-way, unrelated samples" design. If both IVs used related samples, it would have a "two-way, related samples" design. If one of the IVs used unrelated samples and one used related samples, the experiment would have a "two-way, mixed" design, for designs involving both types of IV are described as having **mixed designs**. Using this convention, the designs that we talked about in Chapter 10 were *one-way* designs.

So, to label your design correctly using this method, first count how many IVs there are in your design. If there is one IV, it will be a *one-way* design. If there are two, it will be a *two-way* design. With three it will be a *three-way* design, and so on. Once you have determined this, then work out for each IV whether it uses related samples or unrelated samples. If all the IVs use related samples, then it is a *related samples* design. If all the IVs use unrelated samples, then it is an *unrelated samples* design. If there is at least one of each type of IV, then it is a *mixed* design. The logic extends to "five-way" experiments, "six-way" experiments, and so on. However, my advice is that you restrict yourself to experiments with a maximum of three IVs (Section 13.6).

If you have been taught to use different labels for your IVs than the ones that I am using in this book, then use these to label the design. For example, you might call your design a "two-way, within-participants" or a "three-way, between-participants", and so on. If so, just substitute the label that you have been taught to use for the ones I am using.

When writing your report you will need to specify the number of levels on each of the IVs and what these levels were. With mixed designs, you will need to make clear which of the IVs used related samples and which used unrelated samples. (See Chapter 3 for an example.)

Another way of labelling these designs is to refer to them by describing the number of levels on each of the IVs. For example, the design in Table 13.2 could be described as a "2×2 related samples" design if you had used only related samples IVs. If you had used only unrelated samples IVs, it could be described as a "2×2 unrelated samples" design. If you had used one of each type of IV it could be described as a "2×2 mixed" design. Likewise, a three-way design involving one unrelated samples IV and two related samples IVs with three, three, and four levels respectively could be referred to as a "$3 \times 3 \times 4$ mixed" design, and so on.

Again, when writing your report you will need to make clear which IVs had which number of levels and what these levels were. With mixed designs, you will need to specify which of the IVs used related samples and which used unrelated samples.

? **SAQ 45**   Below you will find a list of studies that have more than one IV. Go through each in turn and attempt to name these designs using *both* of the conventions outlined above.

(a) An accident researcher is interested in the effects of different levels of alcohol (0, 2, 4, or 8 standard unit measures of wine) on driving performance. Over the course of several weeks, she varies the quantity of alcohol given to a group of participants on different occasions. She then examines whether the impact of the alcohol varies with the person's gender and the length of time since they passed their driving test (passed in the previous 6 months, in the previous 7–18 months, or more than 18 months previously).

(b) An occupational psychologist is interested in the effects of different types of physical stressor (in this case heat, noise, or light) and the nature of the task (demanding or undemanding) on blood pressure. He exposes different groups of participants to the different types of stress, and measures their performance on both types of task.

(c) A psychologist interested in personality wishes to examine the effects of gender and extraversion (extravert or introvert) on public speaking performance.

(d) Another accident researcher is interested in the effect of listening to in-car audio on driving performance. Using a driving simulator, she varies the driving conditions (easy, moderate, or difficult), the nature of the material listened to (talk or music), and the volume at which it is played (low, moderate, or loud), on the driving performance of a group of experienced drivers.

Note that sometimes you will find designs with more than one IV referred to as *factorial designs*, and also come across references to *repeated measures* or to *split-plot designs*. **Factorial designs** are ones that use all the possible combinations of the levels of the different IVs. The designs in Tables 13.2–13.4 are all factorial designs. **Repeated measures** is another name given to designs employing (usually only) IVs with related samples. **Split-plot** is an alternative term for a mixed design that stems from the origins of this research design in agricultural research. Other names may also be used. However, you should never come across (or use) the term "one-way, mixed design".

? **SAQ 46**   Why should you never use the term "one-way, mixed design"?

Summary of Section 13.3

1 You must be able to label accurately designs involving more than one IV.

2 In your report you must make clear for each IV in your experiment whether it used a related or unrelated samples IV, how many levels it had and what these levels were.

3 You can do this succinctly with a basic design statement.

4 This section described two ways of labelling designs that you could use in your report. One involves specifying the number of IVs in the basic design statement (e.g., two-way, three-way, and so on). The other involves specifying the number of levels on each IV in the basic design statement (e.g., 2×2, $2 \times 3 \times 3$, and so on).

5 Designs involving a combination of unrelated and related samples IVs are called mixed designs.

6 Although these methods have been illustrated using the labels for IVs employed in this book (unrelated and related samples IVs) other terms that you may use for these IVs can easily be substituted for these labels in the basic design statement.

13.4 Main effects of independent variables

With designs involving two or more IVs we can test for *interactions* between the different IVs, as well as for *main effects* of each IV. Testing for interactions enables us to test more sophisticated ideas about the ways in which causal variables operate in The Psychological Universe. First, however, let us consider main effects.

The **main effect** of an IV is the effect of that IV on the DV, *ignoring* the other IVs in the experiment. For example, in the experiment in Table 13.2, a significant main effect of alcohol would indicate that driving performance with alcohol differed from driving performance without alcohol. A significant main effect of music, on the other hand, would indicate that driving performance when listening to music differed from driving performance when not listening to music.

One way of thinking about experiments employing more than one IV is to think of them as if they were several experiments being run simultaneously. The number of experiments being run corresponds to the number of separate IVs. There is potentially a significant main effect for every IV in the experiment, irrespective of whether it uses related or unrelated samples. For example, if we ran an experiment involving three IVs, this would be like running *three* experiments simultaneously. We could thus test for three main effects – one for each of the IVs in the design (see Table 13.5 for the main effects in experiments with two and three IVs).

? SAQ 47   How many significant *main* effects could we find in each of the experiments in SAQ 45?

    You can find more about main effects in Section C of the Web site that accompanies this book at **http://mcgraw-hill.co.uk/openup/harris/**.

13.5   Statistical interactions

When we combine IVs in this way in an experiment, however, we get several bonuses. One of the most important of these is that we can test whether our IVs *interact* with each other. When IVs **interact** the effect of one IV is *different* at the levels of the other IV or IVs. For example, in Figure 13.1 you can see that drinking alcohol makes a bigger difference to performance when participants listen to music than it does when they do not listen to music. That is, the *difference* between driving performance with alcohol and with no alcohol is bigger at one level of the music IV (music) than at the other level of the music IV (no music). Therefore, the IVs interact.

Figure 13.2 contains another example of an interaction. Here you can see that the IVs interact to such an extent that the effects of alcohol are actually *opposite* in direction at the levels of the music IV. Here driving is worse among those who have drunk alcohol when they do not listen to music but better among those who have drunk alcohol when they *do* listen to music. (Obviously, I have made these

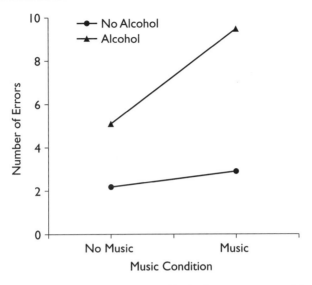

Figure 13.1.   Line graph displaying one type of interaction between two IVs.

effects up!) Again, the IVs interact. That is, the effect of one IV is *different* at the levels of the other.

Both of these are examples of interactions. Had the IVs *not* interacted then, when graphed, the data would have looked more like Figure 13.3. Here the difference between driving performance with alcohol and with no alcohol is more or less the same when participants listen to music as it is when they do not listen to music. Therefore, the IVs do *not* interact.

As a student you can sometimes struggle to understand statistical interactions. Yet, when you first start designing your own studies in psychology, you are in fact naturally very aware of the possibility that variables can interact. Remember those first studies in which you wanted to include all the variables that you could think of? From ethnic background, social class, time of day, gender of participant, gender of experimenter, temperature in the room and what the participants had for breakfast, to how much coffee they had drunk? This reflects your natural, intuitive awareness that these variables may well make a difference to the effects. That is, you were concerned that the effect of the variables of interest may be changed – accentuated, reduced or even eliminated – in the presence of other variables. This is what an interaction tells us – that the effects of an IV are different – bigger, smaller or even eliminated – at the levels of another IV.

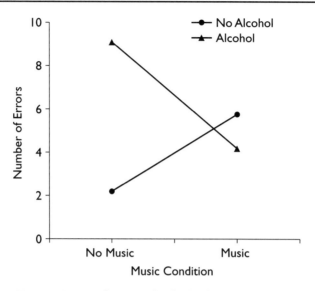

Figure 13.2.   Line graph displaying an alternative type of interaction between two IVs.

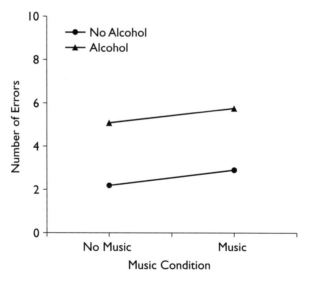

Figure 13.3.   Line graph displaying no interaction between the two IVs.

A statistically significant interaction therefore tells us that the effects of one IV are *inconsistent* at the levels of other IVs. Although it might sound odd to be interested in inconsistencies in the effects of our IVs, we are often very interested in evidence that our IVs interact in this way. You can find out more about interactions in Section C of the book's Web site at **http://mcgraw-hill.co.uk/openup/harris/**. You will also hear more about these effects on your statistics course.

13.6   Analysing designs involving two or more IVs

Designs involving the simultaneous manipulation of two or more IVs are commonly analysed using the statistical test known as **analysis of variance** (ANOVA). You will certainly learn more about ANOVA on your statistics course. With ANOVA you can simultaneously test *all* of the main effects and interactions in your experiment for statistical significance. To help you with this, Table 13.5 lists all of the effects that you can find in designs using two and three IVs. Use this table to check against your statistical output. It will help you to keep track of the effects that you can expect to find in the analysis. Any or all of the effects listed there can be found to be statistically significant in a particular analysis.

Table 13.5
The Potential Main Effects and Interactions in Designs Employing Two and Three Independent Variables

Experiment with 2 IVs	Potential main effects:	IV1
		IV2
	Potential two-way interaction:	IV1 × IV2
Experiment with 3 IVs	Potential main effects:	IV1
		IV2
		IV3
	Potential two-way interactions:	IV1 × IV2
		IV1 × IV3
		IV2 × IV3
	Potential three-way interaction:	IV1 × IV2 × IV3

Note. Section C of the book's Web site contains an expanded version of this table showing the potential main effects and interactions in an experiment with four IVs.

Note that you do not need to know the number of levels or whether the IVs use unrelated or related samples in order to be able to use Table 13.5. You *do*, however, need to know these things in order to analyse the data appropriately. For this reason it is essential that you specify *which* particular version of ANOVA you used in your analysis. So make sure that you include an accurate and sufficiently detailed statement about which ANOVA you used in the RESULTS (see Section 4.6.10).

Finally, be careful about how many IVs you use in an experiment. My advice is to restrict yourself to three at the most, unless you have lots of experience or will receive very close supervision from a tutor. One reason for this is that in such designs controlling for order, matching materials, or obtaining enough participants is difficult. The main reason, however, is that interpreting three-way interactions is hard and interpreting interactions above and beyond three-way interactions (e.g., four-way interactions) is *so* hard that it can make your brain start to feel like it is slowly dissolving.

13.7   Graphing statistical interactions

Graphing significant interactions is a *very* useful aid to interpreting them. This was evident even for the 2×2 designs that I discussed in Section 13.5. It is even more evident when you have more levels on your IVs or more IVs involved in the interaction (or both).

I used **line graphs** in Figures 13.1–13.3 to illustrate the effects. The principal reason for this is that, because they represent inconsistencies in effects, interactions are revealed by deviations from the parallel. This is easy to see with a line graph. Technically, however, I should have used a *bar graph* for these examples, as the IV on the horizontal axis (music) is not quantitative. That is, the conditions *no music* and *music* are absolute, categorical states with no gradations between them. Yet there is a line on the horizontal axis for points between them and this is meaningless. Had I put alcohol on the horizontal axis this would have made sense, as there are sensible gradations between 0 units and 2 units of alcohol. Figure 13.4 is a *bar graph* showing the same interaction as in Figure 13.1. Take the advice of your tutor on which type of graph to use. Whichever you do use, get into the habit of graphing statistically significant interactions to help you to interpret them, and include figures displaying the key ones in your report

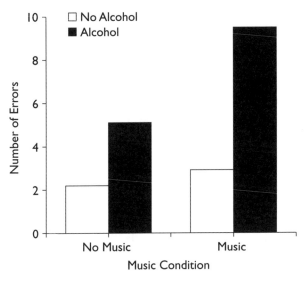

Figure 13.4. Bar graph displaying the same effects as in Figure 13.1.

(see Section 8.5). (You can find advice on how to graph three-way interactions in Section C of the book's Web site at **http://mcgraw-hill. co.uk/openup/harris/**)

Summary of Sections 13.4–13.7

1 In experiments involving more than one IV we can differentiate and test for the main effects of the different IVs and for inter-actions between the different IVs.

2 The main effect of an IV is the effect of that IV disregarding the other IVs in the experiment. There is potentially a significant main effect for each IV in the experiment.

3 An interaction occurs when the effects of one IV are different at the different levels of another IV.

4 It is difficult to interpret interactions between three or more IVs. So, as a general rule you would be well advised to limit the number of IVs that you manipulate in an experiment.

5 You should get into the habit of graphing statistically significant interactions and include graphs of the key ones in your report.

13.8   Watch out for "IVs" that are not true independent variables

Sometimes you will include in your experiments variables that look like IVs but are not true independent variables. These are variables like gender (male or female), personality variables (e.g., optimists or pessimists; people who are high, medium or low in trait anxiety), or differences in attitudes or behaviour (e.g., being for or against abortion; being a smoker or a non-smoker). Variables such as these are not *truly* independent variables because we have not been able to assign participants randomly to the different levels of the variable. That is, participants arrive at our study *already* assigned to the levels of these variables. For example, they come to us *already* as women, or against abortion, or smokers. Thus we do not determine their assignment to groups – it is predetermined.

Take the driving and music experiment. Imagine that instead of alcohol we are interested in gender differences in driving performance and the possibility that gender interacts with listening to music. We take our participants and allocate them randomly to the music on and the music off conditions. We take our participants and allocate them randomly to the women and men conditions. Er, except we cannot. Every time we reach for a human being who is neuter we find that they are already either male or female. Despite our best efforts, we are simply unable as experimenters to control who will be male and who will be female in our experiment. The allocation of participants to the levels of our variable *gender* is predetermined. Whenever we find that this is the case – whenever we are unable as experimenters to allocate our participants randomly to conditions – then we do not have a *truly* independent variable. (Do not confuse this with our control over *which* men and women participate in our experiment. The issue is our inability to control which sex any given participant gets given, not our ability to control who takes part in the experiment.)

This does not mean that we should avoid testing for gender differences or for differences in response between people classified in other ways that are predetermined. On the contrary, we often want to know a great deal about what other responses and variables are associated with being male or female, politically committed or apolitical, being of average or above average IQ, for or against genetic engineering, and so on. The important point is that, even though these variables look like IVs, we must remember when reporting the study and interpreting the findings involving these variables that they are not IVs in the strict sense and that our conclusions must therefore be qualified and cautious.

Why qualified? Because, despite appearances, they are *not* experimental but correlational (see Section 9.2). This means that we cannot assume that they are the *causal* variables when we find changes on the DV associated with levels of this "IV".

Let's take an example. Suppose that you and I are interested in the impact of laughter on physical health. One approach to this would be to measure how much people laugh during a 5-minute interaction and relate this to a measure of physical health, say, how often they visit the doctor in the following 6 months. We could even form two levels on this "IV" by differentiating those who laughed *more* than average (high laughter) from those who laughed *less* than average (low laughter). (Let's do this by splitting them at the median for laughter, putting those above the median into the high laughter group and those below the median into the low laughter group.) Imagine that we find that there is indeed a difference, such that the above average laughter group pay fewer visits to the doctors. Would we be able to conclude that laughter *caused* this difference in visits? No, we would not. There are countless ways in which people who laugh a lot differ from those who laugh little. Take a minute or two to think of reasons why some people may laugh more than others. I bet several of these are also plausible explanations for the difference in doctor's visits between the groups. That is, there are a whole variety of *additional* differences between people who laugh a lot and those who laugh little, any or all of which could be responsible for the differences in health *in addition to* or *instead of* laughing per se. That is, our laughter "IV" is *inevitably* confounded.

This is true of all such variables. They are inevitably confounded. Thus, we can only make suggestions and guesses about causality. It is only when we are free to allocate people to levels randomly that we have the possibility of breaking the natural associations between variables and thus can remove these confounds from our design.

To understand this, imagine that instead of *measuring* the laughter variable and *classifying* participants into high and low laughter groups, we *manipulate* this variable. There are a number of ways that we could do this, but let's keep it simple. Say that we randomly allocate participants to one of two conditions. Those in the *experimental* condition we get to laugh out loud for 1 full minute every 3 waking hours for 5 days. Those in the *control* condition we get to hum a tune of their choice for 1 full minute every 3 waking hours for 5 days. We use the same DV as before and get the same results: the laughter group pays fewer visits to the doctors. If the randomization has worked properly, then there should be no systematic differences between the groups in the variables that confounded the other version of this study: personality, stress, happiness, and so on. We would then be in a position to attribute unequivocally any differences in physical health to laughter.

You will come across many examples of such variables in your reading and will use them in your own studies in psychology. It is perfectly appropriate to use such variables in studies and analyses, provided that you are circumspect in the conclusions you reach. You can run studies with such variables in conjunction with true IVs (e.g., a study on the effects of alcohol and gender on driving). However, if you *only* have such variables in your design, make sure that you are aware that it is *not* an experiment. You therefore need to be able to differentiate a true IV from something that looks like one but is not.

? **SAQ 48**   Look again at the studies in SAQ 45. Are all the variables true IVs? State for each study whether this is the case and which variable(s) are not true IVs.

Because of this, some researchers suggest that we should replace the terms independent and dependent variables when using such variables with ones that do not imply causality. One possibility is to refer instead to the **explanatory** variable and the **response** variable. Other possibilities include **classification** variable, **subject** variable or **predictor** variable instead of IV and **measured** variable or **criterion** variable instead of DV. Your tutor may encourage you to use such alternative labels, so watch out for this issue.

One relevant term that you may also come across in your reading is **quasi-experimental design**. A quasi-experimental design is one that looks like an experimental design but that lacks the critical ingredient – random assignment. Quasi-experimental variables are thus particular versions of these variables that look like IVs but are not really independent variables. Quasi-experimental designs are interesting and useful methods of attempting to conduct experiments in real-life settings where it is not possible to randomly assign participants to treatment conditions. You may learn more about such designs in your methods course.

Summary of Section 13.8

1   Sometimes you will include in your experiments variables that look like IVs but that are not true independent variables.

2   For a variable to be a true independent variable you must be able to randomly assign participants to the levels of your IV or to randomly assign orders of conditions to participants.

3   Quasi-experimental variables are ones in which participants are in different conditions but have not been assigned to these conditions randomly. They are thus a particular class of variables that look like IVs but are not true IVs.

13.9   Some tips to help you to design better experiments and write better reports

This brings us almost to the end. I will spend the final few pages of the book giving you a few tips to help you to design better experiments and, I hope, also to write better reports. You can find some more tips for your later experiments – those that you design as you become more experienced – in Section G of the book's Web site at

 http://mcgraw-hill.co.uk/openup/harris/

13.9.1   The basic rule

A very important rule to remember is that there is no such thing as *the* right way to design an experiment to test a given hypothesis. Although there will be lots of wrong ways, there will usually be several right ways, perhaps many. So, do not feel overawed by the task. Relax! Your task is to design a reasonable, meaningful experiment, free of confounding variables, not to find the "correct" way to design it.

13.9.2   Getting reliable measures of the dependent variable

Would it be fair if your degree classification or grade for any other major qualification were based on a single, end-of-course exam? If I wanted to find out how good you were at something – say, bowling – would it be a good idea to judge you after a single roll? In both cases the answer is, of course, no. A range of factors, not just ability, influences performance on any task. For any single performance, such as one exam, these factors may serve to make you perform below or above par. This is why you tend to be assessed many times on a course.

Well, exactly the same arguments apply to the performance of your participants in an experiment. A common weakness of many student experiments is to measure the participant's performance once. This is unlikely to be *reliable*. If you can, you should take enough measures from a participant to be reasonably confident that you have a *reliable* estimate of their scores on the DV in each condition of the experiment in which they appear. A **reliable** measure would give us a similar value on the DV for a given participant if we had the luxury of assessing him or her under identical conditions on different occasions. A reliable measure is essential if we are going to be able meaningfully to assess the effects of the IV.

Thus, wherever possible, experiments should have more than one *trial* per condition. A **trial** in this context is a basic unit of experimental time. It begins when you present something to the participant and ends when they give you back a response on your DV.

However, as with all aspects of good experimental design, you need to use your common sense. You should have as many trials (i.e., take as many separate measures) of the DV as you need, but not so many as *to induce fatigue or boredom*. The optimum number of measures is one of the things that you can establish during the piloting phase of the study (see below). You should also watch out for situations in which it is not possible to have more than one trial per condition (e.g., when doing so will ask too much of your participants, creates significant carry-over effects, or might reveal too much to your participant about the purpose of the study).

13.9.3 Pilot testing

Once you have designed your experiment, chosen the question you wish to examine experimentally, the IV you wish to manipulate, the DVs you think will best assess this manipulation, decided whether you would be better off comparing the same or different participants, prepared your materials, set up your random sequences, and standardized your instructions, you might think that you are finally ready for the off. However, a little more patience at this stage may well pay dividends later. For, rather than diving straight in to running your study, a sensible procedure to adopt here is to **pilot test** your experiment. That is, to try it out on a few participants first to see whether it makes sense to them, to uncover any serious flaws or problems that might have been overlooked at the design stage and to generally "fine-tune" the procedure. Pilot testing also enables you to familiarize yourself with your role as experimenter so that you are practised and professional by the time you encounter your first participant proper.

Pilot testing can save you a lot of wasted time and effort. It provides you with a golden opportunity to improve the design *before* you have wasted too many participants. It is, therefore, a good habit to get into. Indeed, it will become increasingly important as you take greater responsibility for designing your own experiments.

A pilot test can also reveal whether you have a potential *floor* or *ceiling* effect in your data. For instance, thinking back to the driving and music experiment, we need to set our participants a course on the driving simulator that is neither so difficult that few can do it (**floor effect**), nor so easy that more or less everyone can (**ceiling effect**). Otherwise, we will not be able to assess the effects of manipulating our IV on performance itself. However, it is often difficult to decide on the appropriate level of task difficulty in the abstract. A brief pilot test on a small sample of participants who are *representative of the sample that will take part in the actual experiment* can help with this problem. (It is no good piloting on your relatives and their friends but running the experiment on a sample of students.)

Do do it – even one or two participants may tell you something useful about your study. (Of course, you should run more than one or two if you can.)

13.9.4 The post-experimental interview

Once you have finished collecting all the data you need from a participant, it is often a good idea to spend a few minutes with him or her before debriefing (Section 10.10.2) conducting a **post-experimental interview**. Set yourself up a little interview schedule with gently probing questions to try to find out more about what crossed participants' minds while they did your experiment. This may give you insights into factors controlling their behaviour and the extent to which they were aware of the hypotheses of the experiment. It may help you to interpret your findings and even give you ideas for future research.

If possible, someone who is blind to condition should conduct the interview. Such interviews are an essential feature of pilot tests and can also be useful in the main experiment. Unlike the debriefing, the post-experimental interview is primarily for *your* benefit, not the participants'.

13.9.5 Check and screen your data prior to statistical analysis

After putting all the effort and time into designing the experiment, running it, and collecting the data, an odd thing can happen. You can find yourself suddenly not caring about how accurately the data have been entered into the computer for analysis and just keen (desperate?) to get the analysis done and dusted. When you enter the data yourself this can be because you cannot imagine that you have made a mistake (as *if*). However, it happens even when someone else has entered the data for you. I suspect that it is because you are so close to completion and is part of the general need that we have for closure and for starting the next task on our list. It is important to guard against this tendency, of course.

Whenever you collect any data, whether from an experiment or any other study, you *must* ensure that you have entered them accurately prior to analysis. It is easy to make mistakes when doing something as dull as entering data into a computer. **Check the data** entry in at least two ways. First, get on your screen a frequency count, histogram or bar chart of the IV and the DV, just to check that all the values are ones that make sense (i.e., that they all fall in the right range of values). (Print this out only if you can be sure that it will not cost the earth in paper.) For example, if you find a value of 9 or 33 for a 7-point scale or of 222 for age, you *know* that this is outside the range of possible or legal values. It *must* be a mistake. However, this technique cannot help you spot values that are legal but wrong (for example, giving someone a score of 1 instead of 6 on a 7-point scale). So, second, **proofread** the data by checking that the numbers in the data window for a given participant match those on whatever source was used to input the data (e.g., the relevant coding sheet or questionnaire). If you have lots of participants, do this for about 25 percent of the sample in the first instance, making sure that you sample the data entered early, in the middle and late on. If you discover errors, then check more. If you do not have many participants, check the data for them all just to make sure.

Once you are satisfied that the data no longer contain mistakes, it is a good idea to use graphs and other techniques to check whether the data meet the assumptions of the tests that you hope to use. Look in your statistics textbook for ways of displaying data using histograms, bar charts, scatter plots, stem and leaf plots, and box plots. Most statistical software packages will provide ways of producing such displays and may even contain useful programs to help you with this (e.g., EXPLORE in SPSS for Windows). You will learn more on your statistics course about what to do and what to look out for. The latter include extreme values that unduly influence the means and standard deviations (known in the trade as **outliers**) and any *missing data*. If **screening** your data in this way ever leads you to change or transform the data, make sure that you report what you did and why in the opening paragraph of your RESULTS.

Only once you have done these things should you begin the analyses. You must get into the habit of inspecting your data *before* you compute *any* statistics. Otherwise you risk basing your RESULTS on nonsense.

Summary of Section 13.9

1 Where possible, it is a good idea to have more than one trial per condition – that is, to measure your participant's performance more than once in any given condition of the experiment.

2 A good habit to get into is to pilot test your experiment by trying it out on a few participants *before* you start to record any data. This enables you to spot any flaws in your design and gives you the opportunity to fine-tune the procedure. Pilot testing can save you a lot of wasted time and effort.

3 You must, however, run the pilot test on a sample of participants from the same population as the one you will actually use in the experiment.

4 In some experiments a post-experimental interview with participants can give you useful insights into the variables controlling their behaviour in the experiment. This may help you to interpret your findings and can give you ideas for follow-up studies.

5 Make sure that you check that the data have been entered accurately before analysis. As you become more experienced, learn also how to screen your data thoroughly before analysing it.

13.10 Above all, randomize properly

Finally, here's a note to all you budding experimenters out there: *Randomize properly*! The random assignment of participants to conditions or of orders of conditions to participants is the key to the whole experimental enterprise. At all times and in all experiments use *truly* random procedures for assignment or else the exercise is in danger of being pointless. So, how you go about randomization is a central issue (see Appendix 2). You must take this problem seriously and not do it casually. Think carefully in advance about how you will do the randomization. Use random number generators or tables. Do *not* make the numbers up yourself or use a procedure that can be influenced consciously or even unconsciously. Learn to differentiate randomization *with* replacement from randomization *without* replacement and use the procedure that you require. Subsequently, describe in sufficient detail in your reports the way in which you randomized so that your readers can judge for themselves whether the randomization was effective.

That's it! Good luck. I hope you enjoy finding things out with and about experiments in psychology.

Consolidating your learning

This closing section is designed to help you check your understanding and determine what you might need to study further. You can use the list of methodological and statistical concepts to check which ones you are happy with and which you may need to double-check. You can use this list to find the relevant terms in the chapter and also in other textbooks of design or statistics. The diagnostic questions provide a further test of your understanding. Finally, there is a description of what is covered in the two statistics textbooks paired with this book plus a list of relevant further material that you can find on the book's Web site.

**Methodological and statistical concepts covered
in this chapter**

Ceiling effect
Checking and screening data
Explanatory variable (response, classification, subject, predictor variable)
Factorial design
Floor effect
Interaction effect
Line graphs
Main effect
Measured variable (criterion variable)
Mixed design (split plot design)
Outlier
Pilot test
Post-experimental interview
Quasi-experimental design
Reliability
Repeated measures design
Trial
Two by two (2 × 2) design

Diagnostic questions – check your understanding

1 If we extend the number of levels on an unrelated samples IV are we more likely to face problems with recruiting adequate numbers of participants or with order effects?
2 How many IVs are there in a 2 × 2 mixed design and what type of IVs are they?
3 What is a significant *main* effect?
4 What does it mean to say that two variables *interact*?
5 When is an unrelated samples IV a "true" IV?

You can find the answers at the rear of the book (p. 278).

Statistics textbooks

Σ The books paired with *Designing and Reporting Experiments* have the following coverage:

Learning to use statistical tests in psychology – Greene and D'Oliveira
Greene and D'Oliveira describe how to analyse data from a study with more than 2 levels on an unrelated samples IV using a non-parametric test in Chapter 12 (Kruskal-Wallis test) and a parametric test in Chapter 14 (one-way ANOVA for unrelated samples). They describe how to analyse data from a study with more than 2 levels on a related samples IV using a non-parametric test in Chapter 11 (Friedman test) and a parametric test in Chapter 15 (one-way ANOVA for related samples). They describe how to use ANOVA to analyse data from studies with two IVs, including mixed designs, in Chapters 17–19. These chapters include discussion of how to interpret and graph interaction effects.

SPSS survival manual – Pallant
Pallant describes how to use SPSS to analyse data from a study with more than 2 levels on an unrelated samples IV using a non-parametric test in Chapter 16 (Kruskal-Wallis test) and a parametric test in Chapter 18 (one-way between-groups ANOVA). She describes how to analyse data from a study with more than 2 levels on a related samples IV using a non-parametric test in Chapter 16 (Friedman test) and a parametric test in Chapter 15 (one-way repeated measures ANOVA). She describes how to use ANOVA to analyse data from studies with two IVs, including mixed designs, in Chapters 19 and 20. She has good coverage of interaction and main effects. Pallant describes how to screen and clean data in Chapter 5 and how to check it for violations of statistical assumptions in Chapter 6. She also explains how to use graphs to describe and explore data (Chapter 7) and has coverage of issues to do with reliability and validity in Chapters 1, 8 and 9.

The *Designing and Reporting Experiments* Web site

The book's Web site at **http://mcgraw-hill.co.uk/openup/harris/** has a number of sections that expand on the issues discussed in this chapter. Section C contains further consideration of main effects and interactions, including advice on how to graph three-way interactions and a list of possible main effects and interactions to be found in designs with four IVs. Section F contains advice on things to watch out for with IVs that are not true IVs. Section G contains seven tips for advanced students to further improve their experiments. Section I contains pointers to how to use the Web site for specific advice for those designing and reporting final year projects.

Commentary

This commentary clarifies or expands on issues that I do not have space to cover in detail in the core text. Some of these issues are relevant mainly to students who are studying at a relatively advanced level.

Chapter 1

1 I am tempted to add here that it would be good to see this even in the earliest of reports. When you have only just begun to write reports in psychology, however, at first you need to concentrate on the basics. At this stage, make sure that you have grasped the essentials of those papers centrally relevant to what you have done and do not concern yourself about when they were published. It is no good throwing in an up-to-date reference or two just to impress your marker when you have failed to write about something older but more relevant.

Chapter 2

1 Some of you will be expected to write full introductions in your very first report, however. If you are in any doubt about what is required of you, make sure you check with your tutor.
2 Where your study is not an experiment, you will still invariably have hypotheses and predictions to report (although these are not *experimental* hypotheses). Just as with an experiment, you should state clearly and accurately what the core predictions of your study are.

Chapter 3

1 In some departments or for some studies you may not be required to provide a DESIGN subsection but instead be expected to put this information at the end of your INTRODUCTION section. Check with your tutor whether he or she expects a separate DESIGN section.

2 In some studies, especially those using lengthy questionnaires, there may seem to be a large number of IVs or DVs, or it may be hard to work out which of the variables are IVs and which DVs. Sometimes this is because you are not running an experiment at all but instead have non-experimental data – in which case there *are* no independent or dependent variables. So make sure that you have an *experimental* design before describing your variables as IVs and DVs. For more on reporting non-experimental data or studies involving questionnaires, see Section 3.7 and also Section E of the Web site that accompanies this book at: **http://mcgraw-hill.co.uk/ openup/harris/**

3 Chapter 2 of the *Publication Manual of the American Psychological Association* (APA, 2001) contains detailed guidelines on how to avoid bias in your use of language.

4 A **pretest** is useful. It is designed to enable us to assess whether overall performance in the conditions of our experiment is about the same *before* we introduce the IV. It provides, therefore, a useful check on our randomization. For example, in this experiment our pretest will tell us whether the memory performance of those in the mnemonic and no mnemonic conditions was equivalent before we introduced the mnemonic. In situations in which we suspect that performance among participants might be highly variable at the outset we can sometimes give participants *practice* on the experimental task to get them to a common baseline level of performance before starting the experimental trials. These are called **practice trials**. A **manipulation check** is a measure that tells us something about whether the manipulation had the qualities we presume. For example, by including a manipulation check here we will be able to check whether the participants agree that the easily imaged words were indeed easier to image than were the hard-to-image words. You can find more about *pretests, practice trials* and *manipulation checks* in Section G of the book's Web site at **http://mcgraw-hill.co.uk/openup/harris/**

5 Of course, I go over the gist orally in a standardized way!

Chapter 4

1 You need to do these things when you are testing for statistical significance. If you are *not* testing for statistical significance, then you need to

report instead the probability of the obtained value of your statistic arising by sampling error (this is the probability associated with the statistic), and report and comment on the effect size(s) and relevant confidence interval(s). Once you know how, it is of course a good idea to report the effect size(s) and confidence interval(s) even if you *are* also testing for statistical significance. (If you are confused about any of the above, see Chapter 12.)

2 Among other things, reporting the *exact* probability allows other people to see for themselves how close your results were to being (or to not being) statistically significant. This enables them to make a more informed assessment of your results.

3 This can especially be a problem where you have used a lengthy question-naire and have many responses to report. For advice on what to do when this is the case see Section E of the book's Web site at **http://mcgraw-hill.co.uk/openup/harris/**.

4 Follow this advice until you understand about statistical power. Then you will learn that the outcome of the analysis depends in part on the power of the test. However, until you are quite confident that you understand about power and its implications, it is safer to follow this advice.

5 The paradox is resolved if you think of your reader as someone who in fact knows about psychology in general, but not about the specific area that you investigated in your study. Thus they understand the procedures involved in significance testing, as these are by and large the same regardless of the area of psychology under investigation. However, you still need to explain to them about the psychology relevant to your study.

6 Parametric and nonparametric tests offer you different ways of analysing the same set of data. If you are able to make certain assumptions about your data – e.g., that they come from a normally distributed population – then you can use parametric tests, which are more powerful. If you are not familiar with this distinction, you can find out more about it in Section A of the book's Web site at **http://mcgraw-hill.co.uk/openup/harris/** and in the statistics textbooks paired with this book.

7 However, note also that the more tests of significance that you run on a set of data, the more you run the risk of making a type I error (see Section 11.3). (If in doubt about what to do, see your tutor.)

8 Of course, you should not attempt to use and report any of these statistics without first reading your statistics textbook.

9 Remember that the terms *unrelated samples* and *related samples* are only two of a range of terms you can use to describe these types of IV. You might have been taught to use different terms (see Section 10.2). The terms *pretest* and *manipulation check* are explained in the commentary to Chapter 3. These are also discussed in Section G of the book's Web site at **http://mcgraw-hill.co.uk/openup/harris/**

10 I have assumed here that you have not yet been taught how to conduct these further tests (known as tests of *simple effects*). Obviously, if you do

know how to conduct them, they should be reported here. See Section B of the book's Web site at **http://mcgraw-hill.co.uk/openup/harris/** for more on such tests and how to report them, including an example RESULTS section for this experiment that does contain such tests.

11 Those of you needing to write up a study in Health or Social Psychology using a social cognition model of behaviour can also find in Section B of the book's Web site an example of how to write up a study that uses the Theory of Planned Behavior as a model.

12 Whether you report β, B or both depends on the purpose of your study. I have reported β in the two example sections here, as this is likely to be the one you will most often need to put in your reports. If you are in doubt about what to do, then report both β and B.

Chapter 5

1 Of course, if the designers of the experiment had obtained reports of the number of nightmares experienced by each participant in the weeks leading up to the experiment, they could have been even more confident here. One possibility would have been to allocate participants to conditions based on the number of nightmares they reported experiencing (Section 10.7). Alternatively, after randomization had taken place, they could have tested statistically to see if there was a difference between conditions in the number of nightmares reported by the participants prior to the experiment.

Chapter 6

1 If your department or tutors expect you to adhere strictly to APA guidelines, then your word limit is 120 words!

Chapter 8

1 After a while you will realize that there is a tension between these two guidelines: often you write a passive sentence to avoid using the first person. Which is the bigger sin? Probably the passive, so recast passive sentences into the active voice and then try to recast active sentences to reduce the number of references to the first person. When you have worked out how to do this, let me know how it's done.

2 What I have to say here is about graphs that you put in the report, primarily in the RESULTS, and especially when you are reporting *experiments*. The graphs that you put in the report should not be confused with those

that you use to help you to make sense of your data (Section 13.9.5). Graphs that you use to help you to make sense of the data – such as scattergrams or stem and leaf plots – do not necessarily need to appear in the report.

3 This use of the term "error" may strike you as odd. Let me try to explain. In an ideal world we would expect *all* of the participants in a particular condition of our experiment to get *exactly* the same scores on the DV. The fact that, in reality, they do not we assume reflects "noise" or *error* in our data. The fact that there is any variation in scores within a condition thus indicates the presence of error. Error bars tell us visually something about this spread and thus something about how much error there is. See your statistics textbook for more about this.

Chapter 9

1 Coverage of *qualitative* methods and analysis is beyond the scope of this book.

2 Make sure you are clear about this, as students sometimes make the mistake of equating a confounding variable with any *uncontrolled* variable. A confounding variable is a special uncontrolled variable whose levels vary systematically (*covary*) with those of the IV, such as when more of those in the cheese condition *also* take more sleeping pills.

3 I say here "little or no" difference because you would not expect the two groups to report *exactly* the same number of nightmares even if cheese had no effect on nightmares. We will come back to this in Chapter 11, so you do not need to be concerned about it for now.

4 There are other variants, but this "no effect" null hypothesis is the one we most often test in psychology.

Chapter 10

1 Indeed, there are those who argue that it is unethical to run experiments without having first participated in some.

2 A set of guidelines for ethical practice in psychological research online can be obtained from the Web site of the British Psychological Society.

Chapter 11

1 Be careful here not to make an easy and common mistake. These statistics do *not* tell us the probability that the null hypothesis *is* true. I wish!

Unfortunately, this we can *never* know. Instead, they tell us the probability of getting results like ours (at least as extreme as ours) *assuming* that the null hypothesis is true. Our assumption may be right. Our assumption may be wrong. As you will soon see, in the end we have to make an informed guess about whether our assumption is right or wrong. I will explain more about this later in this chapter. So, for now, just remember that inferential statistics do *not* tell us the probability that the null hypothesis is true. Boy, would life be simpler if they did!

2 The differences between these types of data are described in Section A of the book's Web site at **http://mcgraw-hill.co.uk/openup/harris/** and in the statistics textbooks paired with this book.

3 This will help you decide whether to use a parametric test or its non-parametric equivalent. The assumptions of parametric tests are described in Section A of the book's Web site at **http://mcgraw-hill.co.uk/openup/harris/** and in the statistics textbooks paired with this book.

4 Once you are comfortable with the issues discussed in the next chapter, you can add to this list:

    8 Estimate the *effect size* of the IV.

    9 With results that are not statistically significant, think about the likely *power* of the experiment.

Chapter 12

1 The opposite is also the case. If our studies look like they will be too powerful for our needs, we can take steps to reduce their power. For example, studies involving hundreds or thousands of participants can be so powerful that even relatively tiny and psychologically trivial effects can become highly statistically significant. This can be a waste of resources. It can also lead to confusion over which statistically significant effects are psychologically noteworthy. However, given that effect sizes in psychology are often smaller than we imagine, having underpowered studies is usually more of a problem. As a student, therefore, it is much more likely that you will be in danger of running a study that lacks sufficient power – especially with unrelated samples. A possible exception is if you run a study on the Internet, where your sample size may become quite large. See Section 10.10.3 for a discussion of the ethics of Internet studies.

2 Have you spotted an apparent paradox here? If we know the effect size, then why are we running the experiment? Surely, the whole point of the experiment from this viewpoint is to detect whether there is an effect of the IV on the DV? If we know this already, then why bother to find it out again by running another experiment?

This is a *very* good question. The answer is that you *inevitably* make assumptions about the effect size of the IV whenever you design an experiment in psychology. For example, if you decide to run an experiment with a two-level unrelated samples IV using only 10 participants overall, you are automatically assuming that the effect size is very large. This is because your experiment has little or no chance of rejecting the null hypothesis if the effect size is small or medium. If you decide to run the same experiment with 100 participants overall, however, you are assuming that the effect size may be much smaller than in the 10-participant version. Otherwise, why are you using so many participants? It therefore makes sense to formalize this process and to make calculated estimates of the number of participants that are needed, rather than to do this implicitly.

Making calculated guesses about the likely or possible effect size in our experiment does not beg the question of the *true* effect size: we may be wrong. The effect size may turn out to be bigger than we estimated, smaller, or zero. However, if we estimate sensibly in advance the likely effect size we can at least ensure that our experiment has the power (e.g., has enough participants) to enable us to stand a reasonable chance of rejecting the null hypothesis *if* the effect size is at least as big as estimated.

3 If you are unfamiliar with this distinction, see Section A of the book's Web site at **http://mcgraw-hill.co.uk/openup/harris/** and the statistics textbooks paired with this book.

4 It is easy to work out the percentage variance. Simply multiply r^2 by 100. So, for example, I got the value of 4 percent from calculating $.04 \times 100 = 4$. Thus, with $r = .5$, $r^2 = .25$ and the percentage variance that is shared is 25 percent ($.25 \times 100 = 25$). *Do* think about r^2 when you use Pearson's r. Even some researchers fail to do this, so do not be fooled by what you may find in published papers. I have sat through talks at conferences and even read papers in which the authors reported correlation coefficients that were statistically significant but trivial. Had they looked at r^2 as well, they would not have made this mistake.

5 The reason that the percentages do not add up to 100 is that partial eta squared involves an adjustment to improve the accuracy of the effect size estimate. A consequence of making this adjustment is that the percentages no longer add up to 100.

Chapter 13

1 Every year I get one or two students who take no notice of my warnings that they need to run more participants and end up with an interesting experiment marred by lack of power. The result is that they find themselves lost for things to say in the all-important discussion. So, be realistic at the design stage – it is better to design a simpler study that will have enough participants than a more complex one that will not have enough participants.

2 However, as I say in Part 1, avoid just trotting out the vacuous statement in your DISCUSSION that "our findings would have been significant if we had had more participants." Remember that *any* difference between your conditions will become statistically significant if you use enough participants, no matter how small it is numerically and how trivial it is psychologically. Instead, look at your design and try to assess, if you can, whether your experiment was likely to have been powerful enough to detect any noteworthy effect of the IV on the DV. Section 12.3 has advice on how to do this.

3 Watch out when you use some statistics packages to analyse your data as these may refer to designs that contain *any* related samples IVs as "repeated measures" even if the design also contains unrelated measures IVs. This sometimes misleads students (including graduate students) into describing their design as repeated measures when it has both related and unrelated IVs and is, in fact, a mixed design.

4 You can find an expanded version of this table in Section C of the book's Web site at **http://mcgraw-hill.co.uk/openup/harris/**. However, in using that table be aware that I caution you against designing experiments with more than 3 IVs.

5 This is a *very* common mistake. Very often students write in their RESULTS that they used ANOVA to analyse the data and assume that this is all they need to say. But ANOVA is a family of tests and this is as vague as saying that you observed an animal's behaviour. What type of animal did you observe? You need to be precise, say that you used "one-way analysis of variance for unrelated samples" or "2 × 2 analysis of variance for mixed designs" and so on.

6 This applies to *any* DV you can think of. You will learn about different ways of assessing reliability in your methods course and your statistics textbook. These include such measures as the **test-retest reliability** of a scale or measure – looking to see that the scores on it remain pretty much constant at two different time points when we believe that whatever it is supposed to measure should also remain pretty much constant. If you collect two or more scores of someone's performance, attitude and so on at any given time, you can calculate how well the scores measure the same thing by calculating their **internal consistency**. If they have high enough internal consistency you can then combine them and make a **scale** to measure the performance or attitude. Scales with high internal consistency are generally more reliable than single measures of the same variable. A commonly used statistic for assessing this is known as **Cronbach's coefficient alpha**. Cronbach's alpha ranges from 0 to 1. Scales with Cronbach's alpha of .70 or above are generally considered to be reliable enough. Measures should also of course be *valid* – that is they should measure what they are supposed to measure. You will also learn about different ways of assessing validity in your methods course and your statistics textbook.

Recommended reading

You will find further coverage of most of the statistical issues raised in this book in most statistics textbooks. The texts below are the ones that I know of that I happily recommend. Two of these – Greene and D'Oliveira's *Learning to use statistical tests in psychology* and Pallant's *SPSS survival manual* – are paired with this book.

To those of you who would benefit from a very straightforward and basic introduction to statistical tests with simple "cookbook" guidance for their hand calculation, I recommend either *Learning to Use Statistical Tests in Psychology* by Judith Greene and Manuela D'Oliveira or *Statistics Explained* by Perry Hinton.

Clear and user-friendly coverage is also provided in each of the following: *Research Methods and Statistics in Psychology* by Hugh Coolican, *Statistics for Psychology* by Art and Elaine Aron, and *Statistics without Maths for Psychology* by Christine Dancey and John Reidy. These texts include good coverage of issues to do with power and effect size. *Doing Psychological Research* by Nicky Hayes provides a broad but clear coverage of a wide range of methods in psychology, including qualitative methods.

A useful guide to using the statistical software package *SPSS* for Windows to analyse your data is provided by Julie Pallant in her *SPSS Survival Manual*. The survival manual covers a wide range of analyses and includes material on calculating effect sizes. A good simple and straightforward guide to using *SPSS* for Windows is also provided in *A Simple Guide to SPSS for Windows* by Lee Kirkpatrick and Brooke Feeney.

The following manage to be both authoritative and yet accessible: *Quantitative Psychological Research: A Student's Handbook* by David Clark-Carter and *Fundamental Statistics for the Behavioral Sciences* by David Howell. David Howell also produces *Statistical Methods for Psychology*, which is where I often turn when I am stuck. David Howell also maintains a very useful

Web site at http://www.uvm.edu/~dhowell/StatPages/StatHomePage.html. For those using multivariate statistics a good introductory source is *Reading and Understanding Multivariate Statistics*, edited by Laurence Grimm and Paul Yarnold.

For more on how to write in psychology, *The Psychologist's Companion* by Robert Sternberg is both informative and entertaining. If you want clear and authoritative information on how to lay out your tables in APA format, see *Presenting your Findings* by Adelheid Nicol and Penny Pexman. Of course, the ultimate reference for matters to do with paper writing and layout is *The Publication Manual of the American Psychological Association*.

Appendix 1
Confusing predictions from the null hypothesis with those from the experimental hypothesis

Suppose that you are interested in biological theories of personality. On reading around the area you come across two theories concerning the biological basis of extraversion. Theory 1 predicts that, after exposure to ultrasound, the blood pressure of extraverts will be higher than the blood pressure of introverts. Theory 2, however, predicts that ultrasound should increase the blood pressure of both introverts and extraverts to the same extent. This latter theory thus leads to the prediction that there will be no difference between the blood pressure of extraverts and introverts after exposure to ultrasound.

Now, for personal reasons, you favour the theory that predicts that there will be no difference in the blood pressure of the extraverts and introverts. So, you design an experiment to test this. You expose extraverts and introverts to ultrasound and subsequently measure their blood pressure. (Let us imagine for argument's sake that you obtain ethical clearance and that your experiment is well designed and of sufficient power to detect a small effect.) On analysing the data, you find that there is no evidence of a statistically significant difference in blood pressure between extraverts and introverts following exposure to ultrasound. That is, you fail to reject the null hypothesis in your experiment.

Now you are happy with the outcome. It is evidence against the theory that you oppose. Do not be *too* happy, however – it is not evidence *for* the theory that you favour. Although the evidence is *consistent* with what you would expect under your favoured theory, it does not count as a test of it. This is because findings of no difference are exactly what we would find if ultrasound had absolutely no effect on the blood pressure of extraverts and introverts (which, as far as I'm aware, is the case). That is, in your experiment, the predictions from theory 2 coincide with those under the null hypothesis and are thus not tested by your experiment.

Let us take another example. Suppose that someone argues that babies are brought by storks who drop them down chimneys to their mothers. Suppose, however, that you do not like this explanation. Instead you favour one that proposes that the doctor or midwife brings the babies with them in their bags. Now, you and I can devise a simple test of this. If babies *are* dropped down chimneys by storks, then we would expect to find women having babies only in houses with chimneys – not, for example, in high-rise flats, or houses with chimneys that have been blocked up. However, if the midwife or doctor brings them, then there should be no such difference.

So, imagine that we conduct this study and find that there is no difference in the relative frequency with which babies are born in houses with chimneys and houses without chimneys. This is evidence *against* the stork theory. However, is it evidence *for* the midwife/doctor theory? Really??

The point is that such studies – such experiments – are actually only tests of the ideas that lead us to predict differences. They are not tests of ideas that lead us to predict *no* differences. If you want to test these, then you must create a situation (i.e., design an experiment) in which the ideas you want to test predict a difference at least somewhere between the conditions.

? SAQ 49   There is only one way in which an experiment designed to test an idea that predicts differences between conditions can tell us something about an idea that predicts no differences. Can you imagine when this is?

If you are confused, do not worry unduly. Just remember that *failing to reject* the null hypothesis at the end of your experiment tells you something about the ideas that led to the prediction of a difference and nothing about any ideas that led to the prediction of no difference. If the predictions derived from a theory coincide with those derived from the null hypothesis, then you are not actually testing the theory.

Appendix 2
Randomizing

This is an *essential* skill of the would-be experimenter. Do *not* treat this casually. The capacity of the experiment to allow us to make causal inferences depends critically on assigning participants to conditions or conditions to participants randomly. Make sure that you use a *truly* random procedure, therefore, not one that is even remotely open to conscious or unconscious influence. If you fail to randomize properly you will undo all of the time and effort that you have otherwise spent on the experiment.

There are a number of occasions on which you will need to randomize. One is when you need to allocate different participants to conditions. Another is when you need to randomize the order in which you present the conditions to participants. You may also need to use randomization when preparing your materials. Finally, if you go on to do research, you may eventually find yourself selecting participants randomly from a population.

You will find advice on how to do some of these things below. Note, however, that the basic principle of randomization is the same in all of these cases (although the method by which you realize this principle may differ). Thus, whatever you are randomizing – be it orders or participants or words in a stimulus list – any given item should have an equal chance of selection *at all times* (i.e., the prior selection of one particular item should not affect in any way the chances of any of the other items being subsequently selected). So, for example, if you are selecting orders for your participants, the chances of any given order being selected must not be affected by any selections that you have made previously. Similarly, when assigning participants to conditions, the chances of a given participant appearing in one particular condition should not be affected by previous allocations to that or any other condition.

What this means in practice is that we do not simply sit down and juggle our orders around or assign our participants to conditions in what seems to us to be a suitably random order. Neither do we generate numbers from our heads. Such methods do *not* give us truly random results. Instead, we employ methods that give us truly random sequences and whose results *we obey*, however non-random they appear.

Now, all that is required of these tools is that they make the choice for us in an unbiased way: i.e., that they do not favour some outcomes more than others. Consequently, if used properly, things like (fair) coins, playing cards, dice and so on, can be adequate for the purpose. However, it is sometimes possible to influence consciously or even unconsciously the outcome of a coin toss or dice roll or card selection. Therefore you are best advised to avoid using these things if you can. (You can use, say, a fair coin for some small aspects of the procedure, such as choosing where to start in a table of random numbers.) For most of your randomizing, however, use either *random number tables* or (if you know for sure that it is well designed) a *random number generator* on a computer. The examples below use random number tables.

Tables of **random numbers** can be found at the rear of some statistics textbooks. These tables have been produced by a program that enabled the digits 0–9 to have an equal opportunity of appearing at any given position in the table. So, at any given position, you have no idea which of these digits is likely to appear. Even if the previous twelve digits have all been "7" (which is extremely unlikely, but still possible) the chances of "7" appearing as the thirteenth digit are *exactly the same* as if there had been no "7" among the previous twelve. You can see, therefore, that such tables are ideally suited for the purposes of randomizing.

You can use these digits singly, in pairs, groups of three and so on. The important thing is to make sure that you do not keep entering the tables at the same place. If you do, then you will simply be using the same sequence of numbers and your lists will not differ.

Finally, you should learn to recognize the difference between randomization *without* replacement and randomization *with* replacement. You are already familiar with both. In lotteries or draws for cup competitions, when a number has been selected, it is not put back into the pot to be selected again. This is **randomization without replacement**. With this technique numbers, once selected, are no longer available for reselection. (Consequently, the chances of each of the remaining numbers in the pot being selected will have increased. Nevertheless, the process still meets our requirements for a truly random procedure, for the chances of each of the remaining numbers being selected should still be equal.) In **randomization with replacement**, in contrast, the numbers *are* available for reselection. The previous number selected therefore has the same chance of coming up again. Roulette wheels and fair die use randomization with replacement. These devices have no memories. The number that came up previously has *exactly* the same chance of coming up again on the next spin or roll and *exactly* the same chance as have all the other numbers.

Using the tables

Enter the tables at a random position. Toss a coin to decide whether you will proceed diagonally (heads) or along lines (tails). If tails, toss a coin to decide whether you will move horizontally (heads) or vertically (tails). Then toss a coin to decide whether you will move up or down (if moving vertically) or left or right (if moving horizontally). Proceed similarly if the original toss had returned a head. This procedure is standard for the use of tables.

Allocating participants to conditions

Suppose that we wish to allocate 10 participants to Condition A and 10 to Condition B. One way of doing this is as follows:

Number your participants 1–20, with numbers 1–10 in Condition A and 11–20 in Condition B. Enter the tables and proceed as directed above. Step through the tables reading *pairs* of digits. The order in which you come across these numbers will dictate the order in which you run your participants. For instance, with the sequence

23 53 04 01 63 08 45 93 15 22

the first three participants will be allocated to Condition A (04, 01, and 08), the fourth to Condition B (15), and so on. Once a number has been encountered, however, you should disregard it on future occurrences (randomization *without* replacement). This technique can obviously be extended to more than two conditions.

Allocating orders to participants

Even with a counterbalanced design you must allocate the orders to participants randomly. For example, with our study in SAQ 44(a), we have six different orders. Suppose that we wish to allocate these orders to 12 participants. One way of doing this is as follows. Enter the tables and proceed as directed above. Number the participants 1–12. Step through the tables looking for pairs of digits, allocating the participants to the orders in sequence. For example, with the digits

23 53 04 01 63 08 45 93 15 22

Participant 04 would do order 1, Participant 01 would do order 2, Participant 08 would do order 3, and so on until all 12 participants had received an order. Again, you should disregard repeats of particular numbers (randomization *without* replacement).

Constructing materials

Suppose that you need to randomize the order in which a set of 30 questions appears in a questionnaire. Number the questions, and then step through the random number tables as directed above to obtain the order in which the questions should appear. For instance, with the sequence

23 53 04 01 63 08 45 93 15 22

question 23 would come first, Question 04 would come second, Question 01 would come third, and so on.

To control for order effects you would probably need to produce more than one version of the questionnaire, so you would need to repeat the above process.

Appendix 3
How to use tables of critical values of inferential statistics

In the years prior to the development of statistical software packages, people would use **tables of critical values** of statistics to find the probability associated with their obtained or calculated value of the statistic. These tables contain different values of the statistic – the tabled or critical values – and the probability for each of these values under the null hypothesis. You can still find yourself on occasion needing to use these tables – such as when you have calculated a statistic by hand. This appendix summarizes the procedure involved for those of you who are unfamiliar with the use of these tables.

The tables can be found at the rear of most textbooks of statistics. Sets of tables are also published in their own right. In order to use them, you need to know which statistic you are using and additional information such as the number of observations or participants or the degrees of freedom. Section 4.6 describes the additional information required for some of the statistics that you are likely to use as a student and more information can be found on the Web site that accompanies this book. This information is also contained in your statistics textbook. For significance testing, you will also need to know whether your obtained value needs to be greater than or less than the tabled value. This information is also available on the Web site and your statistics textbook.

Using tables to test for statistical significance

The tables are designed primarily for significance testing and therefore will always contain at least the critical values for the conventional significance levels – 5 percent and 1 percent. To use them to test for statistical significance:

1 Look for the tables containing the distribution of the statistic you are using. These will be described as tables of the distribution of F or t or χ^2 or whatever. Note whether you are using a one-tailed or two-tailed test and the significance level you chose in advance. Most of you, most of the time, will be testing two-tailed hypotheses at the 5 percent level.

 2 Find the additional information necessary to locate the critical value for the test. (For example, look in section 4.6 or Section B of the book's Web site.) Most of the time this will be either the *degrees of freedom* or the *numbers of observations*. Whether the obtained value has to be greater than or less than the critical value for significance will also depend on the test.

3 Locate the **critical value**. These values are called critical values because they are the values that your statistic has to equal or exceed in the relevant direction in order to be statistically significant.

4 The **obtained value** is the value of the statistic you have calculated. If your obtained value differs from the critical value in the direction required for statistical significance, or if it is *equal* to the critical value, then your data are statistically significant. Under these circumstances, *reject* the null hypothesis.

5 If your obtained value differs from the critical value in the direction opposite to that required for significance, then your data are not statistically significant. Under these circumstances, *do not reject* the null hypothesis.

You must be clear about what you are doing at each stage. *First*, you compare your obtained vale with the critical value. For some statistics (e.g., the Mann Whitney U test, the Wilcoxon signed-rank test) the obtained value has to be *less* than (or equal to) the critical value for statistical significance. For other statistics (e.g., χ^2, t, F) the obtained value has to be *greater* than (or equal to) the critical value for statistical significance. However, the *probability* associated with the obtained value will *always* be *less* than (or equal to) the *probability* associated with critical value if the obtained value is statistically significant.

? SAQ 50

Below are a number of results of statistical analyses. Look these up in the appropriate tables. For each of these state whether the result is significant at the 5 percent level, two-tailed.

1 A researcher analysed a set of data using the Wilcoxon signed-rank test and found that $T(22) = 45$. Is this result statistically significant?

2 A researcher analysed a set of data using the Mann-Whitney U test and found that $U(10, 12) = 8$. Is this result statistically significant?

3 A researcher analysed a set of data using chi-square and found that χ^2 $(1, N = 82) = 3.80$. Is this result statistically significant?

4 A researcher analysed a set of data using the independent t test and found that $t(16) = 2.20$. Is this result statistically significant?

5 A researcher analysed a set of data using two-way analysis of variance for unrelated samples and found that for one of the IVs, $F(2, 25) = 5.20$. Is this result statistically significant?

Using tables to establish the probability associated with the obtained value

Statistical software packages have programmed into them the equations for calculating distributions of statistics. They are therefore able to print out the *exact* probability associated with any particular value of the statistic. Unfortunately, when using tables it is unlikely that you will be able to establish the exact probability for your obtained value. Instead, you will most probably find that your obtained value falls between two of the tabled values. The probability associated with your value will therefore also fall between the probabilities for these two values.

For example, in Chapter 11, the obtained value of $\chi^2 = 4.89$ does not appear in the table of values of chi-square (Table 11.2). However, using Table 11.2 (which is in fact a table of critical values of chi-square with one degree of freedom) we were still able to establish an upper and a lower level for the probability associated with $\chi^2 = 4.89$. The value immediately greater than $\chi^2 = 4.89$ in the table is $\chi^2 = 5.02$. This has a probability of $p = .025$. The value immediately less than $\chi^2 = 4.89$ in the table is $\chi^2 = 3.84$. This has a probability of $p = .05$. So, the probability associated with our obtained value lies between $p = .05$ and $p = .025$. (As you can see, this agrees with the $p = .03$ that we obtained from the statistics package, but is less exact.)

You do this the same way with any tables of critical values. However, if your obtained value equals the tabled value (which happens occasionally) then, of course, the probability is *exact*. For it is the probability associated with the tabled value.

Reporting probabilities that are not exact

Although the tables cannot tell us the exact probability associated with our statistic, for statistically significant results we can find out the next *highest* probability and report that our obtained value is lower than that probability. In the case of the above $\chi^2 = 4.89$ with one degree of freedom, we know that the probability associated with this value of chi-square lies between $p = .05$ and $p = .025$. We can, therefore, say that it is *below $p = .05$* and indicate this using the following shorthand: "$p < .05$." The < sign means "less than", so the statement "$p < .05$" is shorthand for "probability less than .05." It is "less than" because the smaller end of the symbol points towards the p. You can, of course, do this for probabilities smaller than this, for example, $p < .01$, or $p < .001$. Probabilities as low as $p < .001$ are striking enough, so there is rarely any need to go below this (e.g., there is no need to report "$p < .0001$").

Alternatively, you might report *both* the upper and lower probabilities. For instance, in the above example you could write $.025 < p < .05$. This tells us *which* probabilities the probability associated with our obtained statistic lies between. Some authors recommend doing this (e.g., Clark-Carter, 2004). See what your tutor thinks.

If the findings are not statistically significant, just change the direction of the sign for your chosen significance level. For example, if you used the 5 percent significance level and your obtained value has a probability higher than this, you can write "$p > .05$." This reads "probability greater than .05," because now the broader end of the symbol points to the p.

Output where $p = .000$

It can be the case that you have probabilities so extremely small that the output from your statistics package does not print out enough decimal places. However, when it prints $p = .000$, this does not mean that there is no probability associated with the outcome! (For example, it may be $p = .00032$.) Under these circumstances you can use the first method described above. For example, you know that $p = .000$ is below $p = .001$, so you can write "$p < .001$." Do *not* put $p = .000$ anywhere in your report, whatever your output says!

Answers to SAQs

SAQ 1

(a) RESULTS; (b) DISCUSSION.

SAQ 2

False. Although this is true of those who mark your reports, it is certainly not true of the person you should have in mind in writing the report: your reader. Write it for someone who is intelligent but unknowledgeable about your study and the area of psychology in which it took place. This is a general rule that applies to all your writing in psychology, including essay writing.

SAQ 3

You could write the INTRODUCTION and the METHOD *before* conducting the study. This is because you report in these sections material that you should have decided upon *prior* to starting the study.

SAQ 4

The DISCUSSION, because it is there that you assess the implications of your findings. It is precisely for their implications that we conduct studies in the first place.

SAQ 5

You should attempt to *substantiate* it. The preferred method of doing this is by *referencing* previous work in the area. You can find out more about how to cite references in Chapter 7.

SAQ 6

The report's conventions are designed to convey information about a study clearly, precisely, and concisely so that interested readers can find the information they need quickly and efficiently.

SAQ 7

In the INTRODUCTION you introduce your *study* to your *reader*. But remember that you must assume that your reader is psychologically naive (Chapter 1). Which means that, as well as telling the reader all about the study you conducted, you must also put it into its context – that is, you must show how your study relates to previous work on the topic.

SAQ 8

Because you must assume that your reader knows nothing about the area of psychology relevant to your study. In order to understand and evaluate your study, therefore, he or she has first to be told about previous relevant work in the area.

SAQ 9

Because the researcher will return in the DISCUSSION to the material summarized in the INTRODUCTION and will reassess this material in the light of the study's findings. To the extent that these findings improve, otherwise illuminate, or qualify the picture presented in the INTRODUCTION, we have made progress.

SAQ 10

Because, as pointed out in Chapter 1, your report reflects the sequence in which you (theoretically) designed the study. The INTRODUCTION, therefore, should provide your reader with an outline of the reasoning that led to the design of your study in the first place. Consequently, it should describe the position that you were in *prior* to running the study and, of course, could have been written at this stage – before the data were collected.

SAQ 11

The INTRODUCTION serves to introduce your study to the reader. There are two aspects to this: first, an introduction to the area of psychology relevant to the study you conducted (in order to tell your reader why you did what you did) and, second, a brief description of your own study (to give your reader an indication of what you actually did).

SAQ 12

An exact replication of a study occurs when it is repeated in *exactly* the same way in order to assess the *reliability* of its findings (i.e., to see if the same results are obtained). The whole point of the METHOD section is to provide readers with sufficient information to enable them to undertake such a replication.

SAQ 13

The DESIGN serves to give the reader a brief, formal account of the precise design employed in your study. This information is essential for anyone who wishes to replicate it.

SAQ 14

Because if they were, ability at the task would be a *confounding* variable. See Chapters 9 and 10 for more on confounding variables.

SAQ 15

Your reader needs to know (1) what kind of participants you sampled and (2) how they were distributed across your experimental conditions. S/he needs to know (1) in order to assess the generalizability of your findings. S/he needs to know (2) in order to establish whether there are any confounding variables arising from the way in which the participants were distributed across the various conditions.

SAQ 16

It is in the form of a list, when it should be in text. It has been labelled APPARATUS, when it contains both apparatus and materials. The precise makes and models of the equipment used are not given. Although a number of pieces of equipment have been used, we are given no idea of how they were linked together – a diagram would have been useful here.

SAQ 17

If there *were* differences between your conditions other than those involving your manipulation of the IV, this would be a confounding variable.

SAQ 18

Because if the instructions vary *between* conditions in aspects other than those involved in manipulating the IV, this would constitute a confounding variable. Similarly, if the instructions vary *within* conditions, this might not only increase the variability within that condition, but again, if uncontrolled, might constitute a confounding variable. Indeed, there is evidence to suggest that participants' behaviour can be strongly influenced by even quite subtle changes in instructions. So if you want to be able to make any sense of the results you obtain, you need to keep the instructions as constant as you can within any given study.

SAQ 19

Your reader needs to be able to satisfy herself or himself that the data you collected are appropriate given the research question, that the inferential statistics you used are appropriate given your data, and that the outcomes of your inferential analyses appear to be consistent with the data as summarized by the descriptive statistics. They need this information in order to evaluate your findings.

SAQ 20

What is wrong: first, we are not told which data are being analysed. Second, the description of the analysis is imprecise – we are not told which type of ANOVA was used. Third, we are not told the value of F, either of the degrees of freedom, the associated probability, or the significance level. Finally, we have no idea what these results really mean. A more appropriate statement would run as follows:

> The data in Table 1 were analysed using one-way ANOVA for unrelated samples with presentation rate (fast, moderate, or slow) as the independent variable. Recall was significantly influenced by presentation rate, $F(2, 15) = 7.45$, $p = .006$.

Indeed, this statement could be improved yet further if it were possible to specify the way in which presentation rate affected recall (e.g., did it improve it, make it worse?).

SAQ 21

The purpose of the DISCUSSION is to enable you to assess the implications of your findings for the area of psychology you have investigated. It is, therefore, the key section of the report, for it is at this stage that we are able to discover how much progress the findings have enabled us to make.

SAQ 22

They alert potential readers to the existence of an article that may be of interest to them.

SAQ 23

What is wrong: For the first reference the "&" is used instead of "and" even though it is a direct reference. No parentheses are used for the 1994, even though it is a direct reference. The list of references within parentheses should come immediately before the full stop, not after it. The list of references within parentheses should be in alphabetical order. There are two references to Bennett and Bennett (1981), neither of which are suffixed. The "and" is used for an indirect reference. Colons, rather than semi-colons, are used to separate the references. Even assuming that the authors of Chopra et al. were described in full the first time or that there are at least six of them, the et al. is in an indirect reference and therefore should be "et al.,". Blake, Perry & Griffith is repeated in full when the et al. should have been used. No page numbers are given for the quotation.

Corrected, the text should read:

> Blake, Perry and Griffith (1994) found that performance on the experimental task improved considerably when participants were in the presence of a group of peers. This contradicted previous findings in the area (Bennett & Bennett, 1981a, 1981b; Buchanan & Livermore, 1976; Chopra et al., 2007; Pike, 1992; Scoular, 1964, 1973). As Blake et al. put it, "it is not clear why this happened" (1994, p. 27).

SAQ 24

The variable we manipulate is called the independent variable. The variable we measure is called the dependent variable.

(a) The IV is the frequency of the words (high, medium, or low). The DV is the participants' reaction time in milliseconds.
(b) The IV is whether the rat had been injected with oestrogen or saline. The DV is change in the body weights of the rats in grams.
(c) The IV is the level of anxiety induced by the programme (high, moderate, or low). The DV is the number of those in each group who take up the opportunity to make a dental appointment.

(d) The IV is the nature of the violence depicted in the programme (realistic, unrealistic, or none). The DV is the mean level of shock that the viewers subsequently give to their victims in volts.

(e) The IV is whether the participants were working alone, or with one, two, four, or eight co-workers. The DV is the number of cereal packets put into boxes during the 20-minute period.

SAQ 25

The IV is whether or not the participant consumed the standard quantity of cheese 3 hours before going to bed. The DV is the number of nightmares reported by the two groups. What we have done here, in essence, is play around with the amount of cheese eaten by the members of the two groups, and looked to see if this has any effect on the incidence of nightmares. Thus cheese eating is the suspected cause and nightmares the measured effect.

SAQ 26

The control condition in our cheese and nightmare experiment is the one in which *no* cheese is given to the participants.

SAQ 27

There are five conditions in this experiment, four of which are *experimental* conditions (Cheddar, Gorgonzola, Brie, and Emmental). The *control* condition has no cheese.

SAQ 28

(a) Three (high, medium, low word frequency). No control condition.
(b) Two (oestrogen, saline injections). Control condition: saline.
(c) Three (high, moderate, low anxiety arousal). No control condition.
(d) Three (realistic, unrealistic, no violence). Control condition: no violence.
(e) Five (alone, one, two, four, eight co-workers). Control condition: alone.

SAQ 29

No. There are in fact two other possible outcomes. This particular piece of folk wisdom might be the wrong way around. That is, instead of giving you nightmares, eating cheese might actually suppress nightmares. In which case we should find that those in the cheese condition report *fewer* nightmares than those in the no cheese condition. On the other hand, it may be that cheese has no effect upon the incidence of nightmares. In which case we should find little or no difference in the number of nightmares reported by the two groups.

SAQ 30

(a) The reaction time of the participants to the high, medium, or low frequency words will not be the same.
(b) The changes in body weight among those rats injected with oestrogen will differ from the changes in body weight among those rats injected with saline.
(c) The number of viewers making dental appointments will not be the same among those who watched the high, moderate, or low anxiety-arousing programmes.
(d) The mean level of shock administered by the participants to the victim will not be the same after viewing programmes that depict realistic, unrealistic or no violence.
(e) The number of packets of breakfast cereal packed by the workers will not be the same when they work alone, or with one, two, four, or eight co-workers.

SAQ 31

Because this would be a confounding variable. If we found a difference between the cheese and no cheese conditions in the number of nightmares, we would not know whether this was caused by cheese or alcohol or both.

SAQ 32

Because the nightmares may not be due to cheese itself but to the act of eating something before going to bed. This may not be as far-fetched as it sounds. In a culture in which there is a belief that eating cheese before sleep can induce nightmares, this belief itself might be sufficient to increase the numbers of nightmares in the experimental conditions. That is, the belief would be **self-fulfilling**. Our current experiment does not rule out this explanation. A control condition involving a cheese-like but inactive substitute would. Beliefs about the effectiveness of the things that we take and consume can be very potent. This is one of the reasons why trials of drugs or treatments include *placebo* conditions. A **placebo** looks like the pill or tablet or resembles the treatment but does not contain the active or key ingredient thought to make the difference.

On the other hand, it may be that eating *anything* too close to going to bed might induce nightmares – that the simple act of eating something is what makes the difference. Our simple design does not rule out this possibility either. Our "placebo cheese" condition would control for both possibilities.

SAQ 33

No. This relationship probably occurs because of a third variable – temperature. That is, as the temperature rises, so more ice cream is consumed and, quite independently, so more people go swimming. As more people swim, so more people die in drowning accidents. So any apparently causal link between these variables is spurious.

SAQ 34

Our original cheese and nightmare experiment had different participants in the two conditions. Hence it had an *unrelated* samples design. We could also have run it by comparing the number of nightmares reported by the same participants on nights in which they had eaten cheese with the number reported on nights in which they had not eaten cheese. This would have been a *related* samples design. The advantage of having the same person in both conditions is that it controls for individual differences in the tendency to experience nightmares. This would be a considerable advantage. However, getting people to sleep sometimes with and sometimes without having eaten cheese would give them strong clues about the nature of the experiment and this might affect the way they responded – a potentially confounding variable.

SAQ 35

(a) Related samples
(b) Unrelated samples
(c) Unrelated samples
(d) Unrelated samples
(e) Related samples

SAQ 36

Otherwise there is the possibility of a confounding variable arising from the non-random assignment of participants to conditions, just as with non-matched participants.

SAQ 37

No. It may be that at other temperatures – for instance, chilled – they *can* taste the difference. Indeed, temperature appears to markedly affect the flavour of a drink, as any beer or wine drinker can tell you. In order to test this possibility, of course, we would need to *manipulate* the temperature variable, rather than hold it constant. So our findings may only hold for the conditions employed in the experiment. Moreover, whether people *in general* are unable to taste the difference, of course, depends on how representative the group of students at this summer school is of the population at large. Also, tap water will vary in flavour from location to location.

SAQ 38

A value of $p = .03$ is nearer to zero than to one. It is, therefore, nearer the impossible end of the continuum. Thus it is an event that is *unlikely* to occur under the null hypothesis. However, note that it does not have a probability of zero. Thus it is *still possible* for it to occur under the null hypothesis – and (sigh!) that's the rub.

SAQ 39

Yes. The probability associated with our obtained value of chi-square, $p = .03$, is less than $p = .05$. It is therefore statistically significant at the 5 percent significance level.

SAQ 40

The probability for a two-tailed t test is twice that for the one-tailed version. The probability associated with $t = 1.73$ with 20 degrees of freedom, two-tailed, is therefore $p = .10$, or 10 percent.

SAQ 41

A type II error – failing to reject a false null hypothesis. Remember, power is the probability of *not* making a type II error.

SAQ 42

(a) 6, 12 and 18 are all possible. Why? Because you need a minimum of six participants to ensure that the design is fully counterbalanced (because there are six possible unique combinations of three conditions). When thinking of the number of participants to run in this experiment, there-fore, you need to think in multiples of six or else the design will not be fully counterbalanced.

(b) Six participants are unlikely to be enough to give you sufficient power to detect an effect of the IV on the DV (see Section 12.2.2). Twelve may also be too few. Eighteen *may* be sufficient, depending on how big an effect the IV has on the DV.

(c) 18 + 6 = 24. So, 24 is the next highest number of participants you could use to ensure the design was counterbalanced.

SAQ 43

(a) 24. Because there are 24 unique combinations of four conditions – see Table 13.1.

(b) 48. (2 × 24). This may well be too many with a related samples IV. Of course, whether this number of participants *is* too many depends, among other things, on the effect size (see Section 12.1).

SAQ 44

Experiment a. As we have three conditions, there are only six different ways in which we can order these conditions. Thus, it is quite feasible to *counterbalance* them. The orders are:

Hi	Med	Lo
Hi	Lo	Med
Med	Hi	Lo
Med	Lo	Hi
Lo	Med	Hi
Lo	Hi	Med

As you can see, therefore, each condition appears an equal number of times in each position, and an equal number of times before and after each other condition – that is, the experiment is counterbalanced.

As we have six different orders, then we need a minimum of six participants for our experiment. Of course we would use more than this. However, our total number of participants would have to be divisible by six. That is, we would have to work in multiples of six participants. So, 18 participants might be acceptable – 17 or 19 would not.

Experiment e. There are five conditions. There are, therefore, 120 different ways of ordering these conditions (5! = 5 × 4 × 3 × 2 × 1 = 120). We would therefore require a minimum of 120 participants to fully counterbalance this experiment. Consequently, we would probably have either to use a method of partial control or otherwise randomize the assignment of orders of conditions to participants. We could randomize by allocating one of the 120 possible orders randomly to each of our participants using randomization without replacement. This method of controlling for order effects does not limit the number of participants that we can employ, so there is no minimum. However, the more we employ, the more effective will be our randomization, and – other things being equal – the more reliable the data.

SAQ 45

(a) The variables are: alcohol, gender, and time since passing driving test. Hence there are three. The first of these, alcohol, is a related samples IV; the other two use unrelated samples. Thus it is a mixed design. One way of describing it is as a three-way, mixed design.

There are four levels on the alcohol IV (0, 2, 4, or 8 measures of wine), two on the gender variable (female or male), and three on the driving experience variable (passed in the previous 6 months, passed in the previous 7–18 months, or passed more than 18 months previously). The other answer, therefore, is a $4 \times 3 \times 2$ (Alcohol × Driving Experience × Gender) mixed design.

(b) The IVs are: type of stress and nature of task. Hence there are two IVs. Stress is an unrelated samples IV, the nature of the task a related samples IV. Thus it is a mixed design. One answer, therefore, is a two-way, mixed design.

There are three levels on the stress IV (heat, noise, or light), two on the type of task IV (demanding or undemanding). The other answer, therefore, is a 3×2 (Stress × Type of Task) mixed design.

(c) The variables are: gender and extraversion. Hence there are two. These are both necessarily unrelated samples variables. Thus it is an unrelated samples design. One answer, therefore, is a two-way, unrelated samples design.

There are two levels on the gender variable (female or male), two on the extraversion variable (extravert or introvert). The other answer, therefore, is a 2×2 (Gender × Extraversion) unrelated samples design.

(d) The IVs are: driving conditions, nature of listening material, and volume. Hence there are three IVs. All of these use related samples. Thus it is a related samples design. One answer, therefore, is a three-way, related samples design.

There are three levels on the driving conditions IV (easy, moderate, or difficult), two levels on the listening material IV (talk or music), and three levels on the volume IV (low, moderate, or loud). The other answer, therefore, is a $3 \times 3 \times 2$ (Driving Conditions × Listening Material × Volume) related samples design.

SAQ 46

Because a mixed design has *at least* one IV that uses related samples and *at least* one IV that uses unrelated samples, it must have at least two IVs. As, by definition, a one-way design has only one IV, you cannot, therefore, have a one-way, mixed design.

SAQ 47

(a) Up to three: alcohol, gender, driving experience.
(b) Up to two: type of stress, nature of task.
(c) Up to two: gender, extraversion.
(d) Up to three: driving conditions, nature of listening material, volume.

SAQ 48

(a) No. Gender and driving experience are not true independent variables because we have not been able to assign participants randomly to be male or female or to have more or less driving experience.
(b) Yes. Both variables in this study, type of stress, and nature of the task, are true IVs. We have been able to randomly allocate participants to both IVs.
(c) No. Neither variable in this study, gender and extraversion, are true IVs. We have not been able to assign participants randomly to be male or female, extravert or introvert.
(d) Yes. All three variables, driving conditions, nature of listening material, and volume, are true IVs. We have been able to randomly allocate participants to all IVs.

Strictly speaking, therefore, I was wrong to describe some of the above variables as IVs in my introduction to SAQ 45.

SAQ 49

If you *reject* the null hypothesis. This means that you have found evidence enough to persuade you that there is a reliable difference between your conditions on the DV. So this is *potentially* evidence *against* the ideas that led to the prediction of no difference. Thus, in this sort of experiment you can only ever find evidence that goes against ideas that predict no difference, not evidence in favour of them.

SAQ 50

1 The critical value of T for $N = 22$ at the 5 percent significance level (two-tailed) is $T = 65$. As the obtained T of 45 is *less* than this, the result is statistically significant at the 5 percent significance level.

2 The critical value of U for $n_1 = 10$ and $n_2 = 12$ at the 5 percent significance level (two-tailed) is $U = 29$. As the obtained value of U of 8 is *less* than this, the result is statistically significant at the 5 percent significance level.

3 The critical value of χ^2 with 1 degree of freedom at the 5 percent significance level is $\chi^2 = 3.84$. As the obtained value of χ^2 of 3.80 is *less* than this, the result is *not* statistically significant at the 5 percent significance level.

4 The critical value of t with 16 degrees of freedom at the 5 percent significance level (two-tailed) is $t = 2.12$. As the obtained value of t of 2.20 is *greater* than this, the result is statistically significant at the 5 percent significance level.

5 The critical value of F with $df_1 = 2$ and $df_2 = 25$ at the 5 percent significance level is $F = 3.39$. As the obtained value of F of 5.20 is *greater* than this, the result is statistically significant at the 5 percent significance level. (Note that df_1 refers to the degrees of freedom for the *numerator* of the F ratio, df_2 refers to the degrees of freedom for the *denominator* of this ratio. With tables of the distribution of F you have to make sure that you read the columns and rows correctly and do not confuse df_1 and df_2.)

Answers to diagnostic questions

Chapter 2

1 A variable is something – anything – that *varies*, that can take different forms or values. You can find more about this in Section 9.1.

2 The variable we manipulate in an experiment is called the *independent* variable. You can find more about independent variables in Section 9.1.1.

3 The variable we measure in an experiment to assess the effects of the manipulation is called the *dependent* variable. You can find more about dependent variables in Section 9.1.1.

4 The prediction of no difference comes from the *null hypothesis*. You can find more about the null hypothesis in Section 9.1.4.

5 A *nondirectional* prediction is a prediction that there will be a difference somewhere between the conditions in your experiment, but says nothing about the *direction* of this difference. In contrast, a *directional* prediction states in which direction the difference will be. You can find out more about these different types of prediction in Section 9.1.4.

Chapter 3

1 In a *related* samples IV, the *same* group of participants appears in every level of the IV. You can find more about this in Section 10.1.

2 In an *unrelated* samples IV, a *different* group of participants appears in each level of the IV. You can find more about this in Section 10.1.

3 A *mixed* design has both related samples *and* unrelated samples IVs. A mixed design therefore has at least two IVs. You can find more about this in Section 13.3.

4 In *random assignment*, participants are allocated to conditions using some truly random procedure. You can find more about random assignment in Section 10.9. Random assignment is a critical feature of an experiment and should not be confused with random selection of participants. You can find more about *random selection* of participants in Section 10.8. You can find out more about *how* to randomize in Appendix 2.

Chapter 4

1 *Inferential statistics* are the statistics we use to help us make inferences about our data, such as when we use a *t* test or analysis of variance to test for differences between conditions, or test whether a correlation coefficient, such as *r*, differs significantly from zero. You can find out more about such measures in Section 11.1.

You should not confuse inferential statistics with *descriptive statistics*. Descriptive statistics summarize the key features of a particular set or sample of data. They include measures of central tendency, such as the mean or median, and measures of dispersion, such as the standard deviation. You can find out more about descriptive statistics in Section 4.1.

In essence, we use *inferential* statistics to make guesses or estimates based on our sample of data about the properties (or *parameters*) of the populations of numbers from which they were sampled. For example, if we assume that the data in the conditions of your experiment came from the same population of numbers – i.e., if we assume the null hypothesis to be true – how likely would we be to get data like yours? Inferential statistics help us to make such inferences. This process is described in Chapter 11, so I recommend you read (or re-read) Chapter 11 if you need to refresh your understanding.

2 Technically, a difference is described as *statistically significant* when the probability of the obtained value of our inferential statistic (assuming the null hypothesis to be true) is equal to or less than our chosen significance level. For example, if the probability associated with our obtained value of *t* or *F* is equal to or less than $p = .05$ and we are using the *5 percent significance level*, our difference would be statistically significant. Under these circumstances we would decide to *reject* the null hypothesis. This does not, however, necessarily mean that our finding is psychologically significant – see Section 11.2.

3 The *5 percent significance level* means that we have chosen to set our criterion for deciding whether to accept or reject the null hypothesis at a probability of 5 in 100 or $p = .05$. If the probability of the obtained value of the inferential statistic (under the null hypothesis) is equal to or less than $p = .05$, we decide to reject the assumption that the null hypothesis is true and describe our finding as statistically significant; however, if the probability of the obtained value of the inferential statistic (under the null

hypothesis) is more than $p = .05$, we decide we do not have enough evidence to reject the null hypothesis. Consequently, we continue to assume that the null hypothesis is true and describe our finding as being not statistically significant. For more on this process, see Section 11.2.

4 A *type I error* occurs if we decide to reject the null hypothesis when we should have accepted it. Our chances of doing this – on average – are equal to our chosen significance level. That is, if we use the 5 percent significance level we will reject a true null hypothesis on average 5 times for every 100 decisions we make. For more on this see Section 11.3.

Chapter 5

1 *Internal validity* refers to the extent to which we can relate changes in the DV to the manipulation of the IV. An experiment high in internal validity is one that lacks confounding variables. See Sections 10.9 for a discussion of internal validity and 9.1.3 for more on confounding variables.

2 *External validity* refers to the extent to which the findings generated by your experiment can be generalized to people and circumstances beyond those directly assessed in your study. The findings from a study high in external validity apply to many settings and many different types of people. See Section 10.8 for a discussion of external validity.

3 A *confounding* variable is a special type of uncontrolled variable, one whose levels change with the levels of an IV. It thus presents a potential rival explanation for any changes produced in the DV when the IV is manipulated. You can find out more about confounding variables and why it is essential to control for them in Section 9.1.3.

4 A *type II error* occurs if we decide to accept the null hypothesis when we should have rejected it. As we decrease our chances of making a type I error – e.g., by adopting the 1 percent rather than the 5 percent significance level – so we increase our chances of making a type II error. For more on this see Section 11.3.

Chapter 9

1 A variable is something – anything – that *varies*, that can take different forms or values. You can find more about this in Section 9.1.

2 The variable we manipulate in an experiment is called the *independent* variable. You can find more about independent variables in Section 9.1.1.

3 The variable we measure in an experiment to assess the effects of the manipulation is called the *dependent* variable. You can find more about dependent variables in Section 9.1.1.

4 The prediction of no difference comes from the *null hypothesis*. You can find more about the null hypothesis in Section 9.1.4.

5 A *nondirectional* prediction is a prediction that there will be a difference somewhere between the conditions in your experiment, but says nothing about the *direction* of this difference. In contrast, a *directional* prediction states in which direction the difference will be. You can find out more about these different types of prediction in Section 9.1.4.

Chapter 10

1 In a *related* samples IV, the *same* group of participants appears in every level of the IV. You can find more about this in Section 10.1.

2 In an *unrelated* samples IV, a *different* group of participants appears in each level of the IV. You can find more about this in Section 10.1.

3 In *random assignment*, participants are allocated to conditions using some truly random procedure. You can find more about random assignment in Section 10.9. Random assignment is a critical feature of an experiment and should not be confused with random selection of participants. You can find more about *random selection* of participants in Section 10.8. You can find out more about how to randomize in Appendix 2.

4 *Internal validity* refers to the extent to which we can relate changes in the DV to the manipulation of the IV. An experiment high in internal validity is one that lacks confounding variables. See Section 10.9 for a discussion of internal validity and 9.1.3 for more on confounding variables.

5 *External validity* refers to the extent to which the findings generated by your experiment can be generalized to people and circumstances beyond those directly assessed in your study. The findings from a study high in external validity apply to many settings and many different types of people. See Section 10.8 for a discussion of external validity.

Chapter 11

1 *Inferential statistics* are the statistics we use to help us make inferences about our data, such as when we use a t test or analysis of variance to test for differences between conditions, or test whether a correlation coefficient, such as r, differs significantly from zero. You can find out more about such measures in Section 11.1.

2 Technically, a difference is described as *statistically significant* when the probability of the obtained value of our inferential statistic (assuming the null hypothesis to be true) is equal to or less than our chosen significance level. For example, if the probability associated with our obtained value of t or F is equal to or less than $p = .05$ and we are using the *5 percent*

significance level, our difference would be statistically significant. Under these circumstances we would decide to *reject* the null hypothesis. This does not, however, necessarily mean that our finding is psychologically significant, see Section 11.2.

3 The *5 percent significance level* means that we have chosen to set our criterion for deciding whether to accept or reject the null hypothesis at a probability of 5 in 100 or $p = .05$. If the probability of the obtained value of the inferential statistic (under the null hypothesis) is equal to or less than $p = .05$, we decide to reject the assumption that the null hypothesis is true and describe our finding as statistically significant; however, if the probability of the obtained value of the inferential statistic (under the null hypothesis) is more than $p = .05$, we decide we do not have enough evidence to reject the null hypothesis. Consequently, we continue to assume that null hypothesis is true and describe our finding as being not statistically significant. For more on this process, see Section 11.2.

4 A *type I error* occurs if we decide to reject the null hypothesis when we should have accepted it. Our chances of doing this – on average – are equal to our chosen significance level. That is, if we use the 5 percent significance level we will reject a true null hypothesis on average 5 times for every 100 decisions we make. For more on this, see Section 11.3.

5 A *type II error* occurs if we decide to accept the null hypothesis when we should have rejected it. As we decrease our chances of making a type I error – e.g., by adopting the 1 percent rather than the 5 percent significance level – so we increase our chances of making a type II error. For more on this see Section 11.3.

Chapter 12

1 *Effect size* refers to the size of the difference between means or (more generally) the size of the relationship between two variables. With a well-designed experiment we can assess whether the IV has a small, medium or large impact on the DV. With a correlation we can assess whether the two variables have a small, medium or large relationship or "strength of association". For more on effect size, see Section 12.1.

2 The *power* of an experiment is its capacity to detect an effect of the IV on the DV of a specified size (e.g., small, medium, or large) when such an effect actually exists. In other words, it is the capacity of an experiment to detect a specified effect size in a sample of data, if we assume this size of effect exists in the population from which the data has been sampled. For more on power, see Section 12.2.

3 An experiment with a power of .80 has an 80 percent chance of detecting a specified effect size in a sample of data, assuming that this effect exists in the population. For more on power, see Section 12.2.

4 *Power calculations* are calculations made before the study is run to estimate its power to detect effect sizes of different sizes. This can alert us to the need to change its power. For more on power calculations, see Section 12.2.1.

5 Practically, we could increase power by (a) adding more participants to the experiment (b) where possible, replacing unrelated samples IVs with related samples IVs and (c) analysing our data using a parametric test. For more on increasing power, see Section 12.2.2.

6 25%. It is easy to work out the percentage variance: square the value of r to obtain r^2 and then multiply r^2 by 100. For example, with $r = .5$, $r^2 = .25$ and the percentage variance $= .25 \times 100 = 25\%$. See Section 12.3.1.

Chapter 13

1 We are more likely to face problems with recruiting participants. There are no order effects with unrelated samples IVs. For more on this see Section 13.1.

2 There are two IVs, each with 2 levels. We can tell this from the "2 × 2" element of the design description. One of the IVs uses related samples and one of the IVs uses unrelated samples. We can tell this from the "mixed design" element of the design description, as we know that mixed designs use both types of IV. For more on this, see Section 13.3.

3 A significant *main effect* occurs when the scores on the DV differ statistically significantly at the levels of an IV (when averaged over any other IVs in the experiment). For example, we had a significant main effect of instruction in our mnemonic experiment (Section 4.6.10) with those in the mnemonic group recalling more items ($M = 15.65$) than did those in the no-mnemonic group ($M = 12.40$). You may find that any or all of the IVs in your experiment have significant main effects. For more on main effects, see Section 13.4.

4 When two variables *interact* the effect of one IV is *different* at the levels of another IV. For example, we had a significant interaction in our mnemonic experiment between the imageability of the words (easy or hard to image) and whether or not our participants had been instructed to use the mnemonic (see Section 4.6.10): the effect of the mnemonic IV was bigger when the words were easy to image than it was when the words were hard to image. For more on interactions, see Section 13.5.

5 When you have been able to randomly assign participants to the different levels of the IV. For more on this, see Section 13.8.

References

American Psychological Association. (2001). *Publication manual of the American Psychological Association* (5th ed.). Washington, DC: American Psychological Association.

American Psychological Association. (2002). *Ethical principles of psychologists and code of conduct.* Retrieved from http://www.apa.org/ethics/code2002.html

American Psychological Association. (2007). *APA style guide to electronic references.* Washington, DC: American Psychological Association. Available from http://www.apastyle.org/elecref.html

Aron, A., & Aron, E. (2005). *Statistics for psychology* (3rd ed.). Upper Saddle River, NJ: Prentice-Hall.

British Psychological Society (2006, March). *Code of ethics and conduct.* Leicester: The British Psychological Society.

Clark-Carter, D. (2004). *Quantitative Psychological Research: A Student's Handbook* (2nd ed.). Hove: Psychology Press.

Cohen, J. (1988). *Statistical power analysis for the behavioral sciences* (2nd ed.). New York: Academic Press.

Coolican, H. (2004). *Research Methods and Statistics in Psychology* (4th ed.). London: Hodder & Stoughton.

Dancey, C. P., & Reidy, J. (2004). *Statistics without maths for psychology* (3rd ed.). London: Pearson.

Glassman, W. E., & Haddad, M. (2004). *Approaches to psychology* (4th ed.). Maidenhead: Open University Press.

Greene, J., & D'Oliveira, M. (2006). *Learning to use statistical tests in psychology* (3rd ed.). Maidenhead: Open University Press.

Grimm, L. G., & Yarnold, P. R. (Eds.) (1995). *Reading and understanding multivariate statistics.* Washington: American Psychological Association.

Hayes, N. (2000). *Doing psychological research.* Maidenhead: Open University Press.

Hinton, R. P. (2004). *Statistics explained* (2nd ed.). London: Routledge.

Howell, D. C. (2007a). *Statistical methods for psychology* (6th ed.). Belmont, CA: Wadsworth.

Howell, D. C. (2007b). *Fundamental statistics for the behavioral sciences* (6th ed.). Belmont, CA: Wadsworth.

Kirkpatrick, L. A., & Feeney, B. C. (2007). *A simple guide to SPSS for Windows, Version 14* (8th ed.). Belmont, CA: Wadsworth.

Murphy, K. R., & Myors, B. (2004). *Statistical power analysis* (2nd ed.). Mahwah, NJ: LEA.

Nicol, A. A. M., & Pexman, P. M. (1999). *Presenting your findings: A practical guide for creating tables*. Washington: American Psychological Association.

Pallant, J. (2007). *SPSS survival manual: a step-by-step guide to data analysis using SPSS version 15*. Maidenhead: Open University Press.

Sternberg, R. J. (2003). *The psychologist's companion* (4th ed.). Cambridge: Cambridge University Press.

Index of concepts

Index of concepts